INTERNATIONAL BUSINESS EXPANSION INTO LESS-DEVELOPED COUNTRIES: THE INTERNATIONAL FINANCE CORPORATION AND ITS OPERATIONS

James C. Baker, DBA

SOME ADVANCE REVIEWS

"Will certainly be recognized as a major contribution to the study of the institutions dealing with development finance. The book is well-written and full of valuable information. The chapters dealing with the IFC's involvement in various regions contain a tremendous amount of information. . . . This is simply an outstanding book."

Sharif N. Ahkam, DBA
Assistant Professor of Finance
Graduate School of Business and Administration
Duquesne University

"This is the most comprehensive book describing IFC role and activities. The author has a futuristic approach and this book should be useful to countries needing IFC assistance in their privatization efforts. The best part of the book is the analysis and description of more than thirty projects financed by the IFC around the globe."

M. Anaam Hashmi, DBA
Associate Professor of International Business and Finance
Mankato State University

International Business Expansion into Less-Developed Countries
The International Finance Corporation and Its Operations

INTERNATIONAL BUSINESS PRESS
Erdener Kaynak, PhD
Executive Editor

New, Recent, and Forthcoming Titles:

International Business Handbook edited by V. H. (Manek) Kirpalani

Sociopolitical Aspects of International Marketing edited by Erdener Kaynak

How to Manage for International Competitiveness edited by Abbas J. Ali

International Business Expansion into Less-Developed Countries: The International Finance Corporation and Its Operations by James C. Baker

Product-Country Images: Impact and Role in International Marketing edited by Nicolas Papadopoulos and Louise A. Heslop

The Global Business: Four Key Marketing Strategies edited by Erdener Kaynak

Multinational Strategic Alliances edited by Refik Culpan

Market Evolution in Developing Countries: The Unfolding of the Indian Market by Subhash C. Jain

International Business Expansion into Less-Developed Countries
The International Finance Corporation and Its Operations

James C. Baker, DBA

International Business Press
New York • London • Norwood (Australia)

Published by

International Business Press, an imprint of The Haworth Press, Inc., 10 Alice Street, Binghamton, NY 13904-1580

Library of Congress Cataloging-in-Publication Data

Baker, James Calvin, 1935-
  International business expansion into less-developed countries : the International Finance Corporation and its operations / James C. Baker.
       p.   cm.
  Includes bibliographical references and index.
  ISBN 1-56024-201-9 (acid free paper)
  1. International Finance Corporation. 2. Investments, Foreign — Developing countries. 3. Development banks. I. Title.
HG3881.5.I56B35   1992
332.6'73'091724 — dc20   91-23251
                                                                                      CIP

Dedicated to those around me: Jean, Jan, Jeff, Jolie, and my mother, and to Dr. Robert Kamienski, a heart surgeon who may have made this project possible.

ABOUT THE AUTHOR

James C. Baker, DBA, is Professor of Finance and International Business at Kent State University where he has taught since 1971. He has also lectured at Columbia University, George Washington University, and the Pacific Asian Management Institute at the University of Hawaii. Dr. Baker's research has covered a wide variety of interests in international business, international financial management, and international banking and he has written or co-written many books on these and related topics. He has been active in a number of academic and professional organizations devoted to international business issues, including the Academy of International Business, the International Management Division of the Academy of Management, the Association for Global Business, and the Cleveland World Trade Association.

CONTENTS

List of Tables and Figures

Preface

This work is about the only global development finance institution which invests in and promotes private sector projects *without government guarantees*. This institution, the International Finance Corporation (IFC), began operations in 1956 with only $78 million of subscribed and paid-in capital, and invests in projects located in less-developed countries which are members of the IFC.

During the half century since the end of World War II, the process of development finance has become quite sophisticated and many changes in development assistance have been adopted. The emphasis on reconstruction of war-torn countries in West Europe and Asia during the first decade after the end of World War II was carried out primarily by funds from the World Bank, then known as the International Bank for Reconstruction and Development, and by financial assistance through bilateral aid from the United States manifested in the form of Marshall Plan aid.

The aid trend then moved to financial aid to the low-income countries which needed social overhead capital or infrastructure to support industrial growth in such economies. During this period, an obscure global development finance institution was born from informal debate carried on at international meetings and conferences as well as during cocktail receptions in Washington, D.C. This was the IFC, a unique global institution which finances private enterprise projects in less-developed countries without the usual government guarantees required by the World Bank and other multilateral institutions.

This organization was necessary, so it was said, to assist the development of private enterprise needed to plug into the social infrastructure which had been erected during the early post-war period. Without such private enterprise, countries would have little use for the infrastructure.

In the 35 years since it began operations, the IFC has become a very successful institution in a wide variety of private sector development activities. This success story is the subject of this book and so will not be discussed here. Since 1956, the IFC has grown in many ways. By mid-1991, it had 135 members and $2.3 billion of total capital. During the past decade, it has expanded its services tremendously and is capable of competing successfully with several functions of Wall Street investment banks. Its operations and success stories are analyzed in this treatise as are some of its problems.

The IFC is a favorite topic of the author, who first learned of this institution in a graduate course in International Finance 29 years ago. The professor was Lee Nehrt. Professor Nehrt was an institutionalist and fostered in his students a desire to know more about the various international financial institutions operating at that time and the reasons for their existence. The author of this book examined the first six years of IFC operations during that classroom experience. The IFC was sufficiently interesting to have held his attention since then and the results have been an earlier book, *The International Finance Corporation: Origin, Operations, and Evaluation* (New York: Praeger, 1968), a number of articles and conference papers about the IFC, and, now, this book.

The work of the IFC cannot be fully measured and evaluated. The vast bulk of the projects it has assisted have been successful in achieving many development goals for their host countries and their market value is impossible to measure. But the book values discussed throughout this book are impressive when one considers the relatively small size of the original IFC. The trend set into progress by the IFC during the past four to five years is even more impressive. Growth of the IFC's operations should be even more impressive in the decade ahead.

This study of the IFC is especially timely because of the importance placed on its operations by the present and immediate past U.S. Administrations. The Reagan Administration praised the IFC as a significant institution which operates according to the supply side economic policy so popular with that administration. During 1991, the IFC was also cited favorably by President George Bush's Administration during the attempt by the IFC to double the size of its subscribed capital from member countries. The U.S. Government, in fact, is on record in recommending that the World Bank also direct assistance toward the private sector of LDCs. This recommendation, if adopted, would represent a major policy change by the Bank.

Several persons and institutions must be acknowledged for their assistance in the completion of this monograph. Lee Nehrt planted the seed for the early interest in the IFC. Several officials of the World Bank and the IFC have given me their time during interviews for the 1968 book and during 1990 for this book. They were extremely helpful. Correspondence has been received from executives with several companies discussed in the book. This information was very useful. The editorial staff at The Haworth Press has been quite helpful, as have comments by anonymous reviewers of the manuscript. Several graduate research assistants have given their time to this project. Among these, Mohamed Hasan, Dan Borgia, and Sayuri Criss should be mentioned for their excellent research assistance. The Kent State University Research Council furnished data collection and travel funds for research on the project. Others have contributed to this project whose names have been omitted but whose assistance made the project possible. I gratefully acknowledge their assistance. This project might have been impossible without the surgical skills of Dr. Robert Kamienski, who replaced the author's aortic valve at the Akron General Medical Center in 1988. Finally, it goes without saying that I owe much to my wife, Jean, and my immediate family who have seen little of me, especially during the last six months of the project, and found it necessary to make a lot of domestic decisions without much input from me.

As in most research and writing projects, errors may be present. To none of the above do I attribute any errors found in the text. I fully accept the blame for such.

James C. Baker
Kent, Ohio

Chapter 1

Global Development Institutions

INTRODUCTION

From the end of World War II until 1990, two global wars have been fought. One has been the political war between East and West which may have shifted to one between the West and the Moslem world – given the effect of Glasnost and Perestroika in 1989-90 and the Persian Gulf incident involving the invasion of Kuwait by Iraq in 1990. The other is the ongoing economic war between North and South that U Thant, the late former Secretary-General of the United Nations, once characterized as more relevant than the war between East and West (Thant, 1963).

Economies have been classified for operational and analytical purposes according to their gross national product (GNP) (World Bank, *World Development Report*, 1990, p. x). The "North" essentially includes the high-income economies, those whose GNP per capita was $6,000 or more in 1988 as well as a few of the middle-income economies whose per capita GNP was higher than $2,200. The former would include the United States, Japan, and the West European nations. The latter includes Brazil and some Asian nations such as the Republic of Korea and Taiwan.

The "South" essentially includes all middle-income countries with per capita GNP of between $545 and $2,200 and those low-income economies whose per capita GNP is less than $545. Thus, the higher-income economies seem to be geographically located north of the Equator while those middle- to lower-income economies are south of the Equator. Most lower-income, or developing, economies can be characterized as having relatively high population growth rates and relatively high infant mortality rates. In general, developing economies (LDCs), as compared with industrialized economies, are agrarian societies or produce extractive minerals whose prices rise less slowly in world markets than do the prices of their imports, generally of industrial products. Thus, the terms of trade do not favor LDCs. This phenomenon exacerbates their poverty. In terms of the world's population that can be characterized as poor, most are located in South Asia and sub-Saharan Africa.

Although some progress has been made in the developing world in the last 50 years, some of the problems remain persistent. The United Nations published a document outlining proposals for a "Development Decade" in the 1960s and it pointed out that higher standards of living were suppressed because of the "higher rates of population growth in developing countries than in wealthier countries" (United Nations, 1962, p. 7). Countries such as Kenya still encounter devastating population growth rates approaching 4 percent, despite the implementation of birth control programs. Robert Theobald wrote that rapid development would only occur if the industrialized nations gave aid to the LDCs. The amount of aid given to LDCs has not kept pace with the growth of GNP in the industrialized countries and much has been spent by the latter on military goods, especially by the United States and the former U.S.S.R. while fighting the Cold War.

An examination of recent analyses of world economic growth shows that it moderated to "a more sustainable pace" in 1989, according to the International Monetary Fund (IMF) (IMF Financial Support, 1990). Growth in the developing countries was 3.25 percent in 1989, compared with 4.25 percent in 1988. Reasons for the slower growth in LDCs in 1989 include slower world trade growth, higher international interest rates, and lower prices for some non-oil commodities. Total external debt of LDCs changed very little from 1988 to 1989. Such debt totaled $1,235 billion in 1989, about one-third of combined gross domestic product of LDCs.

GLOBAL DEVELOPMENT INSTITUTIONS

Since the end of World War II, bilateral and multilateral economic assistance institutions have been established for the purpose of reducing the poverty of LDCs. Many of the industrialized or high-income economies have disseminated economic assistance—

foreign aid — through central government agencies such as the Agency for International Development (AID) in the United States or the Development Assistance Committee of the Organization of Economic Cooperation and Development (OECD), an organization comprised of mostly European nations, along with Canada, United States, and Japan.

Several multilateral international financial institutions have been established to assist the economic development of LDCs. Among these are the International Monetary Fund (IMF), the World Bank Group agencies — World Bank, the International Finance Corporation (IFC), and the International Development Association (IDA), and regional multilateral agencies including the Inter-American Development Bank (IADB), the African Development Bank (AfDB), the Asian Development Bank (ADB), Islamic development institutions, and European Community development institutions.

The International Monetary Fund (IMF)

The IMF was established at a conference held in 1944 in Bretton Woods, New Hampshire. Delegates to this conference were highly supportive of the United Nations and believed a global financial institution was needed to provide liquidity to the war-torn and underdeveloped nations of the world which had not recovered from either the deflation of the Great Depression nor from World War II.

In 1946, member nations of the IMF subscribed foreign exchange and gold reserves to this agency to establish a pool of $8,800 million from which nations with short-term balance of payments imbalances could draw to obtain relief (International Monetary Fund, 1946). Currently, the IMF has available funds, or total quotas, amounting to SDR 90.1 billion (1 SDR = U.S.$1.369359) for this purpose. The IMF has proposed a 50 percent increase in these quotas to about SDR 135.2 billion. As of August 1990, 151 nations were currently members of the organization ("Members' Quotas Guide," August 1990). IMF is headquartered in Washington, D.C., and its President has always been a foreigner, usually a European.

The IMF was established for the following purposes: (*Encyclopedia of Banking and Finance*, p. 56).

1. to promote international monetary cooperation through a permanent institution that provides the machinery for consultation and collaboration on international monetary problems;
2. to facilitate the expansion and balanced growth of international trade, and to contribute thereby to the promotion and maintenance of high levels of employment and real income and to the development of the productive resources of all members as primary objectives of economic policy;
3. to promote exchange stability, to maintain orderly exchange arrangements among members, and to avoid competitive exchange depreciation;
4. to assist in the establishment of a multilateral system of payments in respect to current transactions between members and in the elimination of foreign exchange restrictions which hamper the growth of world trade;
5. to give confidence to members by making the general resources of the IMF temporarily available to them under adequate safeguards, thus providing them with the opportunity to correct maladjustments in their balance of payments without resorting to measures destructive of national or international prosperity;
6. in accordance with the above, to shorten the duration and lessen the degree of disequilibrium in the international balances of payments of members.

In 1968, the IMF was authorized by its member nations to create a new international currency called Special Drawing Rights or SDRs. This "paper gold," as it was referred to, became a supplement to the international reserves held by IMF. Each member was given SDRs in relation to its total subscription of reserves. SDRs have not replaced the dollar or gold but have become an addition to the stock of international money (Moffitt, p. 33). Although SDRs have become well accepted and some international debt instruments have been denominated in them, they have never become a panacea to the world's monetary problems because they were "too late, too small and too timid in [their] conception to save the system." Most of them were allocated to the five major members of IMF: United

States, Great Britain, France, former West Germany, and Japan (Moffitt, p. 33).

Since 1982, the international country debt problems have pushed IMF into another area of focus. It now plays a key role in designing austerity programs and advising countries with severe sovereign debt problems. In fact, IMF has become almost an international policeman in this area, forcing countries to act more responsibly in their monetary and fiscal policies. One of the first such countries whose economic policies were affected was Argentina when it was bailed out by loans from other Latin American countries as well as the United States in 1984. In helping countries alleviate their debt problems, IMF also works closely with the Bank for International Settlements (BIS) as well as with commercial banks which are creditors of these LDCs.

The most recent operations of IMF show that 49 member countries had 51 arrangements with IMF and 87 nations were using its resources—more than half its membership ("Members' Quotas Guide," August 1990). The IMF committed SDR 11.3 billion to member countries in 1989 in the form of stand-by, extended, structural adjustment, and enhanced structural adjustment facility arrangements. These commitments represented a 6-year high in 1989/90. Members withdrew SDR 4.4 billion in 1989 while repaying SDR 6.0 billion. Thus, IMF credit outstanding fell to SDR 22.1 billion in 1989/90 from SDR 23.7 billion in the prior year. The average IDA credit is granted with a grace period of 10 years, maturity of 38.3 years (40 years for IDA-only and least developed countries as classified by the United Nations, and 35 years for other recipient countries), and a service charge of 0.75 percent on the unpaid balance (Stern, June 1990, p. 20).

In its three decades of operations, the IMF has provided 2,183 credits through December 1989, totaling $54,784 million to 86 countries. Of these, $38,021 million have been disbursed and $16,763 million have yet to be disbursed. Since 1985, the agriculture and rural development sector has received the largest amount of IMF credits, receiving more than one-third of IMF commitments. By geographical region, African and Asian nations have received the vast majority of IMF credits, nearly 90 percent on a combined basis (Stern, p. 21). As usual, the United States has shared the heaviest burden of IMF funding, contributing 42.34 percent of the initial 1961-1964 funding, 25 percent of the eighth replenishment for 1988-1990, and 21.61 percent of the ninth replenishment for 1991-1993 (Stern, p. 23).

The World Bank Group

The World Bank Group, headquartered in Washington, D.C., includes the World Bank, the International Finance Corporation (IFC)—the topic of this book, the International Development Association (IDA), as well as more recently established operations—the International Centre for Settlement of Investment Disputes (ICSID) and MIGA, the Multilateral Investment Guaranty Agency. The latter two agencies are not considered global development agencies, although they play important roles in this area, and, thus, will not be discussed in this section.

The World Bank

The World Bank was established in 1944 at the conference in Bretton Woods, New Hampshire, in which the IMF was also established. These two global financial agencies were "designed to be central institutions in a world free of war and destructive economic nationalism" (Acheson, Chant, and Prachowny, p. 14). The World Bank, or Bank as it will be referred to in this study, was originally named the International Bank for Reconstruction and Development, in light of its two major objectives: reconstruction of war-torn areas and economic development of low-income nations (Acheson et al., p. xix). The Bank represented a new experiment in international finance, i.e., an international financial agency supported by the credit of its member nations, each of which would have a voice in the Bank's investment policies (*Business Week*, October 6, 1956, p. 132).

Charter members of the Bank had to be United Nations and IMF members. The bank was originally capitalized with authorized capital of $10 billion subscribed by member nations (Rotberg, 1973, p. 10). The Bank, as of the end of FY1990, had total subscribed capital amounting to $125.3 billion. With the acceptance of Angola to membership, the World Bank now has 152 members (World Bank, *Annual Report*, 1990).

The Bank makes loans to LDCs only for social overhead capital projects and whose payment of principal and interest must be guaranteed by the recipient government. Bank loans are characterized as hard-term loans in that they are for relatively short periods to maturity — generally, 15 years — and the interest payments are relatively high — currently variable-rate interest rates on Bank loans are in the 10-12 percent range. The Bank made $15.18 billion in loans in FY1990 and, of this, a total of $13.9 billion was disbursed (*World Bank and IDA Annual Report*, 1990, p. 13). Overall, it has a loan portfolio which has been disbursed and is outstanding which amounts to $89.1 billion, made to 91 countries and a total of $49.2 billion of loans approved but not yet disbursed (*The World Bank: A Financial Summary*, p. 7).

The Bank obtains its funds in a number of ways. Its present capitalization, presently $125.3 billion, is not used for development loans except in the case of a dire emergency. Most of its funds are obtained by floating Bank bonds on the international bond market. These debt instruments carry the highest rating because of the excellent operational history of the Bank, its conservative lending policies, and because it does not lose money on its own loans since recipient governments must guarantee repayment. Its borrowings total $86.5 billion in 23 currencies or currency units, with about 94 percent of the debt at fixed rates with medium- to long-term maturities. The Bank limits short-term and variable rate borrowings to 15 percent of its total debt (*The World Bank: A Financial Summary*, p. 10).

The Bank also sells some of its loans to other financial institutions, such as private commercial banks, thus encouraging private sector participation in the development process. Finally, repayment of principal and interest on its loans also furnishes funds for the Bank.

The Bank has been a highly successful international development finance institution in its 45 years of operation. However, it has not been without criticism. Some believe it is a giant bureaucracy not totally in control. Its current President is Barber Conable, a former member of the U.S. House of Representatives. The President of the

Bank has always been an American, nominated by the President of the United States — thus, politics plays a role in the appointment — whereas the President of the IMF has always been a foreigner, generally from Europe. Conable, in his first few years, created controversy at the Bank by restructuring its organization and reducing its staff.

Some believe the Bank has little effect where emergency relief is needed, that constraints are present in structural adjustment lending, and that, although its Articles of Agreement are non-political, it is highly influenced by major shareholders, e.g., the United States (Please, 1984, p. 85). In addition, the Bank tends to have technocratic problems. Because of the awesome financial power of the Bank, technocrats play a significant role in the definition of development, thus resulting in Bank support for project issues which are too technical (Please, p. 90; Morris, 1963).

In addition to these criticisms, the Bank is quite conservative in its operations. Aside from the government guarantee requirement for its loans, the Bank maintains a relatively high degree of liquidity, currently holding $17.2 billion in actively managed investments in government and agency securities and deposits in selected banks (*The World Bank: A Financial Summary*, p. 7). This represents more than 15 percent of its subscribed capital. It also maintains $16.7 billion of paid-in capital available for lending and reserves. Nearly two-thirds of this is in reserves and accumulated net income — unallocated (*The World Bank: A Financial Summary*, p. 11). Finally, the Bank has callable capital which is a direct, unconditional obligation of member countries amounting to $116.3 billion (*The World Bank: A Financial Summary*, p. 11).

The 1990 *Annual Report* of the World Bank shows that the area receiving the highest amount of Bank loans was Asia with 30.9 percent of FY1990 loans. Latin America and the Caribbean received 28.8 percent, Europe, Middle East, and North Africa received 21.3 percent, and Africa received 19.0 percent, respectively ("World Bank Expects 1991 Lending," September 24, 1990). When compared with its historical overall allocations, these data show that the Bank has changed its lending policy with regard to certain regions in recent years. Overall, its disbursed and outstanding loans by regional distribution show that Latin America and the

Caribbean region have received 36 percent of Bank loans, Asia has received 32 percent, Europe, Middle East, and North Africa have received 22 percent, and Africa has received only 10 percent (*The World Bank: A Financial Summary*, p. 5). Its commitments in FY1990 were $20.7 billion, compared with $21.4 billion in FY1989. Actual loan disbursements to LDCs in FY1990 amounted to $13.9 billion.

The International Finance Corporation (IFC)

Since IFC is the subject of this study, suffice it to say at this point that it is the only fully global financial institution which gives economic assistance to the private sector without the requirement of a government guarantee. It was established in 1956 and is part of the World Bank Group. The President of IFC is also President of the Bank. The IFC is managed by an Executive Vice-President. As of the end of FY1990 (June 30), IFC had committed funds totaling $14.4 billion to more than 1,000 projects in more than 90 countries, as well as a number of regional investments in Africa, Asia, and Latin America, and global investments in five other projects. Such investment on the part of IFC is catalytic in nature and, thus, has resulted in projects whose total book value is $43.1 billion. The market value of these operations would be much greater.

The International Development Association (IDA)

IDA was formed as part of the World Bank Group in 1960 as a means of making development loans with soft terms to LDCs (Weaver, 1965). In fact, IDA makes very soft loans. Its loans carry no interest and are for a period of 50 years. No principal payments are due for the first 10 years and the loan is then paid off at the rate of 2.5 percent annually for the next 40 years. An administrative service fee of 0.75 percent on the unpaid balance is charged annually. Recipients of loans must be members of the Bank and the loans—for social overhead capital projects with the same high financial and technical standards as World Bank-financed projects—must be government-guaranteed. To be eligible for an IDA loan, the member country must be a low-income country. At present, more than 50 such countries, with per capita incomes of less than

$970, are eligible to receive IDA funds and these countries have a combined population of 2.5 billion ("Donors Agree to Provide," January 8, 1990). In reality, the cutoff income is $580 per capita because of the large demand for IDA funds. IDA presently has commitment authority of $251.5 billion and 138 members (*World Bank and IDA Annual Report*, 1990, pp. 13, 204).

IDA was established with original capital of $1 billion subscribed by member nations. Because of its payment terms, its capital has had to be replenished nine times ("Donors Agree . . . ," p. 8). Each time, IDA has had to appeal to member nations to subscribe more capital. Thus, IDA remains the most controversial of the World Bank Group institutions because of its terms and frequent need for refinancing. The ninth replenishment calls for 32 nations to provide $15.5 billion over the next three years ("Donors Agree . . . ," p. 8). However, it has made $52.7 billion in cumulative commitments to the lowest-income countries (*World Bank Annual Report*, 1989, p. 11). These are nations whose economic development would be highly restricted without funds with terms such as those offered by IDA.

REGIONAL DEVELOPMENT BANKS

Other international financial agencies have been established to make investments in LDCs, but do not operate globally. These agencies may have global membership, but their assistance is restricted to a regional geographic area. The major examples of such institutions are the Inter-American Development Bank (IADB), the African Development Bank (AfDB), the Asian Development Bank (ADB), the Islamic Development Bank (IDB), the agencies of the Organization for Economic Cooperation and Development such as the Development Advisory Committee (DAC) and the Technical Assistance Committee (TAC), the European Investment Bank, other Arab institutions such as the Arab Fund for Economic and Social Development (AFESD), and private groups such as ADELA and PICA. These will be discussed in the following sections.

The Inter-American Development Bank (IADB)

The IADB was established in 1959 by agreement concluded by a committee of the Organization of American States (OAS) and became operational along with the Alianza por Progreso program of the President John Kennedy administration ("Inter-American Development Banking Lending Soars," April 16, 1990; Inter-American Development Bank, *Annual Report 1989*). This program stemmed from a number of incidents, including hostility toward Vice President Richard Nixon during a 1958 Latin America trip, Castro's takeover in Cuba, and the formation in 1960 of the Latin American Free Trade Area (LAFTA) and the Central American Common Market (CACM). The initial subscribed capital of IADB was $1 billion, 55 percent from Latin American nations (De Witt, 1977, pp. 3-5). Its head office is located in Washington, D.C.

The IADB finances projects in Latin American and Caribbean countries. Its major objective is to promote the economic development of its regional develor member countries by encouraging the establishment, expansion, and modernization of private enterprises. It also finances public enterprise (Business International, November 1987, p. 13).

The IADB's main functions are as follows (Inter-American Development Bank, 1985, p. 1):

1. to promote the investment of public and private capital in Latin America for development purposes;
2. to use its own capital, as well as funds raised in financial markets and other available resources, for financing high-priority economic and social projects in the region;
3. to encourage private investment in projects, enterprises and activities contributing to economic development and to supplement private investment when private capital is not available on reasonable terms and conditions;
4. to cooperate with the member countries in orienting their development policies toward a better use of their resources, while fostering greater complementarity of their economies and growth of their foreign trade;
5. to provide technical cooperation for the preparation, financing

and execution of development plans and projects, including the study of priorities and formulation of specific project proposals.

The IADB is mandated to assist private enterprise by the *Agreement Establishing the Bank* (Inter-American Development Bank, 1985, p. 4). It does so by making loans to local private firms for development projects and to local credit institutions to assist them in helping to finance industrial and agricultural credit programs. The IADB is also able to subscribe to shares and to participate in capital issues of Latin American businesses. It also indirectly supports private enterprise by lending to projects which expand or upgrade the region's energy, irrigation, transportation, communications, and marketing systems. It also has promoted the establishment of an Inter-American Investment Corporation which supplements the IADB's activities in support of the private sector in Latin America.

Its cumulative total of lending approvals at year-end 1989 amounted to $41.6 billion for 1,801 loans. Total value of these projects is estimated to be $122 billion. Its loans go mostly to low-income areas of its regional focus and 28 percent have been directed to the energy sector, 22 percent to the agriculture and fisheries sector, and 13 percent to both transportation/communications and industry/mining, respectively ("Inter-American Development Bank Lending," p. 117).

In 1989, IADB lending operations increased dramatically. IADB loans increased to $2.6 billion from $1.7 billion in 1988. Such loans financed 29 projects in 15 Latin American and Caribbean countries. The total cost of these projects was $6.1 billion, the remainder being provided by the borrowing countries.

The African Development Bank (AfDB)

The African Development Bank Group includes the African Development Bank, the African Development Fund—a soft-loan subsidiary, and the Nigerian Trust Fund. The AfDB was established in 1964 by the Organization of African Unity (OAU) and is headquartered in Abidjan, Ivory Coast. It had total capital of $5.82 billion at year-end 1985 (African Development Bank, *Annual Report 1985,*

p. 9) and has 75 members, 50 of which are regional or African nations and 25 of which are non-regional nations (African Development Bank, *Annual Report 1985*, p. 70). The largest share of the AfDB Group's approvals has gone to the agricultural sector (31 percent), followed by public utilities (23 percent), transport (19 percent), and industry (14 percent) ("African Development Bank Report," June 26, 1989; African Development Bank, *Twenty-Five Years of Development Financing*, 1989). AfDB has industrialized members but restricts its loans and grants to the regional area of Africa.

In recent years, the AfDB policies have emphasized commitments which have been concerned with environmental considerations toward such areas as soil resources for agricultural production, water resources for household and irrigation purposes, plant resources for food, fodder, energy, soil protection, and climate. Lending policies have also begun to focus on equity participation in national and regional development banks and other financial institutions and on telecommunications (African Development Bank, 1985, p. 42).

The AfDB approved $2.9 billion in loans and grants in 1989, an increase of 31.2 percent over approvals in 1988. Policy-based loans accounted for 20.2 percent of Group loans and grants, including lending for structural adjustment. Projects accounted for 76.6 percent of Group lending. In 1989, lending was fairly evenly divided among the various sectors with about 1/3 going to transportation and agriculture and some 20 percent going to multisector and public utilities, respectively ("African Development Bank Lending," July 30, 1990).

The Asian Development Bank (ADB)

The Asian Development Bank (ADB) ("Asia-Pacific Region's Growth," May 15, 1989; Asian Development Bank, *Annual Report*, 1989) began operations in 1966 and is headquartered in Manila, The Philippines, and its major purpose is to foster economic growth and contribute to the acceleration of economic development of the developing member countries of Asia, collectively and individually (*Encyclopedia of Banking and Finance*, 1983, p. 56).

It had total capital of $16.2 billion and 47 members comprised of 32 Asian and 15 non-Asian nations at year-end 1985 (Asian Development Bank, *Annual Report 1985*). However, it restricts its financial assistance to LDCs in the Asian region. Cumulative lending by ADB at year-end 1988 was $25 billion for 846 projects in 29 developing member nations. Total ADB lending in 1988 was $3.1 billion, compared with $2.4 billion in 1987. The five largest ADB borrowers were People's Republic of China, India, Indonesia, Pakistan, and the Philippines. The largest share of ADB loans in 1988 went to the non-fuel minerals sector (26 percent), with 21 percent directed to the agricultural and agro-industry sector, 20 percent to transportation and communications, 18 percent to energy, and 14 percent to social infrastructure. On a cumulative basis, 30 percent of ADB lending has been to the agricultural and agro-industry sector. In early 1988, ADB established the Japan Special Fund with which Japanese funds are used to cofinance or finance technical assistance projects and equity investments.

The ADB's principal functions have been to: (1) make loans and equity investments for the economic and social advancement of developing member countries; (2) provide technical assistance for the preparation and execution of development projects and programs and advisory services; (3) promote investment of private and public capital for development purposes; (4) respond to requests for assistance in coordinating development policies and plans of member countries. The ADB assists private enterprise specifically by guaranteeing or making direct loans to private ventures in Asian/Pacific countries, by helping to develop local capital markets, and by underwriting securities issued by private enterprises. Its investment criteria and procedures are so strict that each project takes about one year for approval. Every project goes through a post-evaluation process after conclusion of the investment by ADB.

The Islamic Development Bank (IDB)

The IDB is an Arab institution with 43 Arab member countries and was originally capitalized with $2.4 billion. Saudia Arabia is the largest contributor and, along with Libya, United Arab Emirates, and Kuwait — a nation invaded and taken over by Iraq at the time of this writing — contributes the bulk, 65 percent, of the IDB's funds. The institution operates according to Islamic lending principles, especially with regard to usury and does not charge interest on its loans. It participates in the income of each investment and makes a service charge. It recycles oil revenues into investments, primarily in the Arab world. In 1986, the IDB allocated $724.85 million for economic assistance (Business International, November 1987, pp. 25-28; Kuhn, 1982).

The Arab Fund for Economic and Social Development

The oldest multilateral Arab world development institution is the Arab Fund for Economic and Social Development (AFESD), having been established in 1968. AFESD has $1.4 billion in capital, its membership is restricted to Arab nations, and it invests only in Arab countries. AFESD actively searches for projects and assumes responsibility for project implementation by conducting feasibility studies, contracting, controlling quality, and supervising the work schedule of its projects.

The European Investment Bank

The European Investment Bank (EIB) was established by the European Community (EC) in 1958 (Business International, April 1987, pp. 26-27). It offers funds for certain public and private projects in the poor areas of EC nations as well as in other nations associated with the EC, primarily former African colonies. Two-thirds of EIB lending is made to designated development regions in the EC, specifically Ireland, Italy's Mezzogiorno, and Northern Ireland. Another 15 percent of EIB lending is made to non-EC countries with which the EC has a signed association or cooperative agreement, e.g., African, Caribbean, and Pacific countries.

The EIB has adopted an unofficial minimum size of its loans. This ranges from ECU2 million to ECU80 million, although some projects have received twice as much. Most EIB loans range from ECU2-16 million and cover only a portion of the cost of the investment projects. Terms of these loans are usually 7-12 years, or up to 20 years for infrastructure projects. In 1986, the EIB provided ECU7.07 billion in loan approvals, up from ECU6.78 billion in

1985. The cost of total projects assisted by the EIB in 1986 amounted to ECU22.8 billion. Private companies may obtain loans directly or via intermediary local banks or financing institutions. The EIB finances loans by borrowing on world capital markets. The interest rates charged by the agency are close to the average rates for current borrowing costs in regular commercial markets. Its credits are expressed in the borrower's national currency. However, they may be repaid in any of the EC member states' currencies.

The Organization for Economic Cooperation and Development

The OECD is an organization comprised of Western European nations, Canada, United States, and Japan. It concentrates on research and cooperative ventures which will encourage economic development. Two agencies were established to furnish economic assistance to LDCs. These are the Development Advisory Committee (DAC) and the Technical Advisory Committee (TAC).

The European Bank for Reconstruction and Development (EBRD)

The discussion of regional development banks would not be complete without mentioning the European Bank for Reconstruction and Development (EBRD). The Agreement which established the EBRD was concluded in May, 1990, and created a new financial institution whose mission is the development of Central and Eastern Europe. This Agreement was signed by representatives of 40 nations, the European Investment Bank, and the European Community.

The creation of this institution is unique for a number of reasons. It is the first multilateral development bank which will have both the United States and the former U.S.S.R. as actual members. It is the first international financial institution not limited to European countries and gives an absolute majority to Western European members, insuring that the majority will remain in their hands. And it will limit its assistance to a small number of countries and will condition explicitly its assistance on the application of specified political principles.

PRIVATE DEVELOPMENT INSTITUTIONS

Private Regional Groups

Two private regional development groups should be mentioned in this discussion for their work in private sector development in certain regional developing areas. These are the Atlantic Development Group for Latin America (ADELA) and the Private Investment Company of Asia (PICA).

ADELA

ADELA was formed in 1964 and has some 230 shareholder banks or companies. Each shareholder, primarily international commercial banks, subscribes to $500,000 in equity in the institution. Primarily, it is a joint venture in which all shareholders have equal shares. ADELA is headquartered in Luxembourg and is an international private investment company dedicated to socioeconomic development in Latin America. Its objective is to strengthen private enterprise by providing capital and entrepreneurial and technical services.

PICA

PICA is also a private investment company but its emphasis is development of private enterprise in the Asian developing countries. It is financed in the same manner as ADELA and its shareholders also contribute $500,000 each in the same manner as the shareholders of ADELA.

NATIONAL DEVELOPMENT BANKS

Most LDCs have development banks which are predominantly controlled or wholly-owned by the governments of these countries. Some of these place development financing emphasis on general projects while some focus on specific industrial sectors. One key criticism of development banks is that many of them perpetuate economic stagnation by financing statist rather than free-market solutions. In other words, many of them build up the public sector at the expense of the private sector. This criticism is the primary reason why so many development finance companies (DFCs), predominantly privately-owned development finance institutions, have been established in LDCs. The International Finance Corporation has supported the DFC concept and this relationship will be discussed in detail in Chapter 5.

CONCLUSIONS

The overview presented in this chapter has included a thumbnail sketch of the major international development finance institutions which have been created during the past 50 years. One institution has been omitted since it is the focus of attention of this book. This is the International Finance Corporation (IFC), an affiliate of the World Bank Group. Some of the agencies analyzed in this chapter make some of their investments in private-enterprise projects. Most of the loans or grants by these institutions are directed at social infrastructure projects. Most require a host government relationship of some kind with the project financed. IFC is the only development financial institution with global membership which makes investments *only* in private enterprise projects *without government guarantee.* This makes IFC a very unique institution, not to mention one of the most interesting and exciting of the development agencies.

Chapter 2

The International Finance Corporation: Origin and Background

INTRODUCTION

The focus of this chapter is on the evolution and background of the international financial institution that is the subject of this book — the International Finance Corporation (IFC). Few students of development finance will deny that IFC is the most exciting of the agencies devoted to financial assistance of LDCs. The literature affirms this belief and the employees of the organization, when interviewed by the author, confirm this fact. Nearly all such interviewees certainly had the educational background and professional expertise to command much higher paying employment in some area of commercial or investment banking. However, they have chosen to remain with IFC and to work longer hours than their average counterparts in the private sector for lower average salaries. Thus, the coverage of the IFC operations may be colored with such enthusiasm as demonstrated by IFC officials.

During the Bretton Woods Conference at which the IMF and the World Bank were established, delegates dreamed of another and quite unique international financial institution — a global agency which would be devoted to the development of private enterprise in the lower income countries. It is somewhat amazing that an institution as exciting as the IFC was fostered from the establishment of such a conservative development finance institution as the World Bank. Raymond F. Mikesell described the evolution of the World Bank from its very conservative beginnings in his essay, "The Emergence of the World Bank as a Development Institution" (Acheson et al., 1972, pp. 70-71). For example, Bretton Woods delegates adopted the original principal for the World Bank of limited paid-in subscriptions and severe limitations on their use. Most of the Bank's funds were to be obtained in the private capital markets so the Bank adopted very conservative lending policies in its early years. By 1950, the Bank had made loans to LDCs amounting to only $350 million, whereas the U.S. Export-Import Bank made $800 million in loans to LDCs. Once the role of U.S. foreign aid declined, the Bank became relatively more important.

Shortly after the World Bank began operations, the debate among development economists became concerned with the lack of a development institution whose role would be to promote and foster private enterprise in LDCs. Those who advocated such an institution believed that it would be futile for the World Bank to develop the social infrastructure of LDCs if these countries lacked a private sector which could plug into the electric utilities, transportation, communications, and other such facilities developed with World Bank funds.

The Bank represented a large step forward in channeling development finance to LDCs but a gap in financing private enterprise became recognized in the late 1940s. Private investment was the catalyst which added dynamism to economic development everywhere except in nations where such investment was completely state-controlled. The private sector in LDCs needed capital and the World Bank was unable to furnish it.

The private sector in LDCs nearly always derives benefits from foreign direct investment (FDI). Among the several benefits provided host countries may be found the following:

1. additional equity capital;
2. transfer of patented technologies;
3. access to scarce managerial skills;
4. creation of new jobs;
5. access to overseas market networks and marketing expertise;
6. reduced flight of domestic capital abroad;
7. more rigorous appraisal of investment proposals;
8. diffusion of improved techniques;
9. long-term commitment;
10. action as a catalyst for associated lending for specific projects (Marsden, 1989, pp. 1-2).

An agency, thus, which could encourage FDI to flow into LDCs was deemed necessary so that these benefits of FDI could be made manifest. However, two limitations in the charter which established the World Bank made direct participation in the private sector impossible. First, the Bank was precluded from lending to projects which were not government guaranteed. Second, the Bank was not allowed to invest in equity capital of proposed projects. It was at this point that discussions, formal and informal, began among officials of the United Nations, World Bank, and the U. S. Government about institutional arrangements which could fill this gap.

THE PROPOSAL

Much of the motivation for the establishment of an international financial institution devoted to development of private enterprise in LDCs was fostered by the U.S. Government. President Harry S. Truman formulated American foreign policy toward economic development with his Point Four program announced during his inaugural address of January 20, 1949, which "placed the policy of the United States on a plane of high principle" (Matecki, 1957, pp. 49-51). In the United Nations, a Subcommission on Economic Development was instructed by the United Nations Economic and Social Council to study general methods for financing economic development (United Nations Economic and Social Council, May 3, 1947). In 1949, this group proposed UNEDA—United Nations Economic Development Administration—to finance low-yield projects which were not self-liquidating, an agency which would be financed with contributions from member countries.

The IFC concept was assisted in 1950 by two events. First, the UNEDA proposal failed to be endorsed by the Subcommission on Economic Development. Second, President Truman commissioned a report—the Gray Report—which set forth proposals for U.S. economic aid including an appropriation of $500 million for basic assistance. Truman asked the U.S. International Development Advisory Board (DAB) to consider the Gray Report and to formulate a strategy for using U.S. resources. The DAB was chaired by the late Nelson Rockefeller, later to become Governor of New York and Vice-President of the United States.

The DAB issued its report entitled *Partners in Progress*, (International Development Advisory Board, 1951) popularly referred to as the "Rockefeller Report." This report was drafted during the national emergency declared because of the Korean War and emphasized international economic development as a major U.S. defense policy interest. It endorsed the Gray Report's proposals of large expenditures for economic assistance and its "belief in the prime importance of private capital" (Matecki, 1956, p. 263).

Several steps which would encourage private investment in LDCs were proposed in the Rockefeller Report. These included tax incentives, bilateral tax and commercial treaties, and underwriting of transfer risks on foreign dollar obligations. The report recommended the establishment of an international financial institution authorized to make loans in local and foreign currencies to private enterprise without government guarantee and to make nonvoting equity investments in such enterprises in participation with local private investors. The name of this institution would be the International Finance Corporation. This was the first reference to IFC using this title. The organization's authorized capital was recommended to be $400 million with a U.S. contribution as high as $150 million. It was proposed that the management of IFC would be carried out by the World Bank and that the United States should take the initiative in developing such an institution.

Later in 1951, the United Nations Economic, Employment and Development Commission recommended to the Economic and Social Council (ECOSOC) that this proposal be considered and in August 1951, the Council debated the issue and adopted a resolution which requested the World Bank to determine the contribution of an International Finance Corporation. In April, 1952, the World Bank responded to the ECOSOC request with a "Report on the Proposal for an International Finance Corporation" which discussed the need for such an institution and its possible role and potential. Rockefeller Report viewpoints were borrowed by the World Bank.

U.S. Government Approval

Since the United States would play a prime role in the establishment of the IFC, the proposal needed full approval from the U.S. Government. At first, the United States opposed the IFC through negative recommendations by the U.S. Treasury Department, the

Federal Reserve Board, and the U.S. Export-Import Bank, particularly after the Eisenhower Administration took office in 1953. These agencies were opposed to the practice by an inter-governmental institution of equity ownership in private firms. American economic standards—from a conservative basis—were in opposition to activities involving business-government partnerships. Second, some believed that an IFC might jeopardize World Bank and U.S. Export-Import Bank lending operations. Third, the U.S. Treasury Department was opposed to the effects of the proposed $150 million contribution on the Eisenhower Administration's budget-balancing policies. Other U.S. Government agencies offered mixed reactions to the IFC idea. The State Department offered lukewarm and limited support. The Securities and Exchange Commission gave the concept complete support.

Differences of opinion also developed within the U.S. business community. For example, the National Foreign Trade Council expressed opposition to the IFC proposal because its members believed that international economic development should be done completely through private enterprise. Other business trade organizations did offer support during public hearings held later in 1955 on the Congressional bill to authorize U.S. support for IFC. These included the American Farm Bureau Federation, the American Bankers Association, and the United States Council of the International Chamber of Commerce (U.S. House of Representatives, July 20, 1955, p. 3; U.S. House of Representatives, July 11 and 14, 1955).

In May, 1953, the World Bank transmitted a report on the status of the IFC proposal to ECOSOC (United Nations Economic and Social Council, May 25, 1953). This report emphasized the following:

1. the United States was still at a stalemate;
2. most underdeveloped countries supported IFC;
3. a few industrialized nations supported IFC;
4. some industrialized nations were unable to contribute to an IFC at that time;
5. the World Bank had noted mixed opinions toward IFC from the business community.

The World Bank issued a second but similar report on June 3, 1954, that the status of the IFC proposal had not changed (United Nations Economic and Social Council, June 3, 1954).

SUNFED

During Summer 1954, another element entered the IFC proposal equation. United Nations members began discussions the focus of which was a new U.N. development finance agency, SUNFED — Special United Nations Fund for Economic Development. This agency, it was proposed, would finance investments in LDCs which were not self-liquidating and which were non-yielding. LDCs began to espouse both SUNFED and IFC.

The IFC idea had been kept alive by the World Bank but since the status of this proposed agency was, at that time, in limbo, support increased for the SUNFED idea. However, the U.S. Government opposed this proposal because the new agency would be controlled largely by LDCs and, thus, would be unable to maintain high performance standards in the distribution of its financial assistance. In addition, it was felt that no shortage existed of capital in relation of the capacity of developing countries to make effective use of it. And, the Eisenhower Administration and its conservative bent did not favor an institution which merely doled out its aid to LDCs (United Nations, 1953, p. 74).

The IFC concept, however, was considered preferable to LDCs and they increased pressure against the U. S. Government's opposition to it. On November 11, 1954, U.S. Treasury Secretary George Humphrey made a surprise declaration that the National Advisory Council would ask for Congressional approval of U.S. membership in an established International Finance Corporation.

Matecki hypothesizes that the IFC proposal may have demonstrated that a concept developed by an international institution as a policy measure can be adopted by a national government as part of that nation's policy (Matecki, 1956, 1957). A major reason for this hypothesis is that both the international institution, i.e., the World Bank in this case, and the nation which responded to the idea, i.e., the United States in this case, were dedicated to the same goal and the method by which it was attained. A further hypothesis formulated by Matecki was that the World Bank developed its own policy and was not subservient to the United States, although the latter was capable of exercising great influence on the idea—once philosophical obstacles were overcome. The World Bank's personnel—international civil servants—include many Americans. These Americans were able to carry out the policy of the World Bank with regard to its international objectives without subverting their U.S. citizenship.

It may also be true that another institution found and operated throughout Washington, D.C. played a major role in forcing the U.S. Government to accept the IFC proposal. This institution is the cocktail reception held in foreign embassies and at international and U.S. government agencies located there. The IFC idea was discussed informally during many of these diplomatic receptions and parties by many officials who had some influence over the proposal. The idea was, thus, kept alive not only in official reports, studies, and agencies but also in these informal discussions and "debates."

Finally, the support of the United States is vital in the establishment of any multilateral international agency. This was especially true of IFC. It may have been that the SUNFED idea was even more distasteful than was the IFC to the advisors surrounding President Eisenhower. SUNFED would have been a financial agency whose members would contribute funds to it and these funds would have been doled out to recipient LDCs. At least the IFC idea included the development of private enterprise in LDCs in a manner which would return income to IFC. Thus, the Eisenhower Administration, especially through the office of the Secretary of Treasury, George Humphrey—a very conservative official—may have caved in for these reasons and supported the IFC proposal.

ADOPTION OF THE PROPOSAL

With the support of the United States, England and Canada changed their positions and advocated support for IFC. On December 11, 1954, the U.N. General Assembly endorsed the IFC concept by a 52-0 vote, with five abstentions, and ordered the World Bank to establish this new organization (International Bank for Reconstruction and Development, May 1955, p. 6). The only abstaining members of the General Assembly were the Soviet Union, Poland, Czechoslovakia, Byelorussian S.S.R., and the Ukrainian S.S.R., nations which still are not members of IFC ("New Steps Toward Establishing," December 1955).

Formation of the IFC

Subsequent to the unanimous vote by the U.N. General Assembly, the World Bank transmitted articles of agreement for the International Finance Corporation to member governments for their deliberation and approval on April 11, 1955. Membership in the IFC was made open to governments which were members of the Bank. The articles of agreement established initial capital for the IFC to be $100 million. The United States was to be the largest shareholder, subscribing $35,168,000, with United Kingdom having the second largest position in the IFC with a subscription of $14,400,000. When at least 30 governments had subscribed at least $75 million of IFC's capital, the institution began to function ("A Step Closer to Fulfillment," June 1955).

The participation of the United States in the IFC was crucial to its establishment. On May 2, 1955, President Eisenhower sent a recommendation to the U.S. Congress that legislation be passed permitting membership of the United States in the IFC. Among his comments were the following:

> The entire free world needs capital to provide a sound basis for economic growth which will support rising standards of living and will fortify free social and political institutions. Action to that end by cooperating nations is essential.
>
> In its own enlightened self-interest, the United States is vitally concerned that capital should move into productive activities in free countries unable to finance development needs out of their own resources. (U.S. House, 1955, pp. 2-3)

Government funds cannot, and should not, be regarded as the basic sources of capital for international investment. The best means is investment by private individuals and enterprises. The major purpose of the new institution, consequently, will be to help channel private capital and experienced and competent private management into productive investment opportunities that would not otherwise be developed. Through the Corporation we can cooperate more effectively with other people for mutual prosperity and expanding international trade, thus contributing to the peace and solidarity of the free world.

During the Summer of 1955, hearings on the authorization of U.S. membership in the IFC began before a subcommittee of the Senate Committee on Banking and Currency for S. 1894 and before the House Committee on Banking and Currency for H.R. 6228. One of the early stumbling blocks with U.S. support of the IFC stemmed from the proposal that it could make capital stock investments. The original articles of agreement did not authorize the IFC to make such investments. However, it could make so-called venture capital investments but could not take capital stock in return. This seemed to be resolved in the explanatory memorandum on the proposed articles of agreement submitted during the hearings on S. 1894 permitting IFC to require a participation in the profits of the company financed with a right, exercisable by any purchaser of the investment from the IFC, to subscribe to, or to convert the investment into, capital shares. This procedure would be required in cases in which an investor would normally take an equity position (U.S. Senate, June 6-8, 1955, p. 15). During these same hearings, U.S. Secretary of the Treasury George Humphrey stated that when the IFC was first proposed as an institution which could make direct equity investments, the U.S. Treasury did not think the practice would be desirable or feasible for an international governmental corporation to invest in common stock and to take the management responsibility that stock ownership entailed. The plan outlined in the articles of agreement eliminating the equity investment and management feature was agreeable to the U.S. Treasury and, thus, the United States gave its full support to the IFC.

During subsequent Congressional hearings, officials of the U.S. Treasury Department, State Department, and Export-Import Bank all testified in support of the IFC. The U.S. Securities and Exchange Commission testified that proposed IFC financing activities did not violate any U.S. securities laws. Business support of the IFC was manifested in testimony by the U.S. Council of the International Chamber of Commerce, the Investment Bankers Association of America, the Washington Board of Trade, the American Farm Bureau Federation, and the American Bankers Association. Opposition to IFC was registered by very few business trade organizations. The only large groups to oppose the idea were the National Foreign Trade Council and the American Paper and Pulp Association. It was pointed out in Senate hearings that many members of the National Foreign Trade Council – a group opposed to the IFC – were also members of the U.S. Council of the International Chamber of Commerce which had supported it (Baker, 1968, p. 27).

Extremely conservative members of the Senate were represented by Senator Homer E. Capehart, Republican from Indiana, who questioned the feasibility of the IFC. These senators advocated the position that American financial institutions, e.g., the U.S. Export-Import Bank, could fulfill the role of the proposed IFC. Capehart's views were not very instrumental because President Eisenhower was authorized to accept membership in and subscribe to the capital of the IFC by Congress on August 11, 1955, as the first step to finalize membership and participation in the IFC by the United States (U.S. Congress, August 11, 1955).

The next step toward American acceptance of the IFC occurred on October 2, 1955, when President Eisenhower issued an executive decree which designated the IFC as a public international organization entitled to the benefits of the International Organizations Immunities Act of December 29, 1945 ("IFC Designated," 1956, p. 634). This law provides that certain privileges, exemptions, and immunities shall be extended to those public international organizations which have been designated by the President by appropriate executive order. These privileges extend to the officers, employees and representatives of member nations of such organizations.

Finally, on December 5, 1955, the United States delivered its instrument of acceptance to the World Bank. The United States became the third country to complete the acceptance procedure. Canada and Iceland were the first two nations to complete the membership process ("U.S. Completes Action," 1956, p. 54). The official date of birth of the IFC was July 24, 1956, the date when the 31st nation approved the IFC's articles of agreement, bringing total subscriptions to $78,366,000. Thus, membership had reached the minimum number of 30 and subscribed capital the minimum of $75 million and the Charter of the IFC entered into force. France and the Federal Republic of Germany were the 30th and 31st nations to join IFC. At that time, 20 other nations had expressed a desire to join the new organization ("Charter of New Finance Corporation," 1956, p. 23). The founding member governments and their initial subscriptions are shown in Table 2-1.

The World Bank announced on July 25, 1956, that the IFC was officially formed. The Bank's Board of Directors named Robert L. Garner to be the new organization's first president. The Board also adopted several enabling resolutions, among them one requesting the IFC's present members to make full payment for their shares of its capital stock, in gold or U.S. dollars, by August 23, 1956 ("International Finance Corporation Begins Operations," 1956, p. 248). Bank personnel, because of their experience, were placed in important positions at the IFC. The treasurer, secretary, director of administration, and director of information of the Bank were appointed to the same positions in the IFC.

The IFC's first chief executive officer was Robert L. Garner. In the first annual report of the IFC's operations, Mr. Garner announced that the agency had obtained 53 members. Major sectors supported by the IFC were the manufacturing, processing and mining fields. The first investments made by the IFC in its initial year of operations were a $2 million investment in Brazil for the manufacture of heavy electrical equipment, the equivalent of $600,000 in Mexico for the manufacture of industrial engineering products, the equivalent of $520,000 in Mexico for airplane engine overhaul, $2.2 million in Chile for copper mining, and $660,000 for the expansion of a lumber business in Australia, a country no longer eligible for support from the IFC ("International Finance Corporation Presents," 1957).

CONCLUSIONS

Cooperation and joint deliberations, formal and informal, among many groups of interested advocates produced a new international financial institution to assist in world economic development — the International Finance Corporation. The idea had originated in the

TABLE 2-1. Founding Members of the International Finance Corporation (July 24, 1956)

Country	Initial Subscription	Country	Initial Subscription
Australia	$ 2,215,000	Guatemala	$ 22,000
Bolivia	78,000	Haiti	22,000
Canada	3,600,000	Honduras	11,000
Ceylon	166,000	Iceland	11,000
Colombia	388,000	India	4,431,000
Costa Rica	22,000	Japan	2,769,000
Denmark	753,000	Jordan	33,000
Dominican Republic	22,000	Mexico	120,000
Ecuador	35,000	Nicaragua	9,000
Egypt	590,000	Norway	554,000
El Salvador	11,000	Pakistan	1,108,000
Ethiopia	33,000	Panama	2,000
Finland	421,000	Peru	194,000
France	5,815,000	Sweden	1,108,000
Germany	3,655,000	United Kingdom	14,400,000
		United States	35,168,000

Note: From "On the Economic Front" by Elba Kybal, 1956, September, *Americas*, 8, p. 14. Copyright 1956 by Americas. Adapted by permission.

World Bank because of a recognition that the Bank's charter limited its investment activities, especially in the area of financing private enterprise in underdeveloped countries without government guarantee and its concomitant government interference. Bank officials believed that a separate institution was necessary to eliminate such limitations.

Approval by the U.S. Government was mandatory for the survival of the IFC concept. Although American policies toward economic development were similar to World Bank policy, the U.S. Government, as a result of its conservative political philosophy, opposed the IFC from the beginning. The United States offered its support only when (1) a dole-type international financial institution, SUNFED, began to gain popularity among many U.N. members and (2) the World Bank dropped the equity investment proposal from the IFC methods of financing.

Some, e.g., Matecki, suggested that an international agency — the World Bank — may have persuaded U.S. Government officials to formulate foreign policy which included support of the IFC proposal. Such a possibility may have been facilitated by the easy access for close communications between World Bank, foreign government, and U.S. Government officials in Washington, D.C., formally through the U.S. Executive Branch and Congress, the World Bank, and embassies, and informally through the many cocktail receptions held in that city. Both the World Bank and the American Administration compromised their positions and this action led to American support. The Eisenhower Administration decided that the IFC would more closely represent the desires of the United States and, thus, with U.S. support, the IFC concept came to life after the ratification of 31 countries with $78.4 million of subscribed capital on July 24, 1956.

Chapter 3

Operations and Administration
of the International Finance Corporation

INTRODUCTION

The IFC entered its 35th year of operations at the time of this writing. At the inception of its operations, planned capital to be subscribed by member nations was $100 million. It officially began operations with 31 member nations and subscribed capital of $78.4 million. Its initial capitalization made it a fledgling development finance agency by today's standards. Today, the IFC is the world's largest multilateral organization which provides financial assistance by means of loans and equity investments to private enterprise in LDCs. It is affiliated with the World Bank and utilizes the Bank's public sector infrastructure development programs to support its investments in private sector projects. However, the IFC operates as a separate, legally independent agency with its own staff and funding.

The IFC has invested in projects in LDCs whose capital cost totals more than $50 billion. These projects have involved more than 2,000 companies and financial institutions in support of more than 1,000 businesses in more than 90 countries. In this chapter, an aggregative analysis of these projects will be presented. But first, the operations and administration of the IFC will be discussed, including its objectives, membership, administration, sources and uses of funds, and the underwriting, standbys, and sales of IFC investments.

IFC operations have also reaped benefits for the industrialized member countries as well. For example, Great Britain entered the 1980s controlling 11.4 percent of the IFC's votes. Government ana-

lysts in that country estimated that during the IFC's first 25 years of
operations, Great Britain gained $10 in export business for every $1
it had subscribed to IFC's capital. Similar comparisons could be
made for other industrialized IFC member countries, including the
United States ("The IFC's Small but Key Role," 1980, p. 50).

IFC's Purpose

IFC's general purpose is:

> to further economic development by encouraging the growth
> of productive private enterprise in member countries, particu-
> larly in the less developed areas, thus supplementing the activ-
> ities of the International Bank for Reconstruction and Devel-
> opment (World Bank) (International Finance Corporation,
> *Articles*, 1956, p. 3).

To implement this purpose, IFC's Articles of Agreement required IFC to:

1. in association with private investors, assist in financing the
   establishment, improvement, and expansion of productive private enterprise which would contribute to the development of
   its member countries by making investments, without guarantee of repayment by the member government concerned, in
   cases where sufficient private capital is not available on reasonable terms;
2. seek to bring together investment opportunities, domestic and
   foreign private capital, and experienced management; and
3. seek to stimulate, and to help create conditions conducive to
   the flow of private capital, domestic and foreign, into productive investment in member countries (International Finance
   Corporation, *Articles*, 1956, pp. 3-4).

When the IFC began operations, it performed several functions in
order to implement these objectives. In addition to the financing of
industrial projects, it has: (1) underwritten shares issued by companies; (2) encouraged financial institutions in capital exporting nations to participate in development projects by selling them investments from its own portfolio; (3) financed private development

finance companies, a type of development bank which is privately owned and whose capital is invested in local private enterprise; (4) appraised investment proposals submitted to the World Bank by industrial and mining companies; (5) advised the management of companies in which it has invested; and (6) assisted these companies in drafting market surveys (Baker, 1968, pp. 290-291). Only the IFC, of all the development agencies, clearly states in its mission that economic development sought by it is to be attained by private enterprise. As we shall see subsequently, the IFC is unique in that it not only invests in private enterprise projects in LDCs, it does so *without* government guarantee. In fact, it will not consider any project in which the least taint of government interference may be present.

In its first two decades of operations, the IFC has added several other services, designed to facilitate the implementation of its general purpose. These include syndications, privatization, development of securities exchanges and development finance companies. These activities will be discussed in Chapter 5. During the 1980s, other activities were initiated, such as the formation of country investment funds — closed-end investment companies whose portfolios include the securities of companies in a specific country, the Africa Project Development Facility, the Caribbean Project Development Facility, the Foreign Investment Advisory Service, Technology Transfer and Project Development, and others. A discussion of these relatively new services is found in Chapter 6.

MEMBERSHIP AND CAPITAL

Members of the IFC must first be members of the World Bank (Syz, 1974, p. 2). Of course, World Bank members, at least originally, had to be members of the IMF. Original capital authorized for the IFC amounted to $100 million in the form of 100,000 shares each having a par value of $1,000. Table 3-1 shows the present list of members with their subscribed capital. IFC subscriptions were allocated on the basis of World Bank subscriptions existing at the time of the creation of the IFC (Syz, 1974, p. 110).

Countries which were not charter members — those 31 members which had deposited instruments of ratification of IFC Articles of

TABLE 3-1. Present Members and Paid-in Capital Stock (thousands of US$)

Members	Paid-in Capital Stock	Members	Paid-in Capital Stock
Afghanistan	$ 111	Cameroon	$ 885
Angola	837	Canada	45,976
Antigua and Barbuda	13	Cape Verde	11
Argentina	19,205	Chile	4,552
Australia	26,751	China	8,122
Austria	9,943	Colombia	4,571
Bahamas, The	142	Congo, People's Republic of the	131
Bangladesh	4,552	Costa Rica	420
Barbados	182	Côte d'Ivoire	1,349
Belgium	27,446	Cyprus	1,209
Belize	50	Denmark	10,487
Benin	67	Djibouti	21
Bolivia	958	Dominica	22
Botswana	64	Dominican Republic	598
Brazil	19,885	Ecuador	1,479
Burkina Faso	432	Egypt, Arab Republic of	6,855
Burundi	100	El Salvador	11
Ethiopia	33	Italy	41,942
Fiji	108	Jamaica	2,157
Finland	8,872	Japan	79,794
France	68,400	Jordan	735
Gabon	931	Kenya	1,529

Gambia, The	35	Kiribati	7
Germany, Federal Republic of	72,861	Korea, Republic of	9,013
Ghana	2,242	Kuwait	4,533
Greece	3,051	Lebanon	50
Grenada	46	Lesotho	18
Guatemala	598	Liberia	83
Guinea-Bissau	18	Libya	55
Guyana	406	Luxembourg	1,209
Haiti	306	Madagascar	111
Honduras	184	Malawi	853
Hungary	5,216	Malaysia	7,668
Iceland	11	Maldives	9
Indonesia	16,131	Mali	116
Iran, Islamic Republic of	372	Mauritania	55
Iraq	147	Mauritius	736
Ireland	729	Mexico	10,306
Israel	1,076	Morocco	4,552
Mozambique	182	Sierra Leone	83
Myanmar	666	Singapore	177
Nepal	306	Solomon Islands	19
Netherlands	31,726	Somalia	83
New Zealand	1,583	South Africa	9,014
Nicaragua	184	Spain	13,175
Niger	131	Sri Lanka	3,594
Nigeria	10,900	Sudan	111
Norway	9,947	Swaziland	404

TABLE 3-1 (continued)

Members	Paid-in Capital Stock	Members	Paid-in Capital Stock
Oman	671	Sweden	13,539
Pakistan	8,626	Syrian Arab Republic	72
Panama	426	Tanzania	724
Papua New Guinea	490	Thailand	5,510
Paraguay	270	Togo	808
Peru	1,777	Tonga	13
Philippines	3,247	Trinidad and Tobago	1,818
Poland	4,090	Tunisia	1,795
Portugal	4,705	Turkey	5,985
Rwanda	306	Uganda	735
St. Lucia	37	United Arab Emirates	1,838
Saudi Arabia	1,444	United Kingdom	68,400
Sénégal	1,106	United States	231,429
Uruguay	1,797	Yemen Arab Republic	360
Vanuatu	55	Yugoslavia	4,169
Venezuela	15,593	Zaire	2,159
Vietnam	166	Zambia	1,286
Western Samoa	20	Zimbabwe	546
		Total	**$1,072,326**

Note. From <u>Annual Report 1990,</u> by IFC, 1990, Washington, D.C.: International Finance Corporation, p. 53.

Agreement before July 24, 1956, which are listed in Table 21, were given the privilege to become members subsequent to December 31, 1956. The IFC was authorized to increase its capital stock by as much as 10,000 shares by a majority vote of members in order to facilitate this privilege. By the time of the inaugural meeting of IFC's Board of Governors in September 1956, some 51 nations had joined IFC and had subscribed a total of $92 million in capital. Guyana, the 83rd nation to become a member of the IFC on January 4, 1967, brought subscribed capital to $99,929,000, almost the original planned capitalization of the IFC (*International Financial News Survey*, 1967, p. 7).

Capital Acquisition Amendment to Articles of Agreement

Since 1956, IFC's capital has grown tremendously. IFC presently has total capital of $5,444 million, including $3,580 million of borrowings and $1,072 million of paid-in capital (update with 1990 Annual Report [IFC, 1990, *Annual Report*, p. 5]). Much of this growth in capital has come from retained earnings from its operations and accumulated earnings at the end of FY1990 amounting to $792 million – more than six times the original subscribed capital of the IFC (update with 1990 Annual Report).

A large amount of this growth in the IFC's capital has been a result of changes in its method of sourcing funds and increases in its share capitalization. One change deals with two amendments to the IFC's Articles of Agreement, 1977 and 1983, increasing the share capitalization of the IFC. One change deals with an amendment to the IFC Articles of Agreement in 1965 permitting the IFC to borrow directly from the World Bank. Finally, the other change relates to a different operating policy adopted in the last few years which permits the IFC to borrow directly on the international capital markets – a change to be discussed in the next section – as well as a doubling of the IFC's authorized shares from 650,000 to 1.3 million.

The original IFC Articles of Agreement had authorized IFC to obtain funds in the international capital markets. However, since IFC's top management was also the top management of the World

Bank and since the World Bank made frequent issues of its very well received and highly rated international bonds on the global capital markets, Bank officials believed that IFC funding in these same capital markets might jeopardize the ability of the Bank to obtain funds in this manner. Thus, the IFC was not permitted to borrow by issuing debt obligations on the open market—until, as we shall see, the last few years.

In order to alleviate the earlier problem caused by Bank management's limitation on the IFC's borrowing power, one of two formal amendments to its Articles of Agreement was made in 1965. At the Annual Meeting of the IFC Board of Governors in Tokyo during September, 1964, the Board stated that an increase in the IFC's financial resources was necessary because of the increased investment activity projected for the coming years. Without this increase, the IFC's purpose, as spelled out in its Articles of Agreement, could not be implemented properly.

The Board recommended a change in the Articles of Agreement (IFC, 1956, Articles, IV (6) and III (6)(i)) to enable IFC to borrow funds directly from the World Bank. This change, essentially a charade, allowed the Bank to continue borrowing funds on the international capital markets without competition from its affiliate, the IFC. The recommendation permitted the IFC to borrow from the Bank an amount not to exceed four times the unimpaired subscribed capital and surplus of the IFC.

Member governments approved the change in 1965. Hearings were held on H.R. 8816 in the U.S. House of Representatives and on S. 1742 in the U.S. Senate. Both Houses passed these bills and President Johnson of the United States signed into law an act enabling the U.S. Governor of the IFC to approve the change. The Articles of Agreement were amended in late 1965, allowing IFC to borrow up to $400 million from the Bank at that time. Implementation of this change enabled IFC to increase its capital in 1966 to more than $500 million available for potential investment. This authorization gave the IFC more flexibility in its investment operations and enabled it to increase its investments, at that time, from $3-4 million per project to as much as $15-20 million. The IFC was able to further diversify its portfolio with this change.

1977 Capital Increase

In 1977, the IFC's Articles of Agreement were amended to increase its capital. The IFC had estimated that each project it financed created 2,000 jobs. Thus, it needed more capital to expand its successful operations. The 1977 change increased the IFC's capital from $110 million to $650 million (Hürni, 1981, p. 462).

1984 Capital Increase

In 1984, the IFC Articles were further amended to permit an increase in authorized shares from 650,000 to 1,300,000 (IFC, 1984, *Annual Report*, p. 4). Discussion had actually centered around a proposal to increase the IFC's shares to 1.4 million in 1983 ("IFC Plans Program Expansion," 1983, p. 6A).

1991 Capital Increase

A third capital share increase was proposed in FY1990 and was implemented during FY1991. This amendment to the IFC's Articles increases the number of shares to 2.3 million and subscribed capital to $2.3 billion, thus permitting the IFC to grow by 12 percent annually for the next seven years (Westlake, 1990, p. 39, and confirmed by an IFC official).

An agreement among IFC member nations was effected in mid-1991 which will result in an increase in IFC's subscribed capital from $1.3 billion to $2.3 billion. This increase in capital will permit increased lending by IFC to projects in LDCs to the extent that annual approvals will increase from $1.5 billion to $4 billion in the 1990s. Since every dollar of IFC loans now results in $6 of total investment, IFC projects on an annual basis should result in total combined investments of $24 billion ("World Bank Funds . . . ," 1991).

Recent Changes in IFC Capital Acquisition

The second major change with regard to sourcing funds began in FY1985 when the IFC began to raise funds directly in the international capital markets to supplement its borrowings from the World Bank. In the two years prior to this, the IFC had borrowed from the

World Bank $100 million in FY1984 and $45 million in FY1983, respectively. However, these borrowings were considered by the management of the IFC to be insufficient to meet the objectives of development finance forecast for the next several years.

Thus, the IFC made a private placement in the international capital market in FY1985 for its first direct borrowing. A total of $129.4 million was raised in this manner in FY1985 and market borrowings rose to $595 million in FY1989. During this five-year period, the IFC borrowed funds using several different financial instruments including small private placements, larger Euromarket debt issues, and public issues supported by credit ratings (IFC, 1989, *Annual Report*, p. 6). During FY1989, the IFC's first public issue of debt was given AAA and Aaa ratings by the two leading debt rating agencies in the United States (IFC, 1989, *Annual Report*, p. 2). According to the publication *Bondweek*, the IFC has expressed a desire to enter the U.S. credit markets, having received these debt ratings (*IFC News Digest*, 1990, p. 22). As such, it is seeking an exemption from securities registration laws, an exemption which must originate from the U.S. Congress through the Subcommittee of International Development of the House Committee on Banking. Since the Asian Development Bank and the Inter-American Development Bank already have an exemption from registration with the U.S. Securities and Exchange Commission, the IFC should have little trouble getting the exemption.

The AAA rating given IFC capital market issues demonstrates how the global financial markets have evaluated the IFC's performance of its operations. This rating should enable the IFC to become an established Euromarket borrower. In addition, the agency should gain even more independence from the World Bank (Wilson, 1989).

IFC's debt arrangements at present typically range in maturity from 5 to 10 years and, because of the top ratings, have been made at interest rates as low as 50 basis points under LIBOR. The IFC made public bond issues totaling $600 million FY1989 and $650 million in FY1990 (Wilson, 1989). Nearly half of the international capital market borrowing was obtained by the IFC's largest capital market debt issue to date, a $300 million Eurobond issue underwritten by a group of international investment banks lead-managed by

Deutsche Bank Capital Markets Ltd. In addition, the IFC borrowed $149 million from the World Bank. These borrowings from the Bank facilitated the IFC's asset/liability management program and, specifically, were used to fund fixed-rate assets denominated in various currencies (IFC, 1990, *Annual Report*, p. 17).

Sources of Funds

In addition to its paid-in subscribed capital, borrowings from the Bank, and debt issues on the international capital markets, IFC has other financial resources available. These include earnings from its investments as well as sales of some of its holdings to other financial institutions.

Earnings and Investment Sales

The IFC has earned interest and dividend income on its investments and has made net profits on the sale of its investments to other private investors. These funds have been set aside in a Reserve Against Losses. On June 30, 1990, this reserve account amounted to $319.3 million, and net income on investments during FY1990 amounted to $157 million (IFC, 1990, *Annual Report*, pp. 15-16). These funds are not ordinarily used for reinvestment but will be available to cover any losses which might occur.

Among the operational principles set forth in its Articles of Agreement is the following:

> the Corporation shall seek to revolve its funds by selling its investments to private investors whenever it can appropriately do so on satisfactory terms.

IFC has implemented this principle since it began operations in 1956 through 1987 by selling 283 loan and equity investments totaling $117 million (Owen, 1988). These investments have been sold to private investors and financial institutions in the United States, Europe, the Middle East, and Asia.

In addition to the sales of investments by IFC, the institution has closed out investments. These have been primarily loan investments in which the principal has been repaid. The funds received from these close-outs have been available for investment in new projects.

For a summary view of the IFC's profitability, see Table 3-2. An analysis of these data shows that during the two most recent fiscal years, the IFC earned money in a variety of ways, although dividends on its equity positions showed no growth. Profits from equity sales actually declined in FY1990 from the record year of FY1989. Most earnings were from active operations in loan interest and fees for services (+ $52.7 million FY1989 to FY1990) and passive operations in short-term cash and securities market investment (+ $40.7 million FY1989 to FY1990) ("IFC Goes Into New Markets," 1990, p. 61).

Uses of Funds

The IFC was founded for the primary purpose of providing financial assistance to private enterprise in LDCs. It does so by investing its funds in private enterprises without the guarantee of the host government, a necessary prerequisite to obtaining a loan from the World Bank or IDA, the other two World Bank Group international financial institutions. No investment will be made in a project

TABLE 3-2. Sources of Gross Income (millions of US$)

	FY1989	FY 1990
Interest and Financial Fees	244.4	297.1
Dividends and Profit Participations	30.8	30.7
Realized Gains on Equity Sales	118.6	90.7
Service Fees	25.3	16.8
From Deposits and Securities	101.5	142.2
Other (losses) Income	(2.1)	7.4
	518.5	584.9

Note. From <u>Annual Report 1990</u>, by IFC, 1990, Washington, D.C.: International Business Corporation, p. 16.

which is guaranteed by the host government, or in which the government has a significant investment, nor will an investment be made in any country where the government in power does not welcome such international financing for its privately-owned companies. Investments are possible only in IFC member countries and only those classified as LDCs. A member country of the IFC must be a member of the World Bank.

The IFC's Articles of Agreement dictate the principles which guide IFC's investment operations and may be summarized as follows:

1. the IFC shall not undertake any financing for which, in its opinion, sufficient private capital could be obtained on reasonable terms;
2. the IFC shall not finance an enterprise in the territories of any member if the member objects to such financing;
3. the IFC shall impose no conditions that the proceeds of any new financing by it shall be spent in the territories of any particular country;
4. the IFC shall not assume responsibility for managing any enterprise in which it has invested;
5. the IFC shall undertake its financing on terms and conditions which it considers appropriate, taking into account the requirements of the enterprise, the risks being undertaken by the IFC, and the terms and conditions normally obtained by private investors for similar financing;
6. the IFC shall seek to revolve its funds by selling its investments to private investors whenever it can appropriately do so on satisfactory terms; and
7. the IFC shall seek to maintain a reasonable diversification in its investments.

Two types of private capital are necessary for industrial growth: business or working capital, and investment or long-term capital. The IFC furnishes both types of capital and its investments act as the catalyst which encourages local and foreign investors to commit the majority of the funds for each project. In general, the IFC prefers to finance the final 20-25 percent of a project, only after the sponsors have exhausted domestic and foreign sources of investment funds. Furthermore, the agency prefers to finance this portion with relatively equal shares of equity and debt investments.

The lending strategy of the IFC is predicated on the fact that its more profitable investments should carry the costly efforts to meet private sector demands in smaller and low-income LDCs. Some 28 percent of the IFC's staff effort is designated for African investments, even though Africa will produce only 17 percent of short-term investment volume (World Bank, *Developing the Private Sector*, 1989, p. 33).

Equity Investment Amendment to Articles of Agreement

When IFC was established, it was prohibited from making investments in the capital stock of an enterprise. This prohibition was the principal reason why the IFC concept was accepted by the U.S. Government. However, its investments were not conventional fixed-interest debt obligations. Some features of both equity and debt were present in these early investments. The term used by the IFC was "venture capital." Some investments were long-term loans with the right to share in the profits of the company. Other loans carried the option to subscribe to share capital. Still other loans were convertible into capital shares when held by investors other than the IFC (IFC, 1960, *Annual Report*, pp. 12-13). The IFC could not exercise either stock option or conversion features of these loans but such loans could be sold to private investors who could exercise such options. These features had made the IFC's investments more marketable before 1961.

During the IFC's first 5 years of operations, its management recognized that the prohibition against equity investments severely hampered its potential in fulfilling its objectives. On February 24, 1961, the President of the IFC announced a desire to amend the Articles of Agreement to permit the institution's investment in share capital. This resolution was presented to the Board of Governors. In the United States, authorization for the American governor to the IFC to approve the resolution was considered in H.R. 6765 and S. 1648 in the House and Senate, respectively (U.S. House, 1961, p. 3).

U.S. Secretary of the Treasury Douglas Dillon, in testimony before the Subcommittee No. 1 of the House Committee on Banking and Currency, presented two important reasons for the necessity of the amendment. First, the use of convertible debentures by the IFC created problems because investors in foreign capital markets, especially those in LDCs, were not very familiar with such an investment instrument. Second, the use of long-term stock options created complex legal problems, especially in the negotiating stages (U.S. House, May 10, 1961, p. 3; Syz, 1974, p. 80). Thus, after short hearings, the United States voted authorization for the change. The amendment was approved by the IFC's Board of Governors in September, 1961.

The first investment by the IFC in the capital shares of a firm where the equity investment was part of the initial commitment was consummated in February, 1962, when the IFC also made its first investment in Spain, a nation then considered a LDC but now a member of the European Community. The equity investment was part of a $3 million commitment in Fabrica Española Magnetos, S.A. (FEMSA), a family business and leading Spanish manufacturer of automotive electrical equipment. The IFC purchased 30 million pesetas in common shares (then about $500,000) (IFC, 1961-1962, *Annual Report*, p. 13).

The amendment to permit the IFC to invest in the equity of its project firms changed the IFC's operations in two other areas. First, it has aided IFC investments in private development finance companies (DFCs). DFCs are privately-owned institutions in some LDCs which essentially perform locally in the same manner as does the IFC but on a much-reduced basis by investing in small-business enterprises which will enhance development in these countries. Second, the sale of investments from the IFC's portfolio also has been aided by this change. Before the change, the financial instruments held by the IFC representing a profit-sharing position in a given project were difficult to spin-off to other financial institutions in conformity with the IFC's objectives. These "ownership positions" did not have the liquidity that ordinary capital shares had and investment banks which might consider purchasing them from the IFC were not familiar with the mechanism.

IFC's Investment Terms

The terms of repayment of loans and the interest rates charged borrowers are matters of negotiation between the IFC and the enterprise but, generally, interest rates are charged at local market rates. The investment agreement between the IFC and the firm is kept strictly confidential. The IFC has no standard terms and negotiates terms which are appropriate for the company concerned as well as for economic and money market conditions in the host country. In FY1990, the IFC made its loans at market rates and maturities, which differ according to the requirements of each project, were from 5 to 13 years, including grace periods which ranged from 2 to 5 years. Interest rates were 62-294 basis points over 6-month LIBOR for variable-rate loans. The IFC also charged the usual front-end and commitment fees (IFC, 1990, *Annual Report*, p. 11). Its investments are generally mixed between straight debt and equity arrangements.

The early investments of the IFC were primarily in the industrial and mining sectors. In its first few years of operations, investments were made in, for example, steel companies in Argentina, Brazil, India, Mexico, and Venezuela; cement and related manufacturing companies in Greece, Iran, Peru, and Mexico; textile firms in Colombia, Ecuador, Ethiopia, Nigeria, and Pakistan; and fertilizer companies in Greece, Peru, and Tunisia. Its next stage of diversification included investments in a grain storage company in Colombia, a hotel in Kenya, and electric utility and telecommunications sectors in other countries (Mendels, 1966, p. 2). In addition, one of the large sectors of investment interest by the IFC in the early years of its operations concerned the DFCs mentioned above.

During its first decade of operations, IFC investments averaged $1-2 million each with generally no investment of less than $100,000. Its largest investment during that decade was about $6 million. The amendment to its Articles of Agreement permitting the IFC to borrow from the World Bank enabled the agency to consider investment commitments of $15-20 million and above.

Investment Criteria

The IFC has adopted a comprehensive set of criteria to use as a guide in deciding what projects will be approved for IFC funding (IFC, 1970, General Policies, pp. 3-5). For instance, the IFC finances only ventures that are profitable and which will benefit the economy of the host country. These are the major investment criteria but other criteria are also used by the IFC. It will not consider projects where private capital on reasonable terms is insufficient. Projects must have participation from local investors and the sponsor(s) must participate. The local government must not object to the project, although the IFC invests only without government guarantee. The concept and sponsorship of the venture must be sound, have management available which is capable and experienced, and a market for the venture's products or services. The financial plan must be realistic. The IFC investment must show prospects of a reasonable return. And finally, the IFC's presence must serve a constructive purpose.

Investment Limits and Project Size

The combined loan and equity investments by the IFC are, as a rule, limited to no more than 25 percent of the project's total cost. Minimum IFC investment is generally $4-6 million although it supports facilities which do invest smaller amounts. In higher-income LDCs, the IFC minimum investment may be $10 million. The IFC may invest for its own account as much as $100 million in a project although no upper limit is practiced.

Use of IFC Funds

The IFC may invest funds in a project which can be used for both foreign and local expenditures including fixed assets, permanent working capital, interest costs during construction, and pre-operating cost.

Equity Investments

The IFC will subscribe to as much as 35 percent of the share capital of a project but will remain a minority shareholder. After the investment has matured, the IFC will usually sell the equity portion of the investment. The IFC does not exercise management control and usually will not accept representation on the boards of directors of project companies unless a need arises. The IFC prefers to make both an equity and a loan investment but it will make only one or the other if necessary.

Loans

The IFC makes both fixed-rate and variable-rate loans at market interest rates. Maturities usually range from 5 to 15 years. The loans are denominated in U.S. dollars or in other major currencies although other arrangements may be implemented. Some loans have grace periods which may range from 2 to 5 years.

UNDERWRITING, STANDBYS, AND SALES OF INVESTMENTS BY THE IFC

New entrepreneurial ventures in LDCs are fraught with many problems. One of the major problems is the near nonexistence in most of these nations of a viable, adequate capital market. Equity funds are not sufficiently available for new business ventures because investors which do have capital are unwilling to incur the risks prevalent in such projects. Investment banking institutions generally have not been established in these areas.

One important function of an investment bank is the underwriting of securities issued by business enterprises. The IFC has performed this function in addition to its own investment operations. It generally attempts to mobilize present local financial sources. In order to develop this function, the IFC has invested in new projects or expansions of existing enterprises which were, at least, partially owned by local investors. The procedure adopted by the IFC includes the use of methods to encourage local participation in the investment proposals which the institution considers. One principal means available to the IFC which has been quite effective in encouraging such local investment has been its underwriting and standby operations.

The IFC's underwriting has greatly assisted investment in these projects because it places the authority, stamp of approval, guarantee, and resources of an international financial institution behind them. Underwriting of securities by the IFC not only encourages local investors to participate but also has facilitated the participation of European commercial banks such as Deutsche and Dresdner Banks of Germany, Banca Commerciale Italiana of Italy, Banque Nationale pour le Commerce et l'Industrie of Paris, and Standard Chartered Bank of London, as well as American financial institutions such as Kuhn, Loeb & Company, Morgan Guaranty Trust Company of New York, Lehman Brothers, and Chase Manhattan Bank (Baker, 1980).

A typical example of the benefits stemming from an IFC underwriting operation is found in the case of Fundidora Steel Company of Mexico, whose shares were underwritten a number of times by the IFC in the 1960s. This case is discussed in more detail in Chapter 7.

In addition to underwriting public offerings of securities, the IFC, as previously mentioned, sells investments from its portfolio to other private investors. Some of these securities are earmarked for purchase only by local investors and, in other cases, commercial and investment banks in the capital exporting countries and development finance companies in the LDCs participate by purchasing debt obligations or equities held by the IFC. The sale of IFC investments have not only enabled the institution to revolve its funds, but have also facilitated one of the IFC's objectives of stimulating the flow of private capital from developed to less developed nations.

One of the IFC's operating objectives is to divest itself of mature equity investments when the recipient corporation is determined to be financially sound. Such a sale of the equity investment by the IFC may be initiated as soon as the project company's shares are listed publicly on a local stock market. Thus, by selling these successful projects, the IFC can recycle its investment funds and expand the focus of the international financial community to development finance ("IFC Goes Into New Markets," 1990, p. 60).

Cumulative Operations

The cumulative operations of the IFC show that in each decade of its activities, growth has been relatively geometric. The number of projects approved by the IFC amounted to only 46 in 1961, increased to 210 by 1971, more than doubled to 588 in 1981, and more than doubled again by 1990 with 1,332 projects approved. The cumulative amount of the IFC's gross investments were only $51 million in 1961 but amounted to $14.4 billion by 1990. Investments held at the end of FY1990, loans made, equity investments, total amount invested, borrowings, paid-in capital, and net income all increased in dramatic fashion from 1961 to 1990. See Table 3-3 for a breakdown of cumulative operations of the IFC from 1961 to 1990.

SUMMARY AND CONCLUSIONS

IFC's operations are unique among development finance institutions in that it makes investments in private sector projects in LDCs which are members of the World Bank without government guarantee.

It is unique for three additional reasons (Hürni, 1981). The IFC: (1) provides equity or risk capital and assists in underwriting new shares, which it can resell; (2) emphasizes financial assistance for private industry in LDCs, having to write off only minimal losses; ("The IFC at Fifteen," 1971, p. 10) and (3) acts as a stimulant for other investors since its share of project investment averages only 20 percent or less.

The agency began with total subscribed capital of only $100 million. Total capital since 1956 has increased to $3,838 million as a result of: (1) the 1965 amendment to its Articles of Agreement permitting the IFC to borrow from the World Bank, (2) the 1977 and 1984 share capital amendments to the IFC Articles, and (3) the change in policy in FY1985 when the IFC began to borrow directly in the international capital markets — assisted greatly by the subsequent top rating given its bonds. The agency's accumulated earnings have risen to more than $600 million.

In addition, the IFC has profited from an improvement in its port-

TABLE 3-3. Cumulative Operations—International Finance Corporation (as of end of FY1990)

	1961	1971	1981	1990
Cumulative Approvals				
Number of Projects	46	210	588	1,332
Amount (gross $s)	51	581	4,063	14,409
Total project costs	231	3,047	18,493	43,083
Syndications	6	124	1,559	3,100
Investments Held End of FY				
Number of firms	37	128	314	495
Loans	35	244	1,374	4,068
Equity	--	106	273	684
Total Amount Invested	35	350	1,647	4,752
Resources and Income				
Borrowings (cumulative)	--	63	509	3,580
Paid-in capital	96	107	392	1,072
Accumulated earnings	11	49	159	792
Earnings				
Net Income	2.2	3.3	19.5	157.0

Note. From International Finance Corporations After 25 Years, by IFC, 1982, Washington, D.C.: IFC, and Annual Report 1990, by IFC 1990, Washington, D.C.: International Finance Corporation, p. 5.

folio in recent years. Its collection rate is above 90 percent and nonaccruing loans, as a portion of its portfolio, have been reduced from 19 percent in FY1986 to 12.5 percent in FY1988. This trend toward an improved portfolio was expected, at that time, to continue in the future (World Bank, 1989, *Developing the Private Sector*, p. 32).

IFC has used its funds to make direct loan and equity investments in a great variety of projects beginning at first in the industrial and mining sectors but branching out in more recent years into other sectors such as utilities, telecommunications, and tourism. Its first equity investment was consummated in 1962 when it invested in FEMSA, a Spanish automotive manufacturing company. This was the first IFC investment in Spain, now considered a developed economy and a member of the European Community.

Original investments by the IFC generally averaged $1-2 million and were made to companies in the industrial and mining sectors. Since its earliest years, the IFC has vastly diversified its investments and, because of the large growth in its capitalization, it now makes average investments of $15-20 million or more. In short, the IFC acts as a venture capital fund, a merchant bank, a financial and managerial consultant, an underwriter, and a dealmaker, in its operations.

Chapter 4

IFC's Project Evaluation Methodology and Portfolio Management and Control

INTRODUCTION

During the 35 years since the IFC was established, it has assisted some 1,000 private enterprises in more than 90 countries. In recent years, it has approved 90 to 100 projects annually in 40 countries with a total project cost of more than $4 billion. The organization has formulated a project application, evaluation, and approval procedure which has facilitated the achievement of its major objective of economic development of LDC member countries by investment in their private sectors.

The procedures used by the IFC to evaluate project proposals will be discussed in this chapter. The discussion will include the initiation of a project study, how the project evaluation is implemented, the criteria for project approval, the role of the IFC Board of Directors, management control of projects, portfolio management, and the accounting and financial reporting procedures.

INITIATION OF A PROJECT STUDY

Requests for IFC financial investment originate from many sources including entrepreneurs in LDCs who desire to establish a new business operation and expand an existing one, from companies which have already received IFC support or which want to enter a new field, from companies and financial institutions in industrialized countries planning to enter joint ventures with sponsors in LDCs, and from governments or government agencies promoting a particular business sector which they want private investors to develop (IFC, *What IFC Does*, 1989).

A local financial institution may notify the IFC that a promising investment should be investigated. An early example of this method of identifying a project is found in the case where the Pakistan Industrial Credit and Investment Corporation (PICIC) informed the IFC in 1965 of the expansion plans of Packages Limited, a successful packaging materials producer. PICIC is a development finance company (DFC), one of the predominantly privately-owned development banks which have been supported by the IFC and discussed in Chapter 5. The IFC's follow-up resulted in an operational investment in Packages of $3,151,662.

Industrial promotion by a financial institution itself is another method sometimes employed by the financial sector to assist new enterprises. The financial institution is limited by the high cost of promotion and the uncertainty of immediate return or of any return at all. In an address by Martin M. Rosen, former Executive Vice President of the IFC, he stated that "projects which simply walk in the front door and present themselves across the counter are usually rather shopworn and not particularly attractive" (Rosen, 1964). Although the IFC's investments today are much larger and financial technology is much more modern, Rosen's characterization of proposals presented to the IFC is still quite accurate.

Application Procedures

An investment proposal to be considered by the IFC may arise from any, or a combination, of these methods. Regardless of the way in which the IFC is informed about the potential project, an application for funds must be made. This application must contain preliminary information which would usually be requested by any other financial investment institution. No standard application form is used by the IFC but certain preliminary information is needed in order to properly evaluate the project. The information required by the IFC is as follows: (IFC, *How to Work With IFC*, n/a; IFC, *General Policies*; Baker, 1968, pp. 60-61).

1. Brief description of the project;

2. Sponsorship, management and technical assistance:
   a. history and business of sponsors, including financial information;
   b. proposed management arrangements and names and curricula vitae of managers;
   c. description of technical arrangements and other external assistance (management, production marketing, finance, etc.);

3. Market and sales:
   a. basic market orientation — local, national, regional, or export;
   b. projected production volumes, unit prices, sales objectives, and market share of proposed venture;
   c. potential users of products and distribution channels to be used;
   d. present sources of supply for products; future competition and possibility that the market may be satisfied by substitute products;
   e. tariff protection or import restrictions affecting products;
   f. critical factors that determine market potential;

4. Technical feasibility, manpower, and raw material resources:
   a. brief description of manufacturing process;
   b. comments on special technical complexities and need for know-how and special skills;
   c. possible suppliers of equipment;
   d. availability of manpower and of infrastructure facilities (transport and communications, power, water, etc.);
   e. breakdown of projected operating costs by major categories of expenditures;
   f. source, cost, and quality of raw material supply and relations with support industries;
   g. import restrictions on required raw materials;
   h. proposed plant location in relation to suppliers, markets, infrastructure and manpower;
   i. proposed plant size in comparison with other known plants;

5. Investment requirements, project financing, and returns;
   a. estimate of total project cost, broken down into land, construction, installed equipment, and working capital, indicating foreign exchange component;
   b. proposed financial structure of venture, indicating expected sources and terms of equity and debt financing;
   c. type of IFC financing — loan, equity, or both, and amount;
   d. projected financial statement, information on profitability, and return on investment;
   e. critical factors determining profitability;
6. Government support and regulations:
   a. project in context of government economic development and investment program;
   b. specific government incentives and support available to project;
   c. expected contribution of project to economic development;
   d. outline of government regulations on exchange controls and conditions of capital entry and repatriation;
7. Time scale envisaged for project preparation and completion.

PROJECT EVALUATION PROCEDURE

The project evaluation procedure involves information drawn from a number of sources and a variety of methodologies (Baker, 1968, pp. 59-62). This information may be submitted by a businessman, a group of businessmen, or the company officials themselves. The application is then given to an IFC investment officer. The IFC employs several investment officers who specialize in a geographical region. The investment officer in whose region the proposed project is located and his staff will be assigned to study the application and accompanying papers.

The investment officer and a committee of colleagues, after studying the application, will decide whether or not the IFC should accept the project and whether further study should be made. The investment officer and executive officers of the IFC may, and in most cases do, travel to the project site for personal observation and investigation. If, after this observation period, the investment officers have decided the investment should be made by the IFC, a report advising acceptance is made to the executive officers of the IFC. The final decision is made at this level before sending the project proposal to the IFC's Board of Directors for final approval. This process will be discussed subsequently.

In a few cases, the decision has been made in a more informal manner (Parmar, personal interview, January 18, 1967). The investment may be approved and papers signed and executed by investment officers while present at the project site. In 1966, for example, the IFC committed funds to the expansion of a cement plant in Malaysia. Mr. Judhvir Parmar, an IFC investment officer at the time and now Vice-President for Investment Operations, studied the application and visited the company. While there, Mr. Parmar was joined by a ranking IFC officer who had been in Asia investigating another proposal and the decision was made to commit the IFC at that time. The papers were signed and executed without their formal presentation to the IFC Board. In this case, the company had demonstrated a good past record, management was excellent, and rapid expansion of the supply of cement in Malaysia was needed. Thus a decision to commit IFC funds was feasible and was subsequently approved, after the fact, by IFC officials in Washington.

All negotiations before and after approval of an IFC investment are kept in the strictest confidence by the IFC. The dealings are financial in nature and the applicant is a private enterprise. Thus, the traditional nondisclosure of financial information is usually practiced in these matters, especially in the LDCs. If the investment proposal is approved by the IFC, the latter will issue a press release informing the public about the general details of the commitment.

CRITERIA FOR PROJECT APPROVAL

Before the IFC will approve a project application, the company or its sponsors must demonstrate to the IFC that the project is sound in three ways. The project must be economically, technically, and financially feasible. These are the major criteria, therefore, which the IFC uses in its study of the project according to the procedure discussed in the preceding section.

First, the project must be economically feasible. Accepted standards have been established in LDCs for the most economic minimum capacity for certain installations, such as, for example, the present minimum daily capacity for an ammonia plant or for a paper mill or for a cement plant. Before economies of scale are possible, these standard minimum capacities are necessary. Exceptions to these established norms have been put into practice. A steel mill with an annual capacity of 200,000 tons was built in Malaysia. Normally, steel mills should produce more than one million tons annually. However, the Malaysia plant was more profitable at a lower output because charcoal was used as a reducing agent. Charcoal actually makes a better reducing agent than does coke and it was then a normal by-product from waste rubber trees in Malaysia (Raj, personal interview, February 23, 1968).

Textile mills, at times, have been representative examples of the necessity for project economic feasibility. One more textile mill added to the hundreds in existence in India or Pakistan might not be practical nor would the establishment of a textile mill in some Central African nations be feasible because these economies might not be able to support even one mill. On the other hand, small entrepreneurial type start-ups such as those discussed earlier utilizing some of the new IFC services — APDF and AMSCo — might contribute to export earnings and use of local resources even though they are mere $100,000 projects.

The second feasibility concerns the technical characteristics of the project. The project must not only benefit the local economy but it must have available the necessary labor skills and raw materials. Managerial skills must either exist, or they must be imported or trained as was necessary in the early cases of Arewa Textiles Ltd. of Nigeria and NPK-Engrais S.A.T. of Tunisia. Japanese interests organized and trained personnel in the Arewa case and Swedish interests developed the NPK-Engrais management. Both projects received IFC assistance and are representative of many projects over the years in which local labor resources were inadequate but were furnished either from abroad or by training local personnel. Again relatively new IFC operations such as APDF, AMSCo, CPDF, FIAS, and the SPPF have added services such as management training, financial advice, and technical services to improve many proposals to the point whereby they are more marketable to foreign investors.

In addition to surveying managerial, labor, and raw material needs, the market for the project's product or service must be analyzed. A local market must exist for the output. The IFC demands a very rigorous market analysis because of lessons learned in its early experience where sales less than those forecast had resulted in lowered profits for companies in which the IFC had committed investment funds.

Third, the applicant seeking an IFC commitment must demonstrate that the project is financially feasible. The financial plan must be realistic in terms of available sources of funds. Provision for such contingencies as cost overruns has been a major consideration since the formative period of the IFC's operations (IFC, *Annual Report*, 1965-66, p. 9). Profitability forecasts and budgeting systems should be sound. During these feasibility studies, the IFC may suggest certain changes which result in improved applications.

Finally, after the project has been analyzed for its economic, technical, and financial feasibility, its sponsors must demonstrate to the IFC that sufficient funds on reasonable terms are unavailable from private sources. What constitutes a diligent search for funds required by the IFC differs from project to project. For example, if the project's sponsors have approached the major financial institutions which are strongest in the regional area and have been turned away, this may be all that is necessary. Such a representative institution might be Barclays of London in the case of a project located in Africa. Also, funds may be immediately available. A long period of time may elapse before the funds may be drawn, as in the case of a line of credit, and, thus, the entrepreneurial push in the project may lose momentum.

Local banks may require tying arrangements which would be too binding. Thus, in one, sponsors may seek out local and international funds from many sources whereas another set of sponsors may inquire at only one or two banks. The IFC may be satisfied that in both cases a diligent search was made.

In some cases, the IFC fills a gap where the project's total needs are not satisfied. In other cases, the IFC will initiate the investment process as a last resort to encourage other investors to act. This was true in the 1962 case of Fábrica Española Magnetos, S.A. (FEMSA), a Spanish manufacturer of automotive electrical equipment. No other funds would have been committed had the IFC not agreed to invest in the company. The IFC has generated such high esteem that the mere rumor that it is interested in the project may elicit international commercial banks as well as local financial institutions to become involved in the project.

Role of the IFC Board of Directors

At the present time, the IFC Board of Directors consists of 22 voting members and 22 alternate members. Most of the Board members have public sector experience. Such makeup is inconsistent with the IFC philosophy of focus on the private sector—focus without government guarantee for its investment commitments. However, it is a fact of life in the LDCs that most high level officials will be from the public sector and that much of enterprise in these countries is state-owned.

The Board members are temporary employees of the IFC and have had much of the IFC's corporate powers delegated to them by the Board of Governors. The Board of Directors is the final arbiter of the IFC's basic policies which flow from its articles of agreement and is composed of six members from leading IFC member countries—China, France, Federal Republic of Germany, Japan, Saudi Arabia, the United Kingdom, and the United States. The remaining members represent up to 15 countries and are elected by these countries. Board members live in Washington and meet frequently, once a week or more often. They must approve all projects. Any project involving an IFC investment of up to $10 million can be accelerated. If the Board wants to discuss it for any reason, the project will be placed before the Board. If they do not wish to discuss it, the project will not need Board approval for an IFC commitment (Hamilton, personal interview, August 22, 1990).

When the feasibility studies have been completed, the IFC has examined the application and has been satisfied that the project is sound in all these aspects, and the funding has been arranged, the

IFC's Board of Directors will then vote to commit funds as discussed previously. For every project approved for IFC investment, a number are rejected. It has been estimated that four or five projects are declined for every one accepted.

Most of the proposals are rejected for a variety of reasons. As many as 40 percent of them are not within the requirements of the policies and charter of the IFC. For example, some may be located in nonmember countries and some may be for straight loans or export financing — something a commercial, merchant, or development bank or an export-import bank might better finance. Some may be applications for funds in an amount below which the IFC's operating standards require. These proposals generally are rejected before the project is evaluated.

The remaining proposals are rejected after evaluation for a number of reasons. For example, some may be in a stage too early for consideration. Some may offer insufficient information, while others may not be approved because they are not feasible from an economic, technical, or financial standpoint, or their sponsors are inexperienced. The project's economic value to its country of locus may be unproven. Many of these projects may be enhanced later by consulting some of the new IFC operations designed to improve projects whose first proposal is rejected but which have merit if changes are made.

The IFC has made a diligent study of its evaluation procedure in order to satisfy the feasibility criteria heretofore discussed. It is still possible for problems to arise after the IFC has made a commitment as some of the case studies in subsequent chapters will demonstrate.

MANAGEMENT CONTROL OF PROJECT PORTFOLIO

Once a project is approved for an IFC commitment, it is included in the IFC portfolio until the investment is sold to a financial institution or, if in the form of a loan, matures. The IFC has adopted a set of procedures for managing and controlling its portfolio in order to insure that its investment operations result in the achievement of the agency's goals. The project itself will be supervised by an Investment Officer responsible for the area in which the project is located. The organization of this project control function within the IFC is shown in Figure 4-1. At the end of FY1990, the IFC reported that its portfolio was composed of loan and equity investments in 495 companies totaling $4,752 million in projects located in 79 countries and six regions. The portfolio consists of $4,068 million in loans and $684 million in equity investments (IFC, *Annual Report*, 1990, p. 13).

Organizational Structure

This organizational hierarchy shows that three major committees report directly to the IFC Board. The Investment Committee makes decisions with regard to project appraisal and investment decisions. Membership in this committee is comprised of top management of the IFC, is chaired by the Executive Vice-President — currently Sir William Ryrie — and meets twice weekly.

The Portfolio Committee is responsible for the review of the IFC's portfolio on a regular basis in addition to effective supervision and evaluation of the portfolio. This committee also measures feedback from the experience gained on investments that have been completed. Its membership is similar to that of the Investment Committee.

The Sales Committee is responsible for sales of investments from the IFC's portfolio. Decisions concerning when to take up rights issues or exercise options are also made by this committee. Its membership is essentially the same as both the Investment and Portfolio Committees.

Seven Investment Departments in which relevant investment officers are housed report directly to the three major committees. These departments are responsible for the supervision and administration of the IFC's portfolio.

Accounting and Financial Reporting

After the IFC has approved the project financing and committed the funds, certain accounting and financial reporting procedures must be followed by the recipient firm as long as the investment agreement is in force between the IFC and the enterprise (Baker, 1968, pp. 65-68; International Finance Corporation, *Accounting and Financial Reporting*, 1964, pp. 1-11; International Finance Corporation, "Part II: Control," n/a, pp. 4-7). Certain financial

FIGURE 4-1. IFC Project Control Function Organization (from "Part II: Control of IFC's Portfolio," unpublished working paper, Washington, DC: International Finance Corporation, date n/a, p. 2)

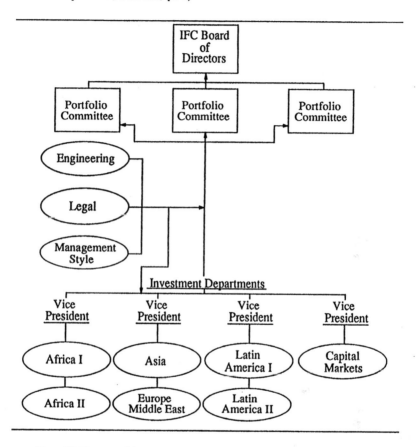

Note (1) These entities perform two roles: (a) they provide technical assistance to the investment departments, and (b) they monitor investment department actions to ensure that these are in agreement with IFC operating policies.

statements and information must be submitted by the company. Specific public accounting standards must be practiced in reporting financial information. Some of the financial statements must be audited by independent public accountants with specific prescribed qualifications, and these audits must be performed according to accepted standards and procedures. These requirements will be elaborated upon in the following sections.

Financial Statements

In addition to the basic financial statements and related company information, the IFC requires an annual balance sheet and income and surplus statements for each year during which the investment is in effect. These statements should show comparative figures for the previous year and should be audited. Quarterly balance sheets and surplus and income statements which show comparative figures for the corresponding period of the previous year are also required. However, an audit of the quarterly statements may not be required.

Income statements should show principal items separately. Such items as net sales, cost of goods sold, expenses — selling, administrative, and general, net operating profit, non-operating income and/or expenses, income taxes, and net income after taxes, should be included although the income statement is not limited to these items. Ratio statements are recommended. These are statements which show each item as a percentage of net sales.

Other information required pertains to statements which elaborate upon significant operating information and give details about non-recurring income and expenses or extraordinary items. Statements should be provided which show operating costs, income, and expenses where these items are relevant to the quantity of a material produced. This requirement pertains to extractive firms where depletion of mineral resources is important. A company with subsidiaries should either submit consolidated financial statements or data which specifically refer to the subsidiary's own statements in addition to those of the parent company.

Public Accounting Standards

The IFC requires that generally accepted accounting principles (GAAP) be recognized when financial statements of its clients are constructed. No attempt is made to prescribe specific principles to be followed but this responsibility is delegated by the IFC to the accounting profession. Accounting principles, however, do vary from country to country, and, therefore, the IFC requires that the accounting principles adhered to in a certain country have some support in practice as well as in theory and that they are used in preparing statements for shareowners, lenders, and other interested parties. Although no international GAAP exists globally, the world-wide accounting profession does attempt to promulgate international accounting standards by means of the International Accounting Standards Committee (IASC) and the International Federation of Accountants (IFAC) (Baker, 1990; Violet and Spring, 1983; Turner, January 1983).

Any differences between statements being presented and those conforming to statutory requirements must be disclosed to the IFC. For example, some countries allow assets to be understated and liabilities to be overstated as long as some system is used. In some countries, property may be carried on the books at replacement cost or some value other than historical cost less depreciation. Some countries allow certain gains and losses to be excluded from the income statement. Among these items may be profits on sale of property, bonuses paid to directors, and income taxes. Foreign exchange losses are handled differently in various countries. If the practices in reporting are generally accepted locally, they may be used in reporting to the IFC. However, full disclosure must be made of the effects such practices will have on financial and operating results. Finally, if conversion of one currency into another is necessary, the conversion method and rates utilized must be disclosed.

The independent public accountant or accounting firm handling the audit must be in good standing and entitled \ practice in its domicile. The accountant or his firm may not have 'ad any financial interest in the audited company nor should the .ccount have been connected in any official manner such as director or officer of the firm during the period covered by the report.

Auditing Standards and Procedures

The annual audit must be sufficient in depth and detail to allow the auditor to express an opinion that the financial statements present a fair and accurate picture of the operations of the company during the reporting period. The auditor must confirm accounts and notes receivable by contacting debtors of the subject company and must witness the physical inventory taking if the amounts of these assets are material. Certain forms are prescribed by the IFC for the auditor's report. A short form contains a discussion of the basic financial information and a long form contains a discussion in detail of the items in the short form. These forms contain the auditor's opinion about the financial condition of the company.

Organization

The organization of the accounting and reporting systems consists of two units, the Management Systems Unit (MSU) and the Portfolio Information and Records Unit (PIRU). The MSU is a small unit with responsibility over the monitoring of all accounting, auditing, and systems matters which concern investments held by the IFC. The accounting and auditing activities must be operated according to standards which are acceptable to the IFC and, therefore, must be handled according to the standards mentioned earlier. The MSU also acts as secretary to the Portfolio Committee, and in this capacity monitors the supervision system to insure that it operates according to objectives required by the IFC's management.

The PIRU has three functions. It: (1) controls all financial and other reporting from IFC projects by requiring project implementation progress reports, quarterly financial reports, annual audited financial statements and auditor management letters, project insurance information, notices and minutes of annual shareholders' meetings, and special reports tailored to particular projects; (2) inputs to a base computer program all audited financial statements in both local currency and U.S. dollars; and (3) carries out a review each six months of the IFC's portfolio for loss reserve purposes.

Reports

Four major reports should be highlighted. They are the annual project supervision report, the annual status report, the project completion report, and the evaluation reports. The annual project supervision report is prepared as an internal management report usually after a recent visit by an investment officer to a project. The annual status report is a brief report for the IFC's Board of Directors containing the important features of the IFC's relationship to the project, a brief description of the project and why the IFC is involved, important financial data for the past five years, and a brief description of the company's current condition and the IFC's proposed future strategy with regard to the investment. The project completion report, written for every project some 4 to 5 years after the IFC's initial investment, compares the projected performance at appraisal with the actual performance of project implementation, to review if the project is meeting the goals intended, to analyze any major variations, and to review the situation for lessons that can be applied to other IFC projects. In short, it is a post-audit report of the project. Evaluation reports are made periodically and cover the IFC's experience following investment in certain industries or regions.

Portfolio Management

The management of the portfolio held by the IFC is comprised of two major activities. These include the annual work program and the manner in which the investment administration is implemented. These activities will be discussed in the following sections.

Annual Work Program

Portfolio management at the IFC is carried out within the Investment Departments and accomplished in the Annual Work Program prepared by each Investment Department and updated every six months. This program covers every investment for which a department is responsible and involves investment officer visits to the projects and monitoring of the preparation of supervision reports or completion reports. An annual status report for each investment is prepared for the IFC Board. Engineers may participate with the investment officer in the project visit if necessary. As part of this program, the MSU prepares a monthly status report for the IFC's top management of the portfolio investments reviewed by the Portfolio Committee.

Investment Administration

Investment Departments are responsible for administering the investments within their own portfolios. This includes the insurance that dividends, interest, and principal repayments by the project companies have been made on time. Reports are made which concern any loan reschedulings, waivers of investment agreement covenants, equity sales, and the exercise of share options and rights issues. Notice is made of any overdue financial and other reports. PIRU bi-annually conducts an in-depth review of each investment in the IFC's portfolio and recommends any additions to or reductions from the IFC's loan loss reserves because of changes in the status of any investments.

Problems

The functions of portfolio management just discussed would normally be divided by several departments in large companies. Generally speaking, after approval of an investment by the IFC, no funds will be committed for 12-18 months. The project will then take, on average, some three years to become mature. The average life of a project is five years. By the time the project is completed, the investment officer who initiated the project will have moved to another department because of the relatively small staff at the IFC. The IFC's staff, thus, is insufficient to keep the same staff which initiated the project on that project until completion. Thus, the management of the IFC believes the necessity exists to combine several functions of portfolio management in the Investment Departments.

Operations in this area at the IFC are carried out in a manner which will alleviate some of these problems. For example, the Investment Department staffs are given regular changes of responsibility for individual projects. New, inexperienced staff members are given periodic interdepartmental transfers so that they receive adequate training by different project managers. The annual review of projects by the Portfolio Committee and the IFC's Board of Directors identifies project problems before they may become severe. And the annual review of selected areas of the supervision system by external and internal auditors and by the IFC's MSU also finds variations from initial objectives before severe problems may occur.

Chapter 5

IFC Programs: Early Years

INTRODUCTION

This chapter includes a discussion of program areas developed by the IFC during its first two decades of operations, which are related to its development finance objectives but which are not direct financial investment operations. These include development finance company (DFC) operations, the Capital Market Department — except for the following activities: country funds development, the Emerging Markets Data Base (EMDB), and the International Securities Group (ISG), activities developed during the 1980s. The chapter concludes with a discussion of the syndication/participation activities of the IFC.

THE IFC AND DEVELOPMENT FINANCE COMPANIES

Three major obstacles to efficient industrialization are found in most countries. First, investment capital is in short supply. Second, the mechanism for channeling existent small savings to feasible projects is absent. Third, entrepreneurs willing to accept risk are difficult to find, especially in LDCs. In order to overcome these obstacles, specialized financial intermediary institutions are needed for mobilizing capital resources and the technical know-how into the productive sector in the industrialization process.

Most countries have established such institutions commonly referred to as "development banks." In fact, nearly every nation has some one or more institutions that fit this description, even the United States where agencies such as the Farmers Home Administration, Federal Housing Agency (FHA), and other similar institutions are in operation. These institutions have the primary purposes of furnishing medium- and long-term capital funds for productive projects and the technical advice necessary to their success in a variety of general and specific economic sectors. Such financial institutions may be privately-owned, government-owned, or joint public-private ventures. They may invest in either the private or public area or in both. Specific development banks may finance only projects in a single business area, such as manufacturing, mining, agriculture, or forestry.

The private development finance company (DFC) is one such institution. DFCs are predominantly privately-owned — a small government participation may be necessary to establish such an institution because of political factors. These finance companies mobilize and channel private savings into productive investments. Such intermediaries may channel foreign and international investment into local projects which could otherwise obtain such capital on their own merits. The management and staffs of DFCs are usually highly experienced, especially in the areas of finance and engineering.

DFCs should possess or be able to obtain the following resources which facilitate their general economic development objectives (IFC, *Private Development Finance Companies*, 1964, p. 3):

1. a supply of long-term capital;
2. management experienced in modern investment techniques and with a knowledge of international and national economic conditions;
3. contacts with foreign private business and financial institutions and public international financial and technical assistance institutions.

Objectives of DFCs

A DFC must formulate its investment policies so as to fulfill a double role, that of being a development institution while at the same time, being a profit-making firm. Therefore, a working relationship between DFCs and international agencies such as those in the World Bank Group is essential to provide an additional source of funds, know-how, and technical services.

The DFC's operational risk incurred in performing its double role is lessened by diversifying its portfolio. This may be done by investing in a broad range of projects which have a wide geographical distribution and in which the investments are balanced between equity commitments and debt obligations (IFC, *Private Development Finance Companies*, 1964, p. 9). The DFC needs to match the duration of its resources with the duration of its investments. Thus, it may make loans with conversion or profit-sharing features (IFC, *Private Development Finance Companies*, 1964, p. 7). Most of these companies will not invest more than half the necessary funds in any project. In short, the DFC operates in a manner similar to the IFC except that it should operate in only one country and at a much lower level of funds invested.

Its management should encourage local investors to participate in its ownership. The ownership should be as broadly based as possible to avert control by a narrow interest and to give the institution a national flavor. It should underwrite security issues and be ready to sell securities from its own portfolio. And it should offer miscellaneous services such as project feasibility studies, economic surveys, and other consultative operations, as well as offering assistance to securities exchanges, devising new forms of securities, and advising government agencies on improving the private sector.

The DFCs are dissimilar to IFC in a few major aspects of their operations and it is these dissimilarities which caused these institutions to fall short of expectations of IFC officials in the early years of its operations. DFCs are principally lending institutions. They seldom, if ever, take equity positions in the companies which are their clients. In addition, they do not have sufficient organizational capacity and bring in outside partners only when they lack the necessary capital. They also primarily dispense public funds. Their share capital is relatively small and they do not generally acquire private funds for reinvestment purposes. BANDESCO, a Spanish DFC which the IFC assisted in the latter's first decade of operations, is one of the few such institutions which funnel private funds into private enterprise projects. BANDESCO accomplished this by acquiring the bulk of its funds from debenture issues which were guaranteed by the credit of large Spanish banks. The role of the DFC in broadening its securities holdings was demonstrated by

BANDESCO's activities in marketing its own shares and debentures (Gustafson, 1968).

Among the important miscellaneous services performed by DFCs are technical and managerial assistance, promotional activities, and assistance to the development of local capital markets by making sales out of its own portfolio, maintaining an orderly market, expanding the number of securities available, developing a trading mechanism, and equity underwriting operations (Gustafson, 1968). A DFC can bring in technical experts from other countries to advise its clients and it may place a representative on the board of the client to assist in managerial affairs.

The DFC may engage in a number of promotional activities in its country. These activities include (Kuiper et al., 1967, p. 17):

1. arrangement of general industrial surveys and feasibility studies for special projects;
2. formulation of specific proposals for new enterprises;
3. assistance in finding technical and entrepreneurial partners for local clients or for foreign investors;
4. investment in share capital and underwriting securities, in order to attract other investors;
5. arrangement of mergers in order to create more economic industrial units;
6. development of a capital market by trying to broaden ownership and by other devices;
7. encouragement of the acceptance of new ideas in the economic sector.

A DFC performs a four-step procedure as a promoter. It will identify a project that appears to be a profitable venture. The finance company will then formulate the project by means of feasibility studies. The project is then initiated and the DFC will consult the services of technical experts, will plan the distribution system, and draft the project's plant blueprints and capital structure. Finally, the project is executed. This final step involves financing, acquiring real estate, closing contracts, and placing orders for machinery and equipment (Kuiper et al., 1967, pp. 17-18). The most important element of this process, and the one which may insure success of the venture, is the DFC's function of making contact between an idea for a project on the one hand and entrepreneurial assistance on the other (Kuiper et al., 1967, p. 24).

A major function of a DFC is the development of a workable capital market in its own region or country (Kuiper et al., 1967, pp. 40-71). The DFC may achieve success in this activity by a number of methods. First, it may assist in creating a much wider distribution of securities ownership by local investors. Second, it may assist the government in the establishment of sound monetary and fiscal policies so that local investors will have more confidence in the local economy. Third, it may encourage cooperation between the public and private sectors. Finally, the DFC should assist in the maintenance of a stable market for securities.

The DFC may implement these objectives by a number of methods. It may market its own shares and debentures. It may assist in upgrading business practices. It may initiate a securities exchange. It may help expand the number and varieties of securities available for investors. It may widen the securities market by underwriting activities, assisting with public issues of other companies' securities, initiating mutual funds, selling securities from its own portfolio, and encouragement of companies to report more adequate and meaningful financial information, resort to higher accounting standards, implement more ethical business practices, and develop more modern financial policies.

The DFC concept does have some limitations (IFC, *Private Development Finance Companies*, 1964, p. 11). In order for the DFC to operate effectively, the private sector development must be consistent with the nation's goals. The absence of this environment in Ethiopia caused the demise of the Development Bank of Ethiopia. The products offered by the DFC – medium-term and long-term loans and equity – must be in demand by local private sector firms. Generally speaking, a clearly defined gap in the capital markets of LDCs can be filled by DFCs.

The World Bank and DFCs

The World Bank had financed DFCs as early as 1950, well before the advent of IFC operations, when it made a $2 million loan to the Development Bank of Ethiopia. By 1975, the Bank had loaned

$2.9 billion to 68 DFCs in 44 countries while the IFC by that time had invested $93 million — $73 million in loans and $20 million in share purchases — in 27 DFCs (World Bank, 1976).

The private DFC model, as described above, evolved from a hybrid of several institutional types including joint ventures of foreign investors, domestic investors, and/or manufacturing companies or business/trade associations. Typical DFCs operated under the profit-making goal but were more complex than this in terms of their developmental goals. They generally have autonomous management and decision-making and were never intended to be wards of the World Bank. Such a model was not applicable in every nation. The Development Bank of Ethiopia, the first World Bank investment in a DFC, encountered serious problems and eventually went out of business (World Bank, 1976).

IFC Operations with DFCs

The IFC began its operations with DFCs in 1961 when it established a Development Bank Services Department to coordinate the activities which developed when it took the initiative in considering proposals submitted to the World Bank Group for financial and technical assistance to private industrial development banks. In August, 1961, the IFC made its first direct investments in DFCs with $2 million loans to each of two Colombian DFCs, Corporación Financiera Colombiana de Desarrollo Industrial in Bogota and Corporación Financiera Nacional in Medellin. These companies had been formed in 1958-1959 by Colombian banks, insurance companies, business firms, and individual investors. The IFC investments were made in the form of notes convertible into common stock. During FY1961-62, the IFC converted $1.5 million of the $4 million total investment into common stock of the two DFCs and this represented the first holding of shares by the IFC since the change in the Articles of Agreement permitting such action had become effective (IFC, *Annual Report*, 1961-62, p. 9). Although the FEMSA investment in shares represented the first direct investment in equity by the IFC, this holding represented the first actual holding of equity by the IFC since the amendment. Since this investment, the IFC has converted the remaining portion of the note into common stock.

Subsequently, the World Bank and the IFC began to collaborate in their efforts to finance the establishment or expansion of DFCs. During FY1962-63, the first such combined efforts took place when commitments were made in the Banque Nationale pour le Développement Economique of Morocco (BNDE), a development bank already established by the Moroccan government and owned jointly by American, Belgian, French, German, and Italian banks, as well as by the Moroccan government. The government held a majority position in the company. In order to qualify for IFC assistance, no finance company may have its ownership controlled by the government. Therefore, a new issue of 10 million shares was made. IFC subscribed to shares amounting to approximately $1.5 million. Thus, the government interest was reduced to a minority position. The World Bank also made a loan at that time to the DFC (IFC, *Annual Report*, 1962-63, p. 6).

Another example of joint World Bank-IFC cooperation resulted in the financing of a development finance company in the Philippines during the FY1962-1963. Through IFC-Filipino efforts, the Private Development Corporation of the Philippines (PDCP) was established. A World Bank loan of $15 million was supplemented with a standby commitment by the IFC covering $4.4 million of capital shares out of $6.4 million offered. The IFC, after encouragement of a number of significant international financial institutions to participate in the equity issue, eventually invested about $205,000. Altogether, 18 private investment firms and banks purchased 30 percent of PDCP's shares. These included 14 U.S. institutions as well as 2 British, 1 German, and 1 Japanese (Bennet, 1965). Included among these financial institutions were Continental International Finance Corporation, an Edge Act subsidiary of Continental Illinois National Bank of Chicago; The American Express Company; The Bank of Tokyo; Deutsche Bank AG; Lehman Brothers; Manufacturers Hanover International Finance Corporation; New York Hanseatic Corporation; and Wells Fargo Bank International Corporation, and Edge Act subsidiary of Wells Fargo Bank (IFC, *Annual Report*, 1962-63, p. 21).

Heavy commitments by the IFC to DFCs continued during the

following year when the IFC made equity investments in firms to which the Bank had made loans. These included the Finnish Industrialization Fund, the Malaysian Industrial Development Finance Limited, and the Industrial Finance Corporation of Thailand. The IFC also invested in shares of the Industrial Development Bank of Turkey and in other DFCs in Colombia, Nigeria, and Venezuela (IFC, *Annual Report*, 1963-64, p. 9).

The IFC has assisted DFCs in a variety of ways in addition to direct investments. The IFC has helped train the staff of these institutions, has assisted them in project analyses and evaluations, has been and is represented on the boards of some of them, and has participated with them occasionally in jointly financing industrial projects. The IFC will accept a position only on the board of DFCs. Its policy has been to decline membership on the board of an industrial firm. The IFC also refers investments to DFCs when the total of funds to be committed is below the IFC's minimum criterion. A list of IFC investments in DFCs which are currently held in its portfolio is shown in Table 5-1. The IFC's current portfolio contains investments in 27 DFCs in 22 different nations plus one regional investment, with combined book value totaling $242.7 million. These investments began as early as 1962 and have involved 68 separate transactions with total original commitments of $299 million (IFC, *Annual Report*, 1990, pp. 76-87).

In summary, the IFC has assisted in industrial development and the strengthening of local capital markets by its investments in DFCs. Means for channeling foreign and domestic capital into small and medium-sized projects have been established by World Bank Group activity in this financial area. The equity investments and underwriting by the IFC have helped to improve the capital markets in LDCs in which these DFCs are located.

IFC Commitments to Selected DFCs

Selected investments by the IFC in DFCs will be discussed in this section. Some of these investments are still held in the IFC portfolio while some have been sold off to the private sector, have matured and paid-off, or have gone out of business. These investments will be examined by geographic sector handled by a specific IFC investment department.

TABLE 5-1. IFC Current Holdings of DFCs (thousands of US$)

	Original Commitment	Cumul. Total	Total Investment Now Held	Cumul. Total
Africa				
Botswana				
Botswana Development Corp., Ltd	$ 607		$ 607	
Kenya				
Development Finance Co. of Kenya				
Ltd.	6,381		4,064	
Liberia				
Liberian Bank for Development				
& Investment	702		70	
Malawi				
Investment of Development				
Bank of Malawi Ltd.	605		70	
Morocco				
Banque Nationale pour le				
Développement Economique	46,690		45,970	
Crédit Immobilier et Hôtelier	67,150		66,199	
Swaziland				
Swaziland Industrial Development				
Co. Ltd.	3,000		3,000	

TABLE 5-1 (continued)

	Original Commitment	Cumul. Total	Total Investment Now Held	Cumul. Total
Tunisia				
Banque de Développement				
Economique de Tunisia	2,305		2,305	
Banque Nationale de Développement				
Touristique	9,081		2,248	
Uganda				
Development Finance Co. of				
Uganda Ltd.	375		376	
Zaire				
Socitété Financière de				
Développement	1,297		1,297	
Regional Africa				
SIFIDA Investment Co., S.A.	<u>3,773</u>		<u>635</u>	
Regional Total		$141,966		$127,376
Latin America				
Colombia				
Corporación Financiera				
del Norte	$ 454		$ 15	
Corporación Financiera				
del Valle	9,784		9,784	

Corporación Financiera			
Nacional	8,042	52	
Ecuador			
Compañia Financiera			
Ecuatoriana	4,589	4,375	
Mexico			
Banca Serfin, S.N.C.	60,000	60,000	
Trinidad and Tobago			
Trinidad and Tobago			
Development Finance Co. Ltd.	469	471	
Regional Total		$83,338	$74,690

Europe and the Middle East

Portugal			
Banco Portuguéz de Investimento	$22,655	$11,410	
Turkey			
Turkiye Sinai Kalkinma			
Bankasi, A.S.	19,742	2,698	
Regional Totals		$44,426	$15,122

Asia

China			
JF Chin Investment Co., Ltd.	$ 3,036	$ 3,036	
Indonesia			
P.T. Private Development			
Finance Co. of Indonesia	483	362	

TABLE 5-1 (continued)

	Original Commitment	Cumul. Total	Total Investment Now Held	Cumul. Total
Korea, Republic of				
Korea Long Term Credit Bank	702		70	
Pakistan				
Pakistan Industrial Credit and				
Investment Corporation Ltd.	3,629		592	
Philippines				
BPI Agricultural Development Bank	976		976	
Sri Lanka				
Development Finance				
Corporation of Ceylon	457		457	
Thailand				
Siam commercial Bank (SCB)	15,000		15,000	
The Thai Farmers Bank Ltd.	5,000		5,000	
Regional Totals		$29,283		$25,493
Worldwide Totals		**$299,013**		**$242,688**

Note. From Annual Report 1990, by IFC, 1990, Washington D.C.: International
Finance Corporation, pp. 78-91.

Latin America

The first IFC investments in a DFC were made to two Colombian
firms in FY1961. These were the Corporación Financiera Colom-
biana de Desarrollo Industrial, of Bogota, and the Corporación
Financiera Nacional, of Medellin. These DFCs had been established in 1958 and 1959, respectively, to furnish medium- and long-

term investment funds to Colombian firms and to develop the Colombian capital market. The companies' stock was originally owned by local banks, insurance companies, industrial firms, and private individuals (IFC, "Press Release," 1961, p. 1). The IFC investments were in the form of notes bearing no fixed interest but convertible into common stock. The IFC converted nearly $4 million of these notes into common shares of the two DFCs, representing the first holding of shares by the IFC since its charter was amended in 1961 permitting such holdings, as discussed earlier in this chapter (IFC, *Annual Report*, 1961-62). The IFC still retains investments in Corporación Financiera Nacional, made in FYs1962, 1963, and 1985, totaling $211,000 in equity.

The IFC joined, in FY1964, with 80 Venezuelan and foreign investors to form C.A. Venezolana de Desarrollo (CAVENDES), a DFC formed to finance industrialization in Venezuela outside the mining and petroleum sectors. The investors included Manufacturers Hanover Trust Company, First National City Bank, a number of U.S. Edge Act subsidiaries, and commercial banks and oil companies of the United Kingdom, Germany, Italy, Netherlands, and the United States, as well as local banks and businessmen (IFC, "Press Release," 1967, pp. 1-2). This DFC was capitalized with $8.1 million of share capital (IFC, *Annual Report*, 1963-64, p. 37). The IFC invested $1.33 million in CAVENDES' shares, a 15 percent share of the ownership (IFC, "Press Release," 1967, p. 2). CAVENDES assisted industrialization of Venezuela by diversification of its commitments outside the petroleum sector and by pioneering the underwriting of new issues in Venezuela (World Bank Group, December 1967, p. 20) in such industries as foodstuffs, paper, textiles, and light metallurgy (IFC, "Press Release," 1967).

In addition to these examples, the IFC currently holds investments in other DFCs located in Latin America in its portfolio. These include Banco Industrial, S.A. in Bolivia, Corporación Financiera del Norte and Corporación Financiera del Valle of Colombia, and Compañía Financiera Ecuatoriana de Desarrollo, S.A. of Ecuador.

As of FY1990, the IFC holds in its portfolio investments in six Latin American DFCs located in four countries whose book value is $74.7 million. The original investments totaled $83.3 million and were made in 15 separate transactions (IFC, *Annual Report*, 1990, pp. 76-87).

Asia

The IFC made investments in four Asian DFCs in its early years of operations. These were (1) Pakistan Industrial Credit and Investment Corporation Limited (PICIC), (2) Private Development Corporation of the Philippines (PDCP), (3) Malaysian Industrial Development Finance Limited (MIDFL), and (4) Industrial Finance Corporation of Thailand (IFCT). The investments in PICIC and PDCP will be discussed in this section.

The first IFC investment in an Asian DFC was in PICIC in FY1962-1963 when it subscribed to 200,000 shares for $449,400. PICIC was established in 1957 to furnish medium- and long-term finance to Pakistani industrial firms in addition to underwriting share offerings and assistance to Pakistani firms in sourcing managerial, technical and administrative services. At the time of the IFC investment in PICIC, the latter institution had approved more than 300 loans totaling over $84 million, held stock in local firms amounting to $2,960,000, had underwritten shares totaling $3,200,000, and helped find $10 million of foreign capital for Pakistani firms (IFC, *Annual Report*, 1962-63, pp. 18-19).

Another Asian DFC assisted by both the IFC and the Bank was PDCP, organized in 1963 to make medium- and long-term loans to Philippine firms, invest in the equity of companies, underwrite new issues, and provide managerial and technical advice (IFC, *Annual Report*, 1962-63, pp. 19-21). PDCP was formed with 500,000 Class A shares subscribed to by local sponsors and the company made a further issue of 1,250,000 Class A shares, 500,000 of which were subscribed to by the IFC, 80,000 to be taken initially with the remainder on a standby basis. An issue of 750,000 Class B shares was also made. The offering was successful but payment by subscribers was slow, creating the necessity for the IFC to pay defaulted balances of $3.72 million in return for the unpaid shares. The total IFC commitment amounted to $4,359,063. The IFC sold its shares on the Manila Stock Market in 1967 at a good profit. PDCP benefited the Philippine economy by its four underwritings and by its investments in industries such as transportation, power, food, textiles, wood and cork, printing and publishing, chemicals, glass, clay and stone products, basic metal products, machinery, electrical machinery, and mining (Rosen, November 7, 1967).

The IFC maintains investments in Asian DFCs in its portfolio. These include Industrial Promotion and Development Company of Bangladesh Limited, JF China Investment Company Limited of China, P.T. Private Development Finance Company of Indonesia, Korea Long Term Credit Bank, PICIC, BPI Agricultural Development Bank of the Philippines, and Development Finance Corporation of Ceylon (Sri Lanka).

In recent years, the IFC has continued to invest in Asian DFCs. The IFC subscribed its pre-emptive rights in two separate share offerings by Korea Investment and Finance Company in FY1989 totaling $4.88 million. The IFC participated in a rights issue in an increase of shares by PICIC. In Thailand, the IFC established a $15 million equity agency line which enabled the Siam Commercial Bank to provide matching equity financing for medium-size Thai enterprises. The IFC also established a similar line of $5 million for the Thai Farmers Bank to enable that bank to provide such financing for Thai entrepreneurs (IFC, *Annual Report*, 1990, pp. 66-73).

As of FY1990, the IFC holds in its portfolio investments in seven Asian DFCs located in six countries with total book value $25.5 million. The original commitments in these DFCs totaled $29.3 million (IFC, *Annual Report*, 1990, pp. 76-87).

Africa

In the formative years of IFC operations, five investment commitments were made in African DFCs. The first of these took place in 1963 when IFC subscribed to shares in Banque Nationale pour le Développement Economique (BNDE) of Morocco. The IFC investment was $1.5 million and the World Bank made a loan to this company at the same time which amounted to $15 million (IFC, *Annual Report*, 1962-63, p. 17). Other IFC investments in African DFCs included the Nigerian Industrial Development Bank (NIDB), the Liberian Bank for Industrial Development and Investment (LBIDI), Banque Ivoirienne de Développement Industriel (BIDI) of Ivory Coast, and Société Nationale d'Investissement (SNI) of Tunisia.

The IFC investments in these DFCs were for different purposes. The BNDE investment was part of a $2 million share increase and included the Moroccan Government, Morgan Guaranty Bank of New York, and banks from France, Italy, Germany, and Belgium. The IFC investments in NIDB, BIDI, and LBIDI were made to assist the establishment of these DFCs. The SNI investment assisted the expansion of this Tunisian DFC and included investments by financial institutions from Italy, Germany, France, and Sweden.

During the decade of the 1980s, the IFC continued to finance African DFCs. In FY1984, the IFC increased shareholdings in LBIDI, taking 1/6 of a $900,000 share expansion. During that year, the IFC also increased its shareholdings in Société Financiere de Développement (SOFIDE) with a $580,000 investment and made a first-time investment in the Development Finance Company of Uganda Ltd. by subscribing to shares in the amount of $380,000. The latter investment was part of an $8.5 million rehabilitation program (IFC, *Annual Report*, 1984, pp. 24-25).

The IFC presently holds investments in 11 African DFCs located in nine countries along with one regional DFC investment. The total book value of these investments is $127.4 million and the original commitments totaled $141.97 million (IFC, *Annual Report*, 1990, pp. 76-87).

Europe and the Middle East

During the first decade of IFC operations, four European DFCs received five different investments from the IFC. These were: Teollistamisrahasto Oy (Industrialization Fund) of Finland and the Industrial Development Bank of Turkey, both in 1963; two investments in 1963 and 1964 in Banco del Desarrollo Economico Español, S.A., (BANDESCO) of Spain; and National Investment Bank for Industrial Development, S.A., of Greece in 1965.

Teollistamisrahasto Oy specialized in assisting the financing of small- and medium-sized firms in Finland. This company was expanded five-fold with a $15.6 million financial reorganization in 1963 with assistance from IFC and the World Bank and the Bank of Finland, European and American financial institutions, and local Finnish investors (IFC, *Annual Report*, 1963-64, p. 19).

The IFC does very little investing in Europe and the Middle East and has sold most of its earlier investments in DFCs of this area. It still has three investments in European or Middle East DFCs in its portfolio. These are Oman Development Bank S.A.O.G. in Oman, Banco Portuguêz de Investimento in Portugal, and Turkiye Sinai Kalkinma Bankasi A.S. in Turkey. The book value of these investments is $15.1 million and the original commitments totaled $44.4 million (IFC, *Annual Report*, 1990, pp. 76-87).

Summary

The decision to assist in the establishment of DFCs in LDCs by the IFC may have been, at the least, a minor stroke of genius. Financial assistance of these predominantly privately-owned development banks generally has resulted in a multiplication of the IFC's financial investment in the LDCs in which these financial intermediaries are located. Equity investments by the IFC in DFCs has been utilized by these companies as a base for further borrowings. And investments by DFCs in development projects have had catalytic effects made possible by financing a project which costs several times as much as the DFC investment but which would have been too small for a direct investment by the IFC (IFC, *International Finance Corporation After 25 Years*, 1981, p. 13).

CAPITAL MARKET DEVELOPMENT

One of the requirements spelled out in the IFC's Articles of Agreement recognized that LDCs lacked capital markets necessary to fund, on a long-term basis, the development projects needed by the private sector in these countries. That requirement was that the IFC should seek to stimulate and help create conditions conducive to the flow of private capital, domestic and foreign, into productive investment in the IFC's member countries (IFC, *Articles*, 1956, pp. 3-4). To facilitate this requirement, the IFC established a Capital Markets Department in 1971. This department both advises on and invests in LDC private sector projects and provides comprehensive assistance in the development of financial markets and institutions. It assists local companies to access international capital markets and, in doing so, works closely with other IFC departments as well as the World Bank (Sethness, 1988, p. 32).

The work of the Capital Markets Department may be implemented in a variety of ways. Long-term savings in the low-income LDC may be encouraged in LDCs by assisting the establishment of financial intermediaries such as housing finance companies, insurance companies, and leasing companies. In middle-income LDCs, securities markets have been fostered and developed by IFC support and specialized financial institutions have been established and promoted by the IFC in its capital market operations. These include stock brokerage and money market firms and investment and merchant banks. Advice about corporate financial reporting and disclosure is considered quite important at this stage (Sethness, 1988, p. 32). In higher-income LDCs, the IFC capital market operations include assistance in the broadening of ownership in business enterprises as well as bringing more issuing companies and individual and institutional investors into the local and international securities markets. In addition, the IFC broadens the financial services which can be offered private enterprise in these LDCs. Financial institutions promoted by the IFC to facilitate these objectives include venture capital companies, specialized investment and merchant banks, mutual fund and unit trust management companies and export financing banks (Sethness, 1988, p. 32). In short, the primary objective of the Capital Markets Department is to achieve the mandate of the IFC's Articles of Agreement by mobilizing savings, whether local LDC funds or worldwide finance from industrialized countries, and channeling them into productive private enterprise projects in LDCs.

Activities of the Capital Markets Department

The major activities of this department in the IFC are as follows:

1. advising governments on how to establish a fiscal, legal, and regulatory environment which will support private financial sector development;
2. investment in financial institutions in LDCs and provision of technical assistance and finance;

3. assistance of domestic firms in gaining access to international capital markets by promotion of portfolio investment from abroad;

4. creation of a broad range of financial institutions — such as those discussed above — in LDCs where they are now absent;

5. expansion of the use of debt-equity conversion programs and funds (IFC, "What IFC Does," p. n/a).

Recent activities are characteristic of IFC operations in this area. For example, in FY1990, the IFC approved capital market investments amounting to $423 million in 33 institutions in 14 countries and one region. See Table 5-2 for a listing of these investments. These projects were broken down as follows: 13 were international securities transactions, 11 were on-lending projects, and 10 were institution-building projects. By geography, 13 were in Asia, 7 each were located in Africa and Latin America and the Caribbean, respectively, and 6 were in Europe and the Middle East (IFC, *Annual Report*, 1990, p. 35).

Advisory Services

The IFC, working in conjunction with the World Bank, advises LDC member countries on legal, financial, fiscal, and monetary policy issues as well as regulatory problems. For example, the IFC has advised (1) the Nigerian Government on a privatization program, (2) India on the design of venture capital policies, (3) Jamaica on a financial restructuring and debt conversion program, and (4) centrally-planned economies such as China and Hungary on the development of securities markets (Sethness, 1988, p. 32). During FY1990, activities in this area included coordinated studies for some 40 countries and regions about present and future legal and regulatory apparatus to support capital market development in these countries. The IFC, through the Capital Markets Department, also made comprehensive analyses of the financial sectors of a number of these countries at the request of the governments (IFC, *Annual Report*, 1990, p. 35).

TABLE 5-2. IFC Capital Market Investment Approvals (FY1990, millions of US$)

Company	Country	Activity	Gross Investment	Project Cost
Corporación de Inversiones y Privatización	Argentina	Investment mgt.	.08	388.10
Jardine Fleming Asia Select Ltd.	Asia	Investment fund	11.25	100.00
Compañia de Teléfonos de Chile S.A. *†	Chile	Telecommunications	22.10	110.00
Five Arrows Chile Fund†	Chile	Investment fund	6.00	75.00
Leasing Andino	Chile	Leasing	10.00	10.00
First Hungary Fund	Hungary	Investment fund	7.50	80.00
India Lease Development Ltd.	India	Leasing	3.94	13.37
Infrastructure Leasing and Financial Services	India	Leasing	16.95	16.95
Technology Development and Information Company of India	India	Venture capital	2.87	60.00
Bank Niaga	Indonesia	Agency credit line	7.50	15.00
Bank Umum Nasional*	Indonesia	Agency credit line	10.00	20.00
Nomura Jakart Fund †	Indonesia	Investment fund	3.00	30.00
P.T. Saseka Gelora Leasing§	Indonesia	Leasing	.07	.56
Korea Development Leasing Corporation	Korea	Leasing	.90	46.30

The Leasing and Finance Company

Name	Country	Type		
of Malawi§	Malawi	Leasing	.11	1.08
Banca Serfin*	Mexico	Development finance	6.50	22.00
Bancomer*	Mexico	Credit line	20.00	40.00
Banco Nacional de Mexico (Banamex)*	Mexico	Credit line	60.00	200.00
First International Investment Bank	Pakistan	Merchant bank	.69	4.76
All Asia Capital and Leasing Corporation	Philippines	Leasing	.26	2.30
The First Philippine Fund†	Philippines	Investment fund	20.00	100.00
The Manila Fund†	Philippines	Investment fund	7.00	50.00
Export Development Bank*	Poland	Credit/quasi-equity facility	29.60	60.00
Finantia Capital	Portugal	Investment fund	4.00	30.00
Portuguese Investment Fund†	Portugal	Investment fund	6.00	30.50
Mutual Fund Company	Thailand	Fund management	.26	3.20
ISGEN Leasing	Turkey	Leasing	.23	1.30
Turkish Investment Fund†	Turkey	Investment fund	10.00	60.00
Barclays Bank of Zimbabwe Ltd.*	Zimbabwe	Credit line	20.11	20.11
Merchant Bank of Central Africa Ltd.*	Zimbabwe	Credit line	25.21	25.21
RAL Merchant Bank Ltd.*	Zimbabwe	Credit line	30.21	30.21

TABLE 5-2 (continued)

Company	Country	Activity	Gross Investment	Project Cost
RAL Merchant Bank Ltd.*	Zimbabwe	Merchant bank/		
		credit line	17.85	19.00
Scotfin Ltd.*	Zimbabwe	Credit line	7.50	7.50
Standard Chartered Merchant				
Bank*	Zimbabwe	Credit line	30.21	30.21
Syfrets Merchant Bank Ltd.				
Zimbabwe	Zimbabwe	Credit line	25.21	25.21
		Total	**423.11**	**1,727.87**

* Project undertaken in cooperation with a regional investment department.

† Underwriting

§ As a rights issue under $250,000, this project is not included in the total number of approvals.

Note: Private placements by the Capital Markets Department, which are not shown in this table, came to $328 million in FY1990, including placements of $113 million for the Emerging Markets Investment Fund.

Note. From Annual Report 1990, by IFC, 1990, Washington, D.C.: International Finance Corporation, p. 34.

Domestic Institutions Investment

The IFC has invested in more than 150 financial institutions such as merchant and investment banks, export finance institutions, housing finance institutions, and leasing and insurance companies.

The establishment of Portugal's first leasing company was facilitated by the IFC. Four Korean institutions concerned with money market and securities financing, equipment leasing, and venture capital financing were established with IFC support. The IFC mobilized foreign and domestic support in the formation of the South East Asia Venture Investments Company N.V., an ASEAN company, and the Housing Development Finance Company Ltd. in India. Most of the IFC investments in this area are relatively small equity subscriptions ranging from $200,000 to $1 million and normally make up about 10-15 percent of the equity capital of the company in which the IFC invests.

SYNDICATIONS AND PARTICIPATIONS

The IFC has, from its inception, had two major goals: to finance as much profitable private sector projects as possible given its finite amount of funds available and to encourage as many international financial institutions as possible to participate in the development finance process. One of the IFC's most active programs has been instrumental in the achievement of both of these goals. That program is the syndication of participations by banks and financial institutions around the world in IFC loans (IFC, "How IFC Works With Commercial Banks," date n/a).

Syndication encourages financial institutions worldwide to furnish funds for IFC-financed projects in the private sector of LDCs. The fact that IFC is a sponsor of these projects is an added inducement for the participating financial institution, especially because the project credit risks are shared with the IFC. In fact, the special status of the IFC has insured that no portion of a loan in participation with the IFC has been included in the rescheduling of the foreign debt of any LDC.

The IFC has placed participations in its loans with more than 200 international financial institutions since it began syndication operations. Most of these participations have been by European banks. Japanese banks do participations only if another Japanese company is involved in the project.

The Syndication Procedure

Although one agreement is generally made between the IFC and the borrower, the IFC loan is divided into two parts: one which is the IFC's portion of the loan—subject to IFC's own peculiar terms—and the other part funded by the participating financial institution(s)—with terms agreed to between the borrower and the participants. Finally, the participation will involve a separate agreement between the IFC and each participating institution. The process, in short, has been one of the IFC's most effective catalytic operations.

To encourage a particular bank to participate in a loan, the IFC outlines the project for the bank and follows this with an appraisal report and the principal conditions of the loan including pricing, if the bank shows interest in the participation. The bank is then invited to participate in the loan. The IFC acts as lead manager for the transaction and if a large amount of funds is needed from several banks, either the IFC or the borrower may request one or more banks to assist syndication of the IFC loan.

The IFC administers the loan since it is the lender of record. Thus, it is responsible for collections of principal and interest, distribution of proceeds to the participant, the availability of financial statements and other necessary information to the participant, and insurance of compliance with loan documentation by the borrower.

Results of Syndications

The IFC developed and initiated the syndication process in the early 1960s. Since then, a total of $3.1 billion of IFC investments have been placed with 249 financial institutions, mostly international commercial banks. At the end of FY1990, the IFC was administering a portfolio of syndicated loans for participants totaling $1.1 billion. During FY1990, syndicated loans amounted to $622 million, more than a third of the IFC's total loans approved during the year. A total of 37 financial institutions participated in these syndications, compared with a record 67 financial institution participants in FY1989. The institutions which participated in IFC loans in FY1990 are listed in Table 5-3.

Syndicated loans were quite representative, geographically speak-

TABLE 5-3. Financial Institutions Participating in IFC Projects in FY1990

The Arab Investment Company S.A.A.	Kansallis Osake-Pankki
Bank for Kärnten und Steiermark A.G.	Kreditanstalt for Wiederaufbau (KfW)
Bank for Oberösterreich und Salzburg	
(Oberbank)	Manufacturers Hanover Trust Company
Banque CSIA	NMB Postbank Groep N.V.
Banque Indosuez	Nederlandse Financierings
	Maatschappij voor Ontwikkelings-
	landen N.V.
Banque Internationale à Luxembourg S.A.	Österreichische Länderbank A.G.
Banque Marocaine du Commerce Extérieur	Österreichische Volksbanken A.G.
Banque Nationale de Paris	PKbanken
Banque del l'Union Européenne	Postipankki, Ltd.
Bergen Bank A/S	Raiffeisen Zentralbank Österreich A.G.
Commerzbank AG	Skopbank
Crédit Lyonnais	Société Générale
Crédit National	Standard Chartered Bank
Den norske Creditbank	The Sumitomo Bank, Limited
Deutsche Bank AG	Swiss Bank Corporation
Ecobank Transnational Incorporated	The Tokai Bank, Limited
Girozentrale und Bank der Österreichischen	Union Bank of Finland Ltd.
Sparkassen A.G.	Union Bank of Switzerland
The Industrialization Fund for Developing	Zentralsparkasse und Kommerzialbank
Countries	of Wien

Note. From Annan Report 1990, by IFC, 1990, Washington, D.C.: International
Finance Corporation, p. 37.

ing, in FY1990. In Asia, the IFC syndicated loans in six projects in four countries including one of $100 million as part of the $529 million Vinythai integrated PVC plant and a $30 million loan to Shin Ho Paper Company for a newsprint paper mill and de-inking pulp plant, both in Thailand. In Latin America, the IFC syndicated loans totaling $157 million for nine projects in six countries including a $35 million loan to Oleoducto de Colombia, S.A., a joint-venture company constructing a $321 million oil pipeline in Colombia. In Africa, the IFC syndicated $150 million in loans to three projects in three countries including a $35 million loan, part of a $93 million project to expand the Sansu gold mine complex for Ashanti Goldfields Corporation in Ghana and a $52 million loan, part of a $92 million IFC loan to finance a number of foreign-exchange earning tourism projects (IFC, *Annual Report*, 1990, p. 38).

Chapter 6

IFC Programs: Since 1980

INTRODUCTION

Programs developed by the IFC during the 1980s will be discussed and analyzed in this chapter. These include the International Securities Group; the Emerging Markets Data Base (EMDB); the fee-based and other advisory services such as Corporate Finance Services (CFS) and its privatization and corporate restructuring activities; the Africa programs including the Africa Enterprise Fund (AEF), the Africa Project Development Facility (APDF), and the African Management Services Company (AMSCo); the Caribbean Project Development Facility (CPDF); the Foreign Investment Advisory Service (FIAS); and the technical assistance (TA) and technology transfer [carried out by the Technology and Development Unit (TDU)]. Cases of each of these programs will be included in the discussion.

CAPITAL MARKETS DEPARTMENT

In this section, the discussion will focus on the new services formed by the IFC within the Capital Markets Department. These consist of (1) the operations to establish closed-end investment companies in the emerging LDC markets and which invest in the securities of a single country—the so-called country funds, (2) the Emerging Markets Data Base (EMDB), (3) the work of the International Securities Group (ISG), and (4) Multi-Country Loan Facilities (MLF).

Access to International Markets

Country Funds

The work of the Capital Markets Department in improving capital flows to LDCs through international securities markets has involved the sponsorship and underwriting of closed-end portfolio investment funds which are traded on stock markets in New York, London, and other major financial centers. These include the Korea Fund, first such fund developed by the IFC in 1984. When the IFC sponsored and lead-managed the Korea Fund with First Boston and Lehman Brothers, only a few mutual funds, with total market value of $500 million, had investments in LDCs in their portfolios. By 1990, more than 131 new-money country funds were being offered to the investing public with an estimated market value of $11.2 billion ("Emerging Markets," 1990). These closed-end trusts, or country funds, have provided investment capital in a way which has lessened the fear by companies in LDCs of takeovers from abroad ("International Finance Corporation: Ryrie Wastes No Time," March 1985). More than 45 of these funds have been developed with the efforts of the IFC representing new capital mobilization amounting to more than $2.5 billion.

The $60 million public offering for the Korea Fund gave American investors the opportunity to invest in Korean stocks with a minimum of red tape. And it met two principal IFC objectives reflected in its charter: to assist LDCs and to make money. The IFC made $600,000 by underwriting the Korea Fund and selling the shares outside the United States (Dumaine, 1984).

The Korea Fund was initiated when the Government of the Republic of Korea asked the IFC to assist the formation and promotion of a closed-end investment fund which would invest in the shares of Korea companies. Wall Street skepticism about whether international investors would invest in a market as youthful as that in Korea and whether the Korean Government could ensure the Fund would not be a vehicle for speculators was overcome when the Fund was well subscribed and traded at a premium to the net asset value. In 1986, a second successful offering of $40 million was made in a similar fund in Korea (Economics Department, 1989, p. 10).

The IFC developed 11 country funds in FY1990 alone which mobilized $1 billion in the international markets, and acted as promoter, underwriter, placement agent, and, when necessary, as investor (IFC, *Annual Report*, 1990, p. 34). These country funds include the Nomura Jakarta Fund in Indonesia, the Portuguese Investment Fund, the First Hungary Fund—the first such investment trust developed in a country previously communist, the Manila Fund in the Philippines, and the Turkish Investment Fund. The IFC has also helped form two other funds in Asia: those in Malaysia and Thailand, to attract foreign investors (Lawrence, 1987).

The IFC has developed other country funds in previous years. For example, it was lead manager of the public offering of the $30 million Thailand Fund in 1986, was co-lead manager of the public offering of the $84 million Malaysia Fund in 1987, and was lead manager of the public offering of the $100 million Thai Fund in 1988 (Gill and Tropper, 1988, p. 30). With the success of these country funds, the IFC held discussions with Templeton Investment Counsel, an organization affiliated with Bahamian-based John Templeton whose firm manages a number of investment funds. Some of the markets which the IFC/Templeton joint venture considered for country funds were Jordan, Chile, and Argentina. Each of these markets is too thin to support a single country fund but a fund covering all three countries might be a good risk (Dumaine, 1984).

Emerging Markets Growth Fund

In 1986, the IFC assisted the establishment of the Emerging Markets Growth Fund (EMGF), a multinational investment fund with a portfolio of companies located in the emerging market LDCs. The EMGF was established with $50 million share capital to be used for investments in publicly-listed shares of companies in LDCs which have attractive growth prospects. It was incorporated in the United States and is managed by the Capital Research and Management Company of Los Angeles. The capital of EMGF can be increased to more than $500 million to be invested in 20-25 countries ("Foreign Portfolio Investment . . . ," 1986).

The EMGF was established to invest no more than 20 percent of its assets in any one country nor more than five percent in any one company. The Fund selected about 200 companies as eligible growth companies and will invest in 25 of these at any one time. One-fifth of its funds can be invested in bonds, money market securities, and other instruments other than equities ("Foreign Portfolio Investment . . . ," 1986).

Summary

Portfolio investors worldwide have increased their demand for such investment vehicles. According to an IFC review, during the second half of the 1980s, the emerging securities markets outperformed all industrialized countries' stock indices including the Tokyo Nikkei average. In fact, four of the top five performing markets were in LDCs in 1989 ("Emerging Markets," 1990). On the other hand, four LDC markets, Korea, Pakistan, Jordan, and Venezuela, were among the five worst performing markets in 1989.

Some of these markets are quite large in some respects. India's market has 6,000 companies listed but has a relatively small daily trading volume of $120 million. On the other hand, the Korea Stock Exchange, with only 626 companies listed, has daily volume frequently exceeding $600 million. Most of these markets have sufficient liquidity to absorb foreign investment but some analysts have shown concern over the speculative trading and rapid growth in some of these markets.

Regardless of this speculative period among the emerging markets, the country funds seem to, in many cases, be trading at a premium to net asset value, generally the opposite of how closed-end investment funds trade. Thus, this demonstrates that the inflow of foreign money into these markets is in excess of what these markets can currently digest. However, some IFC analysts believe that all markets, including those in New York, Tokyo, and Europe, have periods of scandal and excessive speculation and that such will also happen in the emerging markets. In the long-term, these markets will add diversity to global asset management and will be beneficial for investors worldwide.

Other Types of Funds

In addition to investment fund activities, the IFC has sponsored and invested in privately placed "new money" and debt conversion funds and arranged and participated in direct international issues by private enterprises from LDCs. These include the First Philippine Capital Fund L. P., the Chile Investment Company, and Equitypar of Brazil. The IFC also assisted Two Turkish commercial banks to enter the Eurocommercial paper markets — the first such facilities done for private sector borrowers in LDCs. And the IFC acted as lead manager for a series of floating rate notes (FRN) for the Latin American Export Bank (BLADEX), which obtained the first new money from international capital markets for any private company in Latin America since the inception of the 1982 country debt crisis. Finally, the establishment of the Emerging Markets Data Base in 1988 and the work of the International Securities Group, formed in 1989, will be discussed in the next sections.

Emerging Markets Data Base

The Emerging Markets Data Base (EMDB) was established in 1988 and is a computerized source of information on equity markets in LDCs. It is the first comprehensive data base to provide detailed statistics on stock markets in LDCs. The EMDB includes weekly and monthly information on the stock of some 700 companies from 19 markets, going as far back, in some cases, as 1975. These 19 securities markets are shown in Table 6-1. The IFC calculates two types of indexes, one for prices and one for total returns, which are weighted by market capitalization using a formula based on the chained Paasche method (IFC, *Emerging Stock Markets Factbook*, 1990, p. viii).

The IFC developed the EMDB to supplement its roles in underwriting and private placements in LDC capital market activities. This additional operation furnishes a base for its investment program and advisory operations. As part of this service, the IFC publishes an annual *Emerging Stock Markets Factbook*, a *Quarterly Review*, and a *Bibliography* of reports which cover stock markets in LDCs. In FY1990, EMDB also published *The EMDB Company*

TABLE 6-1. Securities Exchanges Covered – Emerging Markets Data Base

Country	Securities Exchange
1) Argentina	Bolsa de Comercio de Buenos Aires
2) Brazil	Saö Paulo Bolsa de Valores
3) Chile	Bolsa de Comercio de Santiago
4) Colombia	Bolsa de Bogota
5) Greece	Athens Stock Exchange
6) India	Bombay Stock Exchange
	Calcutta Stock Exchange
7) Jordan	Amman Financial Market
8) Korea	Korea Stock Exchange
9) Malaysia	Kuala Lumpur Stock Exchange
10) Mexico	Bolsa Mexicana de Valores
11) Nigeria	Nigerian Stock Market
12) Pakistan	Karachi Stock Exchange Ltd.
13) Philippines	Manila Stock Exchange
14) Portugal	Bolsa de Lisboa
15) Taiwan, China	Taiwan Stock Exchange
16) Thailand	Securities Exchange of Thailand
17) Turkey	Istanbul Stock Exchange
18) Venezuela	Bolsa de Valores de Caracas
19) Zimbabwe	Zimbabwe Stock Exchange

Note. From Emerging Stock Markets Factbook 1990, by IFC, 1990, Washington, D.C.: International Finance Corporation, pp. 67-143. Copyright 1990 by International Finance Corporation. Adapted by permission.

Guide which presents operating data for selected companies in emerging markets. The data base is available on-line from The WEFA Group, a merger of Chase Econometrics and Wharton Econometrics.

International Securities Group

The International Securities Group (ISG) was formed within the IFC Capital Markets Department in 1989 to assist private companies in LDCs to raise funds through international offerings of investment funds and individual corporate securities. The ISG accomplishes this objective in a number of ways including (International Securities Group, n/a):

1. acquisition of market intelligence on the types and terms of securities which can be issued by companies from LDCs and placed in international securities markets;
2. advising companies in LDCs to investigate the long-term advantages of diversified access through securitized financings;
3. serving as a partner with some of the most prominent international investment and commercial banks, to bring companies from LDCs to the international capital markets;
4. serving as an underwriter and/or placement agent for country funds and corporate securities issues.

Essentially the ISG acts in a manner similar to a broker in bringing four important elements of the development process together. These are (1) the corporations in LDCs—which issue securities to international institutional investors, (2) investment banks and securities houses—these institutions provide knowledge of and access to the international markets, (3) international institutional investors—these seek portfolio investment opportunities in LDCs, and (4) LDC governments—which regulate the investment of foreign capital in the domestic private sector. ISG will facilitate the interaction of relations among these four sectors by representing the expansion of the IFC's activities in international capital markets.

The ISG intends to carry out several activities. For example, it will provide specialized technical assistance to LDCs which have begun to experiment with market-oriented institutions. In expanding its advisory services, it will work to improve disclosure standards to protect investors. It has already assisted in the creation of a broad range of financial institutions including investment banks and venture capital companies. ISG will also cooperate with other IFC operations in assisting governments in the use of debt/equity conversion programs.

In its first year of operations, ISG developed an active portfolio of projects involving the bringing of sound companies to the international financial markets to raise capital by issuing debt, equity, or convertible securities. It acted as co-lead manager in the underwriting for public issue of American Depositary Receipts for Compañía de Teléfonos de Chile S.A. in the international capital markets. The issue, registered with the U.S. Securities and Exchange Commission and listed on the New York Stock Exchange, is the first public stock offering by a Latin American company in more than 20 years.

ISG performs a function which may result in the Group working itself out of a job. Rather than continue with the establishment of country funds, ISG officials, when interviewed by the author, gave a preference to finding individual companies whose shares may be promoted in the same manner in which country funds are supported. Such companies are located in emerging countries which are approaching ineligibility for investment by the World Bank and the IFC.

Multi-Country Loan Facilities

Finally, in FY1990, the IFC developed a new instrument designed to mobilize medium-term foreign exchange lending from international financial institutions for small and medium-size projects in some LDCs. This Multi-Country Loan Facility (MLF) permits the IFC and an international bank to provide matching amounts of funds, in foreign currency, to finance projects in specified countries. The commercial bank will identify and appraise the project and will supervise the loan subsequent to commitment. The loan must be approved according to IFC investment criteria and, then, the IFC will act as lender of record for the entire loan. The MLF will combine the advantages of availability of local knowledge and client relationships of major international banks with risk-sharing between the banks and the IFC with provision of foreign exchange for development projects normally too small for IFC investment. During FY1990, this program resulted in three approvals: (1) Chile, Indonesia, Malaysia, and Uruguay with NMB Postbank as the participating institution, (2) Indonesia, Morocco, Pakistan, Sri Lanka, and Turkey with Algemene Bank Nederland as the participant, and (3) Bangladesh, Malaysia, Pakistan, Thailand, and Turkey with Banque Indosuez as the participant (International Securities Group, n/a).

OTHER NEW IFC PROGRAMS

Several other new programs have been developed by the IFC in recent years to facilitate the achievement of its objectives of private sector development finance in LDCs. These new programs include the Corporate Finance Services directed toward financial restructuring and privatization in LDCs, the Africa Project Development Facility, the African Management Services Company, the Caribbean Project Development Facility, the Foreign Investment Advisory Service, the Energy Program, the South Pacific Project Facility, and the Technical Assistance and Technology Service. These programs will be discussed and analyzed in the subsequent sections of this chapter. Case studies will be included.

Corporate Finance Services

The Corporate Finance Services Department (CFS) was established in FY1989 to provide advisory services for corporate structuring. Its principal activities are financial restructuring and privatization. In the latter operation, the IFC is brought into close contact with the LDC governments whose guarantee of IFC projects it will not accept. Before the formation of this department, the IFC had already implemented restructuring and privatization operations but needed to centralize these functions in order to better satisfy the demand for these services.

Corporate Restructuring

Financial restructuring of corporations in LDCs is often necessary before the IFC can make regular investments in such companies. Some of these firms have high debt service and require recapitalization and other improvements before they can respond to
market opportunities. In addition, restructuring may be a necessary
prerequisite for privatization because government-owned enterprises usually need financial restructuring to become private enterprises.

During the two years of CFS operations, the IFC has implemented a number of corporate restructurings, supported by charging
fees. In FY1989, one of the largest restructurings in Latin America
was facilitated by the work of CFS. This operation involved the
Visa Group, a Mexican conglomerate, in a $1.7 billion corporate
restructuring and debt reduction program for its companies: Visa
Holding, Fomento Económico Mexicano S.A. de C.V. (FEMSA),
and Grupo Cermoc S.A. de C.V. Visa is an integrated consumer
products company which includes brewing, soft drinks, and mineral
water production as well as distribution. The Group also owns con-
venience stores, food processing, automotive components manufacturing, hotels, and bio-industries facilities. Visa employs more than
40,000 in Mexico. The restructuring recommended by CFS resulted
in a reduction of Visa's total debt from $1.7 billion to $400 million.
Non-core businesses were sold to retire the debt and some debt was
bought back at a large discount. Some of the debt was rescheduled
and debt-to-equity swaps were used. Bonds were issued in the local
capital market and a private placement raised new equity capital.
This operation represents one of the IFC's most complex restructurings to date (Economics Department, 1989, p. 16).

CFS has carried out other restructuring operations. In addition to
the Visa project in FY1989, the IFC provided a flexible line of
credit to Banca Serfin, a leading Mexican commercial bank, to assist this bank in corporate restructuring of medium-size companies
in Mexico (IFC, *Annual Report*, 1990, pp. 43-44). In FY1990, CFS
assisted the debt reduction/financial restructuring of Philippine Associated Smelting and Refining Corporation (PASAR). This operation may also result in utilization of CFS' privatization advisory

services if one result of the restructuring will be a reduction of the Philippine Government's equity holding in PASAR.

Privatizations

Reality in many LDCs may be public enterprise — government-owned companies. Most of these public enterprises were inefficient and unproductive. However, the average LDC lacked personnel with business skills needed to operate these enterprises. Thus, government ownership seemed to be a means of adapting to such problems.

During the 1980s, many developing countries began to change their policies with regard to government ownership. Privatization became accepted by many of these governments (Nankani, 1988). A number of reasons have been advanced to explain the move to private ownership in the LDCs. Among them are governmental budget problems, less foreign direct investment, and the recognition that LDCs which encouraged private enterprise had higher rates of economic growth ("3rd World Focuses . . . ," 1986).

The Republic of Korea is an excellent example of a country in which a major business sector had a history of state ownership. Its banking system had been dominated for many years by government-owned commercial banks (Euh and Baker, 1990). These banks were inefficient and caused the Korean economy to resort to foreign capital in order to reduce the cost of capital for local firms. Foreign banks began to operate in Korea and to compete very well against the government-owned and operated banks. During the 1980s, the Korean Government began to privatize these banks. Now only a handful are still owned by the Korean Government and these are much more efficient because of the foreign competition.

Another example of the IFC's privatization activities involved a Liberian forestry, timber, and plywood operation which was a profitable private enterprise but went bankrupt after a government takeover in 1980. The Liberian Government wanted to reprivatize the company but no investors showed an interest. The IFC wrote a proposal in which a private company would take over the operation and rehabilitate it. The presence of the IFC in the project made it more attractive to foreign and domestic investors as well as the Liberian

Government. The project increased employment, added export earnings, furnished fiscal gains to the country, and increased the local standard of living (Economics Department, 1989, pp. 13-14).

Evidence is growing that privatization has become an accepted way of life in the LDCs. One recent survey showed that the World Bank had supported 109 projects which accomplished some degree of privatization. For example, 30 of these provided for liquidation of state enterprises, 33 resulted in some type of divestiture, and 21 involved other forms of privatization such as leasing, management contracts, and concessions (Farnsworth, 1989).

Privatization is fraught with many problems, especially in LDCs where the tradition has been for government to own, operate, and control business enterprise. For many years, development officials talked a lot about privatization but did very little about it. However, demand in recent years by LDC governments for advisory services related to privatization encouraged the IFC to expand its activities in this area and to centralize the function in the Corporate Finance Services Department. During FY1989 and 1990, the IFC entered into several privatization operations. Advice has been given to the Pakistani Government to assist in the development of a privatization strategy for several government-owned companies including the Pakistan International Airlines (PIA). The privatization of PIA will be a difficult task because of the heavy use of their national airlines to carry out military cargo operations. The Philippines Government is being advised by CFS in the restructuring and privatization of the Philippines Airlines and, in FY1990, the Philippines Government accepted the IFC's advice. In addition, the IFC has advised the Government of Indonesia about privatization of several govern-ment-owned hotels and the Government of Oman has been advised about the privatization of a private sector gas turbine power station and transmission system (IFC, *Annual Report*, 1989, p. 43).

With democratic rule replacing socialism in many of the Central European nations, the IFC has begun to assist the process of privat-izing enterprise in some of these countries. In Poland, the IFC, through CFS, helped to mold the legislative and institutional models needed to move from socialism and state-owned enterprise to private enterprise. Hungary and Yugoslavia are two other nations whose governments have begun privatization talks with the IFC.

Several other nations have begun to develop a rapport with the IFC in discussions of future privatization operations. Nepal has agreed to accept the IFC's advice in institution-building needed to privatize some areas of the economy. And companies and government agencies in Argentina, Egypt, India, Jamaica, Malaysia, Morocco, Nigeria, Turkey, and Venezuela, among others, have initiated discussions in this area with CFS (IFC, *Annual Report*, 1990, p. 36).

The privatization activity of CFS is bringing great promise in a world in which deregulation and liberalization of economic activities seems to be in vogue. However, it is not without problems. This is one area in which the IFC comes in close contact with government agencies and state-owned enterprises in LDCs. The IFC, of course, makes its investments only in private sector projects and without even a hint of government guarantee. Thus, the attempt to avoid intimacy with governments in its normal activities does not facilitate privatization operations. However, the IFC's goal is to foster private enterprise and one means of doing this is to convert public ownership into private enterprise. In order to achieve this goal, the IFC has to compromise some principles.

Another problem inherent in privatization operations is that projects flow into the IFC several at a time. This flurry is often followed with a gap of reduced activity. Officials of the IFC state that a constant flow of activity is needed in order to maintain skills in this area. Thus, CFS engages in a great deal of selling activities designed to promote its privatization advisory services. In addition, prowess in its project performance encourages word-of-mouth advertising. The IFC, in this area, competes with New York investment banks on privatization projects. With its smaller budget in promoting and implementing its privatization services, the IFC must rely more on excellence in performance to keep the pipelines filled with desirable privatization projects.

The Africa Project Development Facility (APDF)

Africa is a vast continent of many diverse nations ranging from the Arab countries in the north to sub-Saharan nations with French, Belgian, British, Portuguese, Moslem, and other cultural backgrounds, to the industrialized but racially-torn South Africa. For the most part, these nations are all LDCs. Some African nations have very low per capita incomes and, as a result, development finance agencies such as the World Bank, the African Development Bank (AfDB), and the United Nations Development Programme (UNDP) have recognized this and have recently begun to expand development financing in Africa.

As a result of this cooperation among leading development finance institutions, the IFC joined in 1986 with UNDP and the AfDB to establish an IFC-based department to assist African entrepreneurs in developing profitable medium-sized companies. This department is the Africa Project Development Facility (APDF). APDF does not provide funds but does work with entrepreneurs to obtain funds from banks and other sources and assists in staffing the new companies as well as obtaining the necessary technology for the projects assisted. The APDF is a UNDP project. The IFC is executing agency for the facility. The AfDB is regional sponsor. Additional financing will be contributed by 14 major industrialized countries. As of October 31, 1989, these agencies and countries had committed a total of $18.3 million to this facility and had disbursed $15.3 million of this commitment (IFC, *The Africa Project Development Facility*, 1990B, p. 7). During its FY1989, APDF obtained the services of 175 experts from 30 countries to consult on the projects examined by APDF.

Objectives

The major goal of the APDF is to speed up the development in sub-Saharan Africa of profitable companies sponsored by African entrepreneurs in order to generate self-sustaining economic growth and productive employment. All business sectors will be aided but the major focus will be on agriculture-related projects. These projects will be relatively small in nature with investment ranging from $0.5-5.0 million. Even smaller projects may be supported if local country conditions warrant (IFC, *The Africa Project Development Facility*, 1990A, p. 2).

APDF Services

Among the services to be offered by APDF are (1) the formulation and screening of project ideas for African entrepreneurs, (2) the provision of guidance, technical, and consultancy services to African entrepreneurs to promote good ideas, (3) the assistance of these entrepreneurs to select project partners and identify financial sources, (4) advice to foreign investors or financial institutions about investment opportunities in Africa, (5) privatization advice to African entrepreneurs when feasible.

Operations

One APDF team is located in Nairobi to cover East and Southern Africa and one is located in Abidjan to cover West and Central Africa. These teams have staffs of 8 to 10, quite small by any standard, but they have experience in development finance, commercial and merchant banking, and relevant private sector business. They are familiar with requirements and policies of various multinational and national government agencies. An Advisory Board meets annually and reviews policies and offers guidance on operations. Its members are from the private sector in Africa and from the APDF sponsors and donor countries. After staff identifies and assesses projects and proposals, those are selected for assistance which will have significant impact on the local economy.

Selected APDF Projects

Three cases can be characterized as representative of APDF projects. The first case, Yarley Cosmetics in Botswana, concerns a company based on a business plan developed by APDF. The firm will manufacture Afro Haircare Products. The sponsor has management experience in the hairdressing salon business. Yarley is a $450,000 project which has created 15 new jobs and its exports will furnish foreign exchange for Botswana. The second case, African Roses in Nigeria, is a flower export project located in Kaduna. It produces roses for the European market. The project will cost $1.4 million. A French firm is technical partner and financing was provided by a consortium of Nigerian banks. The third case, Chrismill

Farms, Ltd., of Tanzania, is a $2 million project which will result in non-traditional exports. Pineapples for export to Europe and the Persian Gulf area will be grown on a 995-hectare farm. APDF assisted with farm plans and market development. A second stage of the project may result in the construction of processing facilities to produce concentrate and juice.

Another representative APDF project consisted of assistance to two women entrepreneurs to negotiate purchase of a retail clothing business in Nairobi. The sponsors will design, make, and sell professional and formal wear for women using local materials through Kwanza Clothing. This $100,000 project will replace Kenyan imports of such clothing (IFC, *Annual Report*, 1990, p. 40).

The African Management Services Company (AMSCo)

Two problems have been identified as hindrances to economic development, especially of the private sector, in Africa. These are: the weakness of many private enterprises and the slow progress in the privatization of many government-owned enterprises. Both of these problems stem from the lack of qualified and experienced management personnel in Africa. To alleviate this shortage, the IFC formed the African Management Services Company (AMSCo) in early 1989. This new agency was formed with the cooperation of the UNDP and the AfDB.

Operations

AMSCo brings together management expertise, public sector funding, and private sector investment. It is incorporated in the Netherlands as a Dutch company with 70 percent of its shares held by the IFC, AfDB, the Danish Industrialization Fund for Developing Countries, the Finnish Fund for Industrial Development Corporation, the Caisse Centrale de Coopération Economique of France, the Finance Company for Developing Countries of the Netherlands, the Development Bank of Portugal, the Swedish Fund for Industrial Cooperation with Developing Countries, and the Commonwealth Development Corporation of the United Kingdom. The remaining 30 percent is owned jointly by more than 50 international private companies from some 20 industrialized and developing nations.

These private companies will provide personnel and training to African companies which need such management services. The venture will be a commercial, self-sustaining project, although this goal will take at least two years to achieve. Eight developed country governments will contribute funds to the project. A total of $7 million has already been contributed to AMSCo (IFC, *Annual Report*, 1990, p. 41).

Objective

The major goal of AMSCo is to promote African companies which are profitable and competitive. The executives furnished these companies by AMSCo will train African managers who will succeed the donor managers (IFC, *Annual Report*, 1990, p. 41).

First Year of Operations

During its first year of operations, AMSCo promoted itself throughout Africa by making presentations to several groups of interested publics. A portfolio of projects was developed and the first project was begun: to improve the management of a dairy operation in Senegal (IFC, *Annual Report*, 1990, p. 41).

The African Enterprise Fund

The African Enterprise Fund (AEF) was established in FY1989 to furnish assistance to small and medium-sized firms in sub-Saharan African nations which are members of the IFC and which are too small to receive direct financial assistance from the IFC. The program was established for a 3-year trial period and the IFC's officials predict that $60 million will be invested in projects approved by the AEF. As of the end of FY1990, AEF had invested $7 million in 14 projects in eight African nations (IFC, *Annual Report*, 1990, p. 21). See Table 10-3 in Chapter 10 for coverage on the investment projects approved by AEF in FY1990.

The Caribbean Project Development Facility (CPDF)

The CPDF was established by the IFC in 1981 in conjunction with the UNDP. CPDF has a regional office in Barbados and receives financial support from government agencies in Canada, the Federal Republic of Germany, the Netherlands, the United States, and the United Kingdom, as well as from the IADB, UNDP, and the IFC. The principal goal of CPDF is to assist entrepreneurs in 27 nations of the Caribbean region to obtain debt and equity finance for new or expanding businesses. Thus, it supplements and complements the IFC's on-going investment operations in this area.

CPDF Services

Services offered by CPDF will include: (1) consulting by which CPDF will provide specialized advisory services to examine and advise local firms and businessmen on different aspects of the project, from technical to marketing matters; (2) technical and commercial partners including assistance to a projects' promoter in the selection of possible technical and/or marketing partners and advice on contractual agreements; (3) local conditions including advice to foreign promoters about the local commercial environment, regulations and requirements and assistance in the identification of potential local partners; (4) project evaluation including the preparation of a detailed proposal description and analysis of the investment project to be submitted for consideration by financial institutions; and (5) financing including identification of sources of financing and provision of assistance to promoters in deliberations and negotiations with interested financial institutions ("FIDE, CPDF Sign Agreement," 1990).

Funding and Operations

Funding of CPDF activities comes from a variety of sources. Donors include IADB, the IFC, UNDP, and government agencies in Canada, the Federal Republic of Germany, Japan, the Netherlands, the United States, and the United Kingdom. During the past year, CPDF began operations to fund nine projects with total costs of more than $83 million. Since its inception, CPDF has obtained funds for 52 projects with total costs of approximately $120 million (IFC, *Annual Report*, 1990, p. 42). Of these projects, more than 40 percent have been in the agricultural sector while more than a third have been in the industrial sector with the remainder in the tourism and financial sectors. More than 70 percent of jobs created with the assistance of CPDF are in the agricultural sector in which the investment cost per new job, about $16, is the lowest ("FIDE, CPDF Sign Agreement," 1990).

An FY1990 project in Honduras is representative of CPDF projects. This project is with the Foundation for Investment and Development of Exports (FIDE) which will provide promotional and logistical assistance to CPDF to support its activities in Honduras. Honduran business firms will have an improved channel of access to funding for major investment projects with this agreement. FIDE will serve as a liaison between Honduran firms and CPDF ("FIDE, CPDF Sign Agreement," 1990).

Energy Programs

The Energy Program of the IFC was authorized in 1984 with a primary objective of contributing to the energy supply of LDCs by encouraging international oil companies to expand their activities in LDCs. So far, the IFC has approved 11 investments in nine pure exploration ventures, along with two equity investments in oil exploration and development in the Meleiha venture in Egypt. Total disbursements in these projects amounts to some $46 million. In addition, loans totaling $665 million have been approved for these energy projects with $380 million of this for the IFC's own account and the remaining $285 million syndicated with commercial banks. During FY1990, the IFC entered into four energy projects in four countries by committing $109.45 million in investment funds to projects whose total cost is $422.6 million (IFC, *Annual Report*, 1990, p. 42).

Exploration

The IFC is currently involved in five exploration projects. Among these are the first oil discovery in an IFC venture in the Chirete-olleros project in Argentina in which a well drilled during testing began producing 800 barrels/day. In addition, the IFC made its first ever investment in the country of Guinea-Bissau in an off-shore project in the Anetibene block in partnership with Shell Pecten and Walter International Inc. The IFC has a 15 percent interest in the project.

Development

One IFC investment typical of energy development in LDCs was the FY1990 loan of $70 million to Oleoducto de Colombia in a $321 million project to construct a 476-kilometer crude oil pipeline. The pipeline will increase production and exports of crude oil from Colombia's two major oil producing areas — the Llanos region and the Magdalena Valley. The IFC commitment is for 50 percent of the loan while the remainder of the loan was syndicated among seven commercial banks.

An example of the potential profitability of investments in the energy area by the IFC concerns the Meleiha Exploration and Development Venture in Egypt. Since 1986, the IFC has made two investments totaling $30 million and has received $14 million in revenues from the project. At the beginning of the venture, the size of the oil field was estimated to be 50 million barrels. Proven reserves now stand at 80 million barrels and it is expected that the field will eventually produce about 100 million barrels. The field currently produces 17,000 barrels per day. In addition, a large quantity of gas has been discovered. No gas market exists in the area but the construction of a gas-holding facility may make this find a contribution to Egypt's export earnings.

Foreign Investment Advisory Service (FIAS)

The IFC established FIAS in FY1986 to carry out advisory services related to its investments and, in FY1989, made it a cooperative joint program with the Multilateral Investment Guaranty Agency (MIGA), a World Bank affiliate established in 1988 to promote economic development by encouraging the flow of private foreign direct investment to developing countries through the insurance of such investment against political risks such as expropriation, revolution, war, etc., and the provision of advisory and consultative services to member countries which will enhance the investment climate and promote specific investment opportunities.

FIAS' major role is to provide advice to LDCs on how to adjust policies, regulations, and institutional arrangements which, if implemented, will attract additional foreign investment in priority private sectors. The resulting foreign investment will be structured in such a way as to safeguard national interests which ordinarily may work against needed foreign private investment as a result of policies and regulations adopted by the host government. Again the underlying principle of this activity is the input of investment funds into LDC private sector firms which will increase profitability and enhance development.

FIAS Operations

FIAS is another of the IFC's new activities which comes in direct contact with member governments even though the original philosophy of the organization disdained government guarantee and interference with investment projects involving the IFC. In short, FIAS will not give advice unless requested by a government. When this occurs, FIAS will then analyze and advise on procedures for the promotion, appraisal, approval, and monitoring of foreign investment. In fact, FIAS may assist the requesting government to implement its recommendation (IFC, *FIAS . . . ,* 1990, p. 2).

FIAS provides assistance to IFC member governments in their formulation of policies directed at the promotion and regulation of direct foreign investment as well as policies that will facilitate such investment in specific sectors. FIAS, in providing this assistance, may identify the important aspects of the project which are inherent in the local investment climate such as the legal, accounting, and regulatory framework; the system which provides foreign exchange for imports, debt reduction, and profit remittance to foreign investors — sometimes subject in LDCs to blocked currency regulations; screening and approval procedures; promotional services for potential investors; regulation of technology transfer and intellectual property rights protection — the latter a problem in many LDCs in which a licensing agreement has been transacted between a local licensee and a foreign licensor; availability of finance; and tax reductions and any other incentives of a fiscal nature (IFC, *FIAS*, p. 2).

FIAS will also focus its attention quite narrowly on specific aspects of financial techniques dealing with foreign direct investment, the knowledge of which is in short supply in LDCs. For example, FIAS has the expertise to organize an investment promotion agency, design a debt-equity swap program, or formulate a law to regulate a specific investment activity. The FIAS team is able to draw on the combined expertise of not only the IFC staff but also those of the World Bank and MIGA in the skill areas of economics, law, finance, and technology. The combined FIAS/MIGA staff has "hands-on" experience in working with local and foreign investors and their skills include those concerned with project appraisal, assessment of political risk, legal arrangements between local and foreign investors and between investors and governments, assessment of a country's international comparative advantage in a specific sector, and engineering problems in the technical appraisal of projects (IFC, *FIAS*, p. 7).

FIAS Projects

In FY1988, FIAS initiated an extensive program in sub-Saharan Africa to assist in the formulation and implementation of strategies for attracting additional foreign investment, stimulating domestic investment, and developing export industries. Other local institutions which have been invited by FIAS to cooperate in the African program include the Preferential Trade Area for Eastern and Southern African States, the Economic Community of West African States, the Southern African Development Coordination Conference, and the AfDB (IFC, *Annual Report*, 1988, p. 45).

Specific activities by FIAS in Africa have been implemented in Togo, Senegal, Ghana, Kenya, and Guinea (IFC, *FIAS*, pp. 2-7). In Togo, FIAS convened workshops in Togo and Washington to facilitate the revision of the country's investment code and to establish a work program to develop export-processing free zones as well as to draft and implement regulations and procedures to accompany the new investment code. In Senegal, FIAS assisted the government to identify policy changes and initiative to encourage foreign direct investment in agricultural ventures in the Senegal River Basin. In Ghana, FIAS assisted in the implementation of a new investment code, including the drafting of legal guidelines to simplify the code's application as well as means of streamlining procedures, organizational arrangements, and work programs. In Kenya, FIAS reviewed the work program and training needs, investment reforms, tax regime, incentives, and creation of an investment code for the Investment Promotion Centre (IPC). From this project, an investment policy statement resulted. In Guinea, FIAS reviewed the investment environment for the government and concentrated on incentives, screening and promotion, as well as recommendations to streamline the investment code implementation. FIAS also analyzed Guinea's institutions necessary to support foreign investment and recommended ways to strengthen these institutions. In FY1990, FIAS sponsored, with support from UNDP, a major conference held in Washington, D.C., on the promotion of foreign investment in sub-Saharan Africa. This conference attracted 40 speakers and 200 participants.

In addition to Africa, FIAS has been active in other countries. These have included Indonesia, China, Yugoslavia, Bangladesh, and Thailand. FIAS is presently beginning to focus on Eastern Europe with its problems of lack of investment capital and managerial skills as the process of privatization replaces state-controlled socialist regimes (IFC, *Annual Report*, 1990, p. 44).

FIAS has also initiated activities in Poland and Hungary. In Poland, FIAS has addressed the issues of changing the foreign investment law to reduce government involvement in business decisions, to improve access of foreign direct investment to foreign exchange, revision of tax regulations to provide more effective incentives, and restructuring and strengthening the Polish Foreign Investment Agency in order to improve its ability to promote Poland to foreign investors. In Hungary, FIAS has focused on restructuring and retargeting tax incentives, identification of public enterprises which should be permitted to proceed with privatization and which should be more closely controlled, and overhauling the screening process for foreign direct investment.

Funding FIAS Operations

FIAS operating costs have been underwritten by the IFC, UNDP, and MIGA, and by its own trust fund as well as by fees charged clients for consultations. The FIAS trust fund received contributions in FY1990 from France, Japan, the Netherlands, Switzerland, and the United Kingdom. The U.S. Agency for International Development made a commitment for funds over a number of years for FIAS operations in sub-Saharan Africa (IFC, *Annual Report*, 1990, p. 45).

South Pacific Project Facility (SPPF)

The experience with the project development facilities in Africa since 1986 and the Caribbean region since 1989 prompted the IFC to establish a similar facility devoted to the South Pacific region. Thus, the South Pacific Project Facility (SPPF) was formed to assist in the development of small and medium-sized private enterprises in the South Pacific island nations. The IFC will manage SPPF and will furnish some of the facility's funds while the remainder of its operating funds will be provided by donor countries and multilateral development institutions. SPPF will begin operations in FY1991 based on a chartered life of at least five years. Thus, no case studies were available at the time of writing nor can an evaluation be made of this newest of the IFC's activities.

Technical Assistance and Technology Service

The IFC Engineering Department has supported the agency's commitment to the application of science and technology to development by providing member countries with technical assistance in the context of project development, project appraisal, and the physical restructuring of industrial operations. During FYs1988 and 1989, the IFC centralized some of this activity in two new operations, Technical Assistance (TA) in FYs 1988 and 1989, and Technology Service (TS) in FY1989.

Technical Assistance (TA)

The IFC established seven TA trust funds during FYs1988 and 1989 with more than $5 million contributed by the European Community and government agencies in Canada, Finland, Italy, Japan, the Netherlands, Sweden, Switzerland, and the United States. Total contributions to these funds by these donors amounted to $8.5 million in FY1990.

With these funds together with a $1 million Investment Feasibility Study Facility used by the IFC, a broad range of services can be financed. Among them are sector studies, pilot operations for new technologies, prefeasibility and feasibility studies, training programs, and short-term management support. These programs enable the enhancement of project proposals which the IFC develops into ventures capable of being spun off to banks and other private investors (IFC, *Annual Report*, 1989, p. 48).

One major area of application of technical assistance by the IFC has been in the area of capital markets, especially aspects of regulation of financial and securities markets in addition to international financial flows. During the last two decades, the IFC, through the Capital Markets Department and now by means of the technical assistance trust funds, has researched and advised on financial systems in 28 countries, securities markets in 43 countries, regulatory systems in 28 countries, accounting systems in 9 countries, tax policies in 22 countries, as well as means to increase access to international capital markets in 14 countries (Economics Department, 1989, p. 15).

During FY1990, the IFC supported 22 TA projects which involved co-financing from the trust funds amounting to $2 million. These projects are listed in Table 6-2. Since the initiation of the TA trust funds, 37 projects have been supported. They involve one project which will prepare viable investments in the South Pacific island nations in cooperation with the SPPF, a fisher/fish processing project in Senegal, a pilot metallurgical operation in Peru to refine silver concentrate into dore bars, and feasibility studies for a poplin fabric plant in Tunisia as well as a sewing-thread operation in Egypt.

TABLE 6-2. Technical Assistance (as of the end of FY1990)

Nature of Activity	Technical Assistance Projects	Country
Sector Study	-Fabrication and export of leather goods	Bangladesh
	-Textiles	Global
Project Identification/	-Poplin fabric production	Tunisia
Linking of Partners	-Mangoro pulpwood export	Madagascar
	-Africa/EC integrated trucking operation	Morocco
	-Production of raw silk	Thailand
	-Multi-phase study to identify investment opportunities in selected countries for IFC and foreign and local sponsors in projects providing environmental goods and services	Phase 1-Turkey Mexico, Thailand Phase 2-Malaysia, Poland, Pakistan, Chile Phase 3-Indonesia, Hungary
Feasibility Study	-Compressed natural gas application for commercial vehicles	Bolivia
	-Leasing company	Bolivia
	-Integrated poultry project	Cameroon
	-Soft drinks project	Indonesia
	-Porcelain/ceramic tableware project	Indonesia

	-Complete systems manufacture	
	and assembly line, services,	
	training	Portugal
	-Silk production project	Thailand
	-Environmental impact of	
	polystyrene project	Tunisia
	-Venture capital fund	Zimbabwe
Pilot Plant	-Paddy straw mushroom growing	Indonesia
Project Rehabilitation	-Nickel mining project	Philippines
	-Fishery/fish processing project	Uruguay
Promotional/Technology	-Biotechnology (medical test kits)	Cameroon
Transfer/Technical	-Follow-up seminars on global	
Assistance	automotive study (Brazil, India,	
	Mexico)	Global
	-Pollution control	Poland
	-Fish processing operation	Senegal

Note. From Annual Report 1990, by IFC, 1990 Washington, D.C.: International Finance Corporation, p. 46.

Technology Service (TS)

In FY1989, the IFC established a new Technology Service (TS) on an experimental basis. Through TS, the IFC will act as a broker in technology transfers and will assist businesses in member countries to identify and acquire the technologies needed to begin a new venture or to modernize, expand, or diversify their operations. TS can also assist owners of technologies to locate applications and business partners in LDCs for their technical processes and expertise.

TS has assisted companies in several LDCs (IFC, *Annual Report*, 1990, pp. 45-46). These include Chile, India, Indonesia, Kenya, Mexico, and Pakistan. Among these projects assisted by TS include preparation of a study for an agribusiness company in India which compared the technologies and business potential of by-products that could be produced by biotechnological processes from a material that might otherwise have been underutilized or treated as waste. TS also conducted a search in Brazil for a company interested in manufacturing a computer developed by a Scandinavian firm.

TS services are available on a fee basis for business firms in member countries. These activities may result in an IFC investment although such is not a prerequisite to obtain assistance from TS.

Guaranteed Recovery of Investment Principal (GRIP)

In the mid-1980s, the IFC created the Guaranteed Recovery of Investment Principal (GRIP), a program designed to encourage private investors to participate in projects financed by the IFC even though the risk is considered quite high by the private investor. The program gives the investor a number of alternatives in participating with the IFC. The private investor considering an equity investment in an IFC project gives the funds to the IFC and receives a dollar-denominated debt certificate (GRIP) which the IFC must repay in some stipulated period, for example, 20 years. The IFC then uses the funds to make the equity investment in its own name. When the debt certificate or GRIP matures, the investor may (1) get his funds returned with some profit included, (2) buy the shares by cancelling the debt and paying a pre-arranged premium to the IFC, or (3) extend the GRIP for an additional period. The risk of the investment is shifted from the investor to the IFC by means of the GRIP ("Promote the Private Sector," 1986, p. 54).

Multi-Country Loan Facilities

During FY1990, the IFC developed a new instrument, the Multi-Country Loan Facility (MCLF), designed to mobilize medium-term foreign exchange lending from international financial institutions (IFC, *Annual Report*, 1990, p. 38). These funds will be invested in small and medium-size projects in selected developing countries, such projects normally too small for direct financing from the IFC.

Under the MCLF, the IFC and another international financial institution will furnish matching funds in foreign currency to such projects. The international financial institution will identify and appraise the projects and will supervise any loans made. The loans must be approved by the IFC which then acts as lender of record for the full amount of the loan. The international financial institution's contribution will be in the form of a participation of 50 percent or more of the IFC loan. Thus, the IFC shares in the risk. The international financial institution will use its branch and other commercial networks to gain local knowledge and client relationships. And foreign exchange is obtained for projects too small for direct IFC funding.

During the first year of operations of the MCLF, the IFC approved three loans. These were (1) for a project with NMB Postbank for loans in Chile, Indonesia, Malaysia, and Uruguay; (2) for a project with Algemene Bank Nederland for loans in Indonesia, Morocco, Pakistan, Sri Lanka, and Turkey; (3) for a project with Banque Indosuez for loans in Bangladesh, Malaysia, Pakistan, Thailand, and Turkey (IFC, *Annual Report*, 1990, p. 38).

SUMMARY AND CONCLUSIONS

During the 1980s, the IFC expanded its range of services and activities in line with the expansion of its capital and investment commitments. The growth in IFC investment-related activities has been in direct correlation with the rapidly expanding and diverse number of financial market instruments and services available to investors. The IFC has centralized activities such as financial restructuring and privatizations in a new Corporate Financial Services

Department. It has expanded its Capital Market Department to include the services of an International Securities Group offering advice to a focused group of investors. The worldwide development of country funds and the concomitant worldwide mobilization of more than $11 billion of funds for LDCs has been a major role of this department. The operations of its Foreign Investment Advisory Service will bring the IFC into close contact with LDC governments in advising them about methods for increasing foreign direct investment in their private sector.

Emphasis has been placed on specific geographical areas or on specific investment activities which are in line with changing development philosophies of international financial institutions. For example, the IFC has established new development facilities for Africa, the Caribbean region, and the South Pacific. And operations which were the responsibility of the Engineering Department concerning technical assistance and technology transfer have been centralized in new operations utilizing Technical Assistance trust funds and a Technology Services Department.

With regard to the IFC's advisory services, it has organized these into a more systematic method by replacing its normal project-related advice with advisory efforts that go beyond what is normal in complex projects and advisory services unrelated to project finance. Private sector investors can benefit from the accumulated expertise in the IFC. The key to success of this new policy depends on how well the IFC channels its special expertise for maximum impact (World Bank, *Developing the Private Sector*, 1989, p. 33).

The IFC has continued to promote two major objectives with the formation of these new services. First, these new facilities enable the IFC to promote and fulfill its role of investing in private sector projects in member LDCs without government guarantee or interference. Second, the IFC's objective of involving the international financial community and the industrialized nations to participate in the development process is facilitated by the cooperation from international financial institutions—with their participations in IFC-sponsored projects, and government agencies of industrialized nations—in their role as donors of funds to cover the operating expenses of new IFC operations.

Chapter 7

The International Finance Corporation in Latin America

INTRODUCTION

The discussion in this chapter will focus on the IFC's operations in Latin America. First, a broad aggregative analysis of the IFC investments in the region will be covered. Second, a number of representative cases of IFC investments in Central and South America and the Caribbean will be discussed. These cases will include IFC investments or underwriting activities in Compañía Fundidora de Fierro y Acero de Monterrey, S.A. (Fundidora) of Mexico; Papel e Celulose Catarinense, S.A., of Brazil; Celulosa Argentina; Companhia Petroquimica Camacari (CPC) of Brazil; and Cape Horn Methanol Ltd., of Chile. Finally, the chapter will include coverage of the new IFC operations in this area, including services offered by Corporate Finance Services (CFS), the Caribbean Project Development Facility (CPDF), and the Foreign Investment Advisory Service (FIAS), as well as Capital Market and syndication/participation activity.

Latin America has been the most active area for IFC operations and investments. Many of the original development finance company (DFC) investments by the IFC were Latin American institutions. As of the end of FY1990, the IFC held in its portfolio 162 project investments located in 21 countries and 1 region. The book value of these investments was originally $2,901,759,000. The IFC still holds investments in these projects valued at $2,082,419,000. See Table 7-1 for a breakdown of these investments by country.

TABLE 7-1. IFC Investments in Latin America (held in portfolio end of FY1990, thousands of US$)

Country	# of Projects Held	Original Total IFC Investment	Currently Held
Argentina	27	$496,677	$394,223
Barbados	2	1,550	1,440
Bolivia	4	22,150	20,700
Brazil	40	797,795	570,330
Chile	10	371,211	285,227
Colombia	12	138,602	87,656
Costa Rica	2	5,524	3,072
Dominica	1	700	701
Dominican Republic	6	25,999	15,688
Ecuador	2	4,677	4,463
Grenada	1	6,000	4,500
Haiti	1	1,500	377
Honduras	2	5,275	4,317
Jamaica	6	27,215	21,136
Mexico	25	734,566	482,248
Panama	2	53,627	15,890
Paraguay	2	8,808	3,993
Peru	6	34,248	12,123
Trinidad and Tobago	3	35,810	29,258
Uruguay	4	36,950	25,202

Venezuela	3	80,375	87,375
Regional	1	12,500	12,500
Total	162	$2,901,759	$2,082,419

Note. From <u>Annual Report 1990</u>, by IFC, 1990, Washington D.C.: International Finance Corporation, pp. 78-91.

IFC Investments 1987-1990

During its operational history, the IFC has been extremely active in assisting private enterprise in Latin America and the Caribbean area (IFC, *Annual Reports*, 1987, 1988, 1989, and 1990). This is especially true of the last four fiscal years, 1987-1990. The IFC made 102 investments to projects in this area over these four years. The IFC commitments to these projects totaled $2,401.67 million. In addition, the IFC made 25 Capital Markets approvals during FYs1987-1990 which totaled $203.08 million. Thus, the IFC's total commitments to 127 projects in this area amounted to $2,604.75 million. The total cost of these projects was estimated to be $14,022.23 million, including the Capital Market approvals and $12,916.6 million excluding these operations.

In the early years before the IFC was able to raise significant amounts of capital, its average commitments were generally in the $5 million range and average size of the projects in which the IFC invested was seldom more than $25 million. Analysis of the Latin American projects shows a dramatic increase of both the IFC investment commitment and the project total cost. The average size of the IFC investment in each private enterprise during the 1987-1990 period was more than $23.5 million and the average total cost of each project amounted to $126.6 million. This change in investment ability on the part of the IFC can be seen in Table 7-2 in which the IFC investment approvals for Latin America and the Caribbean area during the most recent year, FY1990, are shown.

TABLE 7-2. IFC Investment Approvals — Latin America and the Caribbean (FY1990, millions of US$)

Company	Country	Activity	Gross Investment	Project Cost
Hidra Oil Development	Argentina	Oil development	30.00	30.00
Petroquímica Ensenada S.A.	Argentina	Petrochemicals	35.00	135.10
Terminal 6 S.A.	Argentina	Port Services	4.00	13.20
Journey's End Caribbean Club Ltd.	Belize	Tourism	1.00	3.00
Banco Industrial S.A.	Bolivia	Development finance	2.12	5.90
Bahia Sul Celulose S.A.	Brazil	Timber, pulp, paper	55.00	897.00
Companhia Minuano de Alimentos	Brazil	Poultry	7.00	28.00
Companhia Vidraria Santa Marina	Brazil	Glass manufacturing	25.00	103.00
Engepol Engenharia de Polimeros S.A.	Brazil	Plastics manufacturing	3.50	11.54
Ripasa S.A. Celulose e Papel	Brazil	Timber, pulp, paper	25.00	146.00
Compañia de Teléfonos de Chile S.A.*†	Chile	Telecommunications	152.10	1,104.40
Compañia Puerto de Coronel S.A.	Chile	Port services	8.00	39.70
Compañia Colombiana de Tejidos, S.A.	Colombia	Textiles	22.50	56.86

Oleoducto de Colombia S.A.	Colombia	Oil pipline	70.00	321.00
San Isidro Free Trade Zone	Domin. Rep.	Industrial services	6.00	15.30
Sociedad Comercializador				
S.A.	Domin. Rep.	Construction materials/		
		cement	.08	.78
Banca Serfin*	Mexico	Development finance	6.50	22.00
Bancomer*	Mexico	Credit line	20.00	40.00
Banco Nacional de Mexico*	Mexico	Credit line	60.00	200.00
Grupo Condumex, S.A.				
de C.V.	Mexico	Manufacturing	50.00	128.00
Grupo Primex, S.A. de C.V.	Mexico	Petrochemicals	20.00	57.50
Indelpro, S.A. de C.V.	Mexico	Petrochemicals	42.00	108.00
Petrocel	Mexico	Petrochemicals	32.00	101.60
Compañia de Minas				
Buenaventura S.A.	Peru	Non-ferrous mining	.60	6.00
Productura de Alcoholes				
Hidratados, C.A.	Venezuela	Petrochemicals	<u>41.40</u>	<u>142.50</u>
		Sub-total	718.80	3,716.38
		Capital Markets approvals	<u>16.08</u>	<u>473.10</u>
		Total	**734.88**	**4,189.48**

* Project undertaken in cooperation with the Capital Markets Department.

† Two projects, on involving loan and quasi-equity financing of $130 million, the other, underwriting of $22.1 million.

Note. From <u>Annual Report 1990</u>, by IFC, 1990, Washington D.C.: International Finance Corporation, p. 30.

SELECTED IFC INVESTMENTS
IN LATIN AMERICA AND THE CARIBBEAN AREA

The remainder of this chapter contains brief detailed case studies of selected IFC investments in this region. The companies in which the IFC has invested were chosen for their representativeness of the type of private sector enterprises which have appealed to the IFC. Some, such as Fundidora, Celulosa Argentina, and Papel e Celulose were early IFC commitments while others, such as Cape Horn Methanol and Companhia Petroquimica Camacari (CPC), were more recent recipients of IFC commitments. Most of these companies are profitable operations and remain clients of the IFC. One, Fundidora, has incurred problems and has been taken over by the Mexican Government.

Mexico and the IFC

Mexico has been one of the World Bank Group's largest customers. In fact, the country has been one of the leading debtor countries during the 1980s. During the IFC's first ten years, Mexican companies collectively were the IFC's second largest customer. During this period, the IFC made 12 investment commitments in Mexican private enterprises totaling more than $21.7 million (World Bank, *World Bank Group in Mexico*, 1967, p. 2). Since its first commitment to a Mexican firm in 1957, companies in several industries have been assisted by the IFC. Among the products manufactured by these firms are high speed twist drills, steel pipes, sodium sulphate, automobile parts, and steel. The first issue of convertible debentures made in Mexico was accomplished when the IFC invested in Tubos de Acero de Mexico, S.A. (TAMSA) in 1962.

Engranes y Productos Industriales, S.A. (Engranes)

The first investment was made in Mexico by the IFC in 1957 to Engranes y Productos Industriales, S.A. (Engranes), a company owned by Mexican and American stockholders, to finance an expansion of manufacturing operations ("IFC Investment in Mexico," 1957). Engranes expanded its operations to manufacture a variety of industrial products and components including machine tooling for the manufacture of automotive and other mechanical parts, a forge shop, and an electric steel furnace. The expansion brought to Mexico for the first time the manufacture of automotive differential gears and universal joints, hydraulic jacks, and rock-drill parts.

Engranes had been formed from three companies in 1953 by H. C. Carney, a U.S. citizen who had gone to Mexico in 1947. These plants were a machine shop which produced gear drives and parts for deep-well water pumps, an iron and non-ferrous-metal foundry which made a variety of castings, and a plate shop which produced tanks and other steel manufactures ("On the Economic Front," 1957).

The IFC made a loan of $600,000 in notes with a maturity of 10 years, half denominated in dollars and half in pesos, both portions at 7 percent, plus contingent interest related to Engranes' future earnings. The IFC also received a 10-year option to convert 40 percent of the investment into shares. This investment was representative of the quasi-equity commitments made by the IFC before its Articles of Agreement were amended to permit the IFC to make direct share investments in private enterprise.

Compañía Fundidora de Fierro y Acero de Monterrey, S. A. (Fundidora)

Among the largest commitments made by the IFC during its early years to a Mexican firm were those made in Compañía Fundidora de Fierro y Acero de Monterrey, S.A. (Fundidora). Fundidora was the largest privately owned steel company in Mexico in the 1960s. Three underwriting commitments by the IFC to Fundidora in 1962, 1964, and 1966 will be discussed in the remainder of this section.

Fundidora, located in Monterrey, was founded in 1900 with a capitalization of $5 million and pioneered in integrated steel production in Latin America. For 50 years, Fundidora was a leading plant in Latin America with 90,000 tons of production emanating from a 300-ton blast furnace in 1903. The Mexican Revolution of 1913-1915 caused a shutdown of the plant but the company eventually regained its pre-Revolution production level, until the world depression began in 1929. By 1932, Fundidora began the unending growth which continued until the 1970s ("Cia. Fundidora," 1960, p. 2). A large iron ore deposit was acquired at Durango in 1920 and expansions added a plant to manufacture steel refractories in 1927, a second blast furnace and enlargement of its open-hearth shop in 1941-1943.

In 1957, Fundidora decided to expand further by increasing capacity from 200,000 tons to 500,000 tons as well as introducing the production of flat steel. At that time, two further expansions were planned for 1962-1965 and 1965-1970 designed to increase capacity to 1 million tons. The cost of the first expansion was estimated to be $100 million. The U.S. Export-Import Bank loaned $42 million to Fundidora and the company performed all construction, installation, and engineering work. The remainder of the funding was raised from capital increases, retained earnings, and other borrowings. The company voted to increase its shares by issuing an additional 458,333 shares. This share issue raised an additional $5.1 million.

The IFC joined with Credito Bursatil, a Mexican investment company, to form an underwriting syndicate for the share issue. This represented the first underwriting of an equity issue by the IFC since its charter was amended to permit such an operation. Shares not subscribed during a rights offering were taken up by the syndicate. Handelsfinanz A.G. of Zurich, Kuhn, Loeb & Company of New York, and Morgan Guaranty International Finance Corporation of New York participated in the underwriting by subscribing to 1/3 of the commitment. The underwriting was one of the largest in Mexico at that time.

Credito Bursatil, the other member of the syndicate was owned principally by Mexico's largest private bank, Banco Nacional de Mexico. Shareowners of Credito Bursatil also included Banque de Paris et des Pays-Bas of Paris, Morgan Guaranty International Finance Corporation, an Edge Act subsidiary of Morgan Guaranty Bank in New York, and Banco Hispano-Americano of Madrid (IFC, *Press Release*, 1962, p. 2). Credito Bursatil's share of the underwriting was 25 percent and IFC underwrote the remainder. In addition, IFC agreed to purchase 128,000 Fundidora shares for its own account, totaling $1.1 million (IFC, *Press Release*, 1962,

p. 2). Thus, the IFC's total commitment amounted to $1,126,400 in operational investments and a $2,942,500 underwriting commitment, for a total of $4,068,900. The shares not subscribed by Mexican investors during the rights offering were taken up by the syndicate and offered to investors in Latin America, Canada, and Europe (IFC, *Annual Report*, 1961-1962, p. 11).

In 1964, a second phase of Fundidora's long-range objective of 1 million tons capacity was required. This phase, designed to increase the company's capacity from 500,000 tons to 750,000 tons annually, required an additional increase in shares outstanding. A new issue of 1,250,000 shares yielded $12,500,000. The company borrowed $28 million from the U.S. Export-Import Bank. Other funds were generated internally and borrowed locally.

The IFC also joined with Credito Bursatil in this expansion by assisting in the largest underwriting in Mexican history. The underwriting syndicate consisted of these two institutions as well as ten other U.S., Mexican, and Swiss financial institutions. The IFC and Credito Bursatil shared equally in the new issue while Kuhn, Loeb & Company, Handelsfinanz A.G., and Morgan Guaranty International Finance Corporation participated in the IFC commitment. Seven Mexican financial institutions participated in Credito Bursatil's commitment. These consisted of Banco Nacional de Mexico, Banco de Comercio, Banco Comercial Mexicano, Banco de Londres y Mexico, Banco Aboumrad, Banco de Industria y Comercio, and Casasus Trigueros y Cia (IFC, *Press Release*, 1964, pp. 1-2).

The new shares were well subscribed by the public during the offering with only 8,540 shares necessary to be taken up by the syndicate. The IFC acquired 34,615 shares at a cost of $346,250 by exercising its rights. Mexican investors then purchased 25,512 shares of the IFC's holdings, reducing the IFC's ownership to 137,103 shares. The total commitment of $6.3 million was the largest made by the IFC to that date (IFC, *Annual Report*, 1964-1965, p. 16).

The third phase of Fundidora's expansion plans was carried out in 1966 when the company made a new share issue of $7.2 million and issued $6 million of convertible debentures. The IFC joined with Credito Bursatil to underwrite the new financing. The two institutions equally underwrote the share issue with Kuhn, Loeb &

Company, Morgan Guaranty International Finance Corporation, with a member of the Banca Commerciale Italiana Group participating in the issue. Kuhn, Loeb participated in the debentures placement with the IFC and Credito Bursatil (IFC, *Press Release*, 1966, p. 1).

The share issue consisted of 750,000 new shares with rights to buy one new share for each six held. The convertible debenture issue carried a 7 percent coupon rate, was denominated in U.S. dollars, matured in 1984, and was convertible into ordinary shares. The new issue was over 99 percent subscribed. The IFC exercised rights to purchase 16,602 shares at a cost of $159,443. The IFC's original commitment in this funding operation amounted to $5,883,746 (IFC, *Annual Report*, 1965-1966, pp. 24-25).

This financial operation strengthened Fundidora's position in the U.S. and European capital markets by enhancing the company's credit standing. The share issue increased Fundidora's stockholders to well over 2,000 and its stock became one of the most actively traded on the Mexican Stock Exchanges. The IFC commitments raised the agency's total participation in Fundidora since 1962 to $16.4 million. However, after participations by other financial institutions and sales of its investments, the IFC held slightly more than $1 million of this investment by the end of FY1966, all in the form of shares (IFC, *Annual Report*, 1965-1966, p. 37).

The expansions by Fundidora contributed greatly to the development of Mexico and enabled the company to become the largest steel producer in that country. The Fundidora plant became one of the most modern in the LDCs. Its shares were recommended for purchase as a growth stock by many investment analysts (*The Ross Report*, 1967). Although Mexican steel production increased in 1964-65, demand for steel in Mexico had to be satisfied by large imports. The Fundidora expansion enabled increased exports of finished steel products, thus reducing the need for foreign exchange.

The increase in Fundidora shares expanded the number of its shareowners by threefold and Fundidora became one of the most active stocks on the Mexico City Stock Exchange. Its convertible debenture issue enabled it to enter foreign capital markets for funds and encouraged several foreign financial institutions to participate in Fundidora's financial needs.

However, in spite of the financial assistance by the IFC and other international financial institutions, Fundidora's relative importance declined in the 1970s. Its productivity decreased as a result of its aging plant and equipment. Rising domestic steel demand offset the relatively low productivity in Mexican steel plants and, as a result, Fundidora continued in the early 1970s to operate at full capacity. By that time, 23 percent of Fundidora was owned by the Mexican Government. The steel industry had increasingly become an sector in which the Government wanted a larger participation (Bennett, 1972). In the 1980s, Fundidora still had one of the best ore mines in Mexico with good reserves but its two blast furnaces and eight open hearth furnaces have aged and become obsolete (Kendrick et al., 1984, pp. 45-46).

In 1977, the Mexican Government announced its plans for Fundidora as well as the two other largest steel makers in Mexico. In order to boost steel production and save investment capital, the Government decided to merge the three major steel producers, Altos Hornos, Sichrtsa, and Fundidora. These producers manufactured 70 percent of Mexican steel. The Government also announced plans to supervise the giant holding company formed by this merger. The new company was called Sidermex, although each of the three companies continued to operate as independent corporations ("Mexico Plans to Merge . . . ," 1977). By the time of this announcement, the Government held 38 percent of Fundidora's shares. This merger may have stemmed from an earlier announcement in 1977 that Fundidora would be unable to pay the principal and interest on $370 million of loans owed to several leading international financial institutions including Bank of America, Grindlay Brandts and Lloyds Bank International. The Government loaned Fundidora $35 million to enable it to meet interest payments ("Mexican Headache . . . ," 1977).

Finally, Fundidora was nationalized in 1980 as a Mexican Government agency as a result of a recapitalization program sponsored by the Government. During 1980, a syndicate of 21 international banks acted as agent for a $300 million Eurodollar loan to Fundidora, needed to finance the development of an iron ore mine ("Bank of America Group," 1980). At present, the IFC does not hold any investment in its portfolio related to Fundidora, having sold its investments in previous years. The Fundidora projects financed or assisted by the IFC, however, can be characterized as among the most significant in the IFC's history and contributed greatly to the economic development of Mexico.

Pulp and Paper Operations in Latin America

The IFC has made investments in a number of pulp and paper projects in LDCs designed to increase export markets for these products, to reduce reliance on foreign imports, and, thus, increase foreign exchange earnings from this sector. Among these projects financed by the IFC were Papel e Celulose Catarinense, S.A.; Celulosa Argentina, S.A.; La Papelera Argentina, S.A.; Celulosa Arauco y Constitución, S.A.; and Celulosa del Pacifico, S.A. These projects are discussed in the following sections.

Papel e Celulose Catarinense, S.A.

One of the leading pulp and paper producers in Latin America is Papel e Celulose Catarinense, S.A. (Papel), of Brazil. The IFC assisted the establishment of this company in 1966 and continues to support the company. In FY1989, the IFC made a $15 million loan to Papel to finance an expansion of its paper production by 144,000 tons annually to complete the vertical integration of the company (IFC, *Annual Report*, 1989, p. 36).

The initial IFC investment approval committed funds to a project whose total cost was $26 million for construction of a new kraft pulp and paper mill located in the Brazilian state of Santa Catarina, south of Saõ Paulo (IFC, *Press Release*, 1966, pp. 1-2). The mill had annual capacity of 47,000 tons of bleached and unbleached kraft paper and 10,000 tons of kraft pulp. Raw materials for the mill came from local logging and saw mill waste while pine plantatations were established by Papel. The mill is now nearly self-sufficient in raw materials.

Sponsors of the project included the Klabin Group in Brazil, a company engaged in production of newsprint, container board, and kraft paper. The Klabin Group had been active in Brazil since 1906 and had interests in several other manufacturing sectors including chemicals and mining.

The Papel project's total cost of $26 million was financed with a $13.2 million share issue and loans totaling $12.8 million. Shares were subscribed as follows: $8.8 million by the sponsors and Montei Aranha, another Brazilian industrial group; $2.9 million by the IFC; and $1.5 million by ADELA Investment Company, S.A., of Luxembourg, an investment company globally owned by international banks and whose operations concentrate on investments in Latin America. In addition, the shareholders agreed to cover production cost overruns up to $1 million in proportion to their holdings. The IFC commitment on overruns amounted to a contingency of approximately $307,881.

Debt financing of the project included a long-term loan from the National Development Bank of Brazil (BNDE) of $5.5 million; a long-term loan of $3.3 million from the Inter-American Development Bank (IADB); and a 10-year, $2.5 million loan from the IFC. In addition, BNDE provided a standby loan of $850,000 and the Klabin Group and the IFC each committed $425,000 standby loans. The Bank of America, New York, Edge Act subsidiary of Bank of America, N.T. & S.A., participated in the IFC commitment (Lobl, 1967).

The loan agreements all matured in 10 years and carried 3-year grace periods. The IFC loan carried an interest rate of 8 percent and the loan from the IADB had an interest rate of 6 percent. Both were denominated in dollars and the IADB loan was guaranteed by BNDE. The BNDE loan carried an interest charge of 12 percent, contained a maintenance-of-value clause to protect the lender against inflation, and was denominated in cruzeiros (Lobl, 1967).

This project was characteristic of the global approach encouraged by the IFC in the investments in which it participated. The mill was financed by international interests. In addition, it consisted of components manufactured in several countries. The pulp mill came from Finland. The steam and power plant was manufactured in Sweden. The paper mill came from Italy.

Ground for the mill was broken in 1966 and building construction began in 1967. The pulp mill went on stream in 1968 while the paper mill began operations in 1969. During the last 20 years, Papel has become one of Latin America's top pulp and paper operations. The early operations of Papel employed over 1,600 workers and raised local per capita income in Santa Catarina, a region with per capita income only half of the national average at that time. With this operation, Brazil required less imported pulp and has realized over the two decades of Papel operations significant foreign exchange savings.

With the Papel investment, the IFC has fulfilled some of its objectives. Foreign private financial institutions have been encouraged to participate and its portfolio was diversified by industry. In addition, the IFC assisted in the promotion of a project which was conceived in 1957 — at the time of the establishment of the IFC — and for which firm orders for machinery were placed with Scandinavian firms. Sponsors and the IADB assisted in the financing of these purchases. The IFC had originally declined the Papel proposal in 1962 because of the poor economic condition of Brazil but later reconsidered the project when the sponsors reapplied for IFC support in 1965. The IFC commitment represented one of the largest single investments the agency made in its first decade of operations. Papel remains attractive to the IFC as an investment vehicle, a fact confirmed by the FY1989 loan made by the IFC to Papel.

Other Pulp and Paper Operations

In addition to the Papel e Celulose project, the IFC remains active in committing funds to timber, pulp, and paper companies in Latin America. The establishment or expansion of such operations has contributed greatly to foreign exchange savings in Latin America. In 1965, the IFC made a loan of $10 million to assist the financing of a $72.5 million expansion project of Celulosa Argentina, S.A., the largest pulp and paper producer in Argentina and, at that time, one of the three largest in Latin America. This project was designed to expand pulp production capacity from 145,000 tons to 245,000 tons per year, and paper production capacity from 188,000 tons to 292,000 tons per year. These production increases resulted in large foreign exchange savings. In 1964, the IFC had invested $2.5 million in La Papelera Argentina, S.A., a company which subsequently merged with Celulosa Argentina (IFC, *Press Release*, 1972, p. 1).

Celulosa began operations in 1929, growing from a small, simple plant at Rosario to become the largest fully-integrated pulp and paper producer in the country, operating six mills in different provinces. It is a public corporation, wholly locally-owned, whose shares are widely held and actively traded on the Buenos Aires Stock Exchange.

The financial plan for the 1972 expansion showed that 49 percent of the funding came from Banco Nacional de Desarrollo (BND), Celulosa's own cash flows, and new share issues. Foreign sources such as the Export Development Corporation of Canada, the U.S. Export-Import Bank, Crocker International Bank, and others furnished 37 percent of the financing. The remaining 14 percent was supplied by the IFC with the Bank of Montreal (Bahamas and Caribbean) Ltd. participating in the loan (IFC, *Press Release,* 1972, p. 2). The IFC still carries $120,000 of loans to Celulosa in its portfolio (IFC, *Annual Report*, 1990, p. 78).

Two other IFC commitments in the pulp and paper industry in Latin America, made recently, are worthy of mention. These were the FY1989 commitments to Celulosa Arauco y Constitución, S.A. and Celulosa del Pacífico, S.A., both located in Chile. The combined total costs of these projects was $1.2 billion and consisted of construction of a new pulp line to produce fully bleached softwood kraft pulp for export in the case of Celulosa Arauco and a new pulp mill to produce fully bleached softwood kraft pulp for the export market in the case of Celulosa del Pacífico. The IFC acted as lead manager for a $55 million syndicated loan to Celulosa Arauco while it played a significant role in obtaining $440 million of financing for Celulosa del Pacífico, a Chilean-American joint venture. The total commitments by the IFC in these projects amounted to $210 million. Half of this amount was syndicated to other international banks while the IFC took an equity position of $10 million in Celulosa del Pacífico (IFC, *Annual Report*, 1989, pp. 36, 67).

Cape Horn Methanol Ltd.

Cape Horn Methanol Ltd. is a company which was formed in the financial restructuring of Cabo Negro Methanol Project. The IFC has made two investment commitments to Cape Horn. The first was a $45 million loan, committed in FY1986 and disbursed in FY1987, to assist the completion of a project to build a self-contained plant on the Strait of Magellan near Punta Arenas with an annual output capacity of nearly 750,000 tons of methanol. The project also included product storage and shipping facilities and the use of a deep-water port to export methanol to the United States, Europe, and Japan. The total project cost was $305 million, making this one of the largest projects in which the IFC has been involved. The IFC also has taken a $5 million equity position in the project and holds a total of $50 million of the Cape Horn investment in its portfolio. A subsequent financing in FY1988 was syndicated with the IFC's assistance. Again, this project will benefit a Latin American country with significant foreign exchange savings by its increased exports to the industrialized nations.

Companhia Petroquimica Camacari (CPC)

CPC is a major vinyl chloride monomer and polyvinyl chloride producer with plants in the Brazilian states of Bahia and Saõ Paulo. In FY1988, the IFC made a $45 million loan toward a project whose total cost was $191.1 million to construct and operate facilities in the northeastern state of Algoas to produce 200,000 metric tons annually of vinyl chloride monomer and 150,000 metric tons annually of polyvinyl chloride. This project became operational in late 1988 and has helped meet the demand for these products for domestic as well as export markets (IFC, *Annual Report*, 1988, p. 62).

SYNDICATIONS, ADVISORY, AND MISCELLANEOUS IFC OPERATIONS IN LATIN AMERICA

During the 1980s, the IFC initiated several new operations to support its investment activities. These were discussed in detail in Chapter 6. This section includes a few selected cases of the IFC's Latin American operations in these new areas. In addition, syndication activities will be discussed in this section.

Syndications

International banks worldwide have been concerned with their exposure to Latin American loans. Thus, syndication activities in the IFC's loans have been difficult during recent years. However, with IFC's presence in Latin American project loans, several large syndications have been arranged. For example, in FY1988, a $74.76 million loan package for a direct-reduction iron plant in Venezuela was arranged as were a $55 million loan package in FY1989 for a major expansion of a pulp plant owned by Celulosa Arauco y Constitución, S.A., in Chile with European banks participating, and syndications totaling $157 million for nine projects in Argentina, Brazil, Chile, Colombia, Mexico, and Venezuela in FY1990 when commercial bank attitudes toward Latin American exposure began to soften. Examples of these most recent syndications were a $35 million loan package for Oleoducto de Colombia, S.A., a joint-venture company for construction of a $321 million oil pipeline in Colombia, and a $15 million package to finance part of a $128 million expansion project for Grupo Condumex, S.A. de C.V., a major Mexican producer of wires and cables.

Corporate Finance Services

The Corporate Finance Services Department (CFS) began operations in FY1990 to assist, on a fee basis, financial restructuring and privatization of companies in member countries of the IFC. It has had few activities in Latin America although it has held discussions with companies and governments in Argentina, Bolivia, Mexico, Paraguay, Uruguay, and Venezuela (IFC, *Annual Report*, 1990, p. 36).

Caribbean Project and Development Facility

The Caribbean Project and Development Facility (CPDF) was formed by the IFC in 1981 to assist entrepreneurs in 27 countries of the Caribbean area to obtain debt and equity funds for new projects or expansions of existing ones (IFC, *Annual Report*, 1990, p. 42). Since its establishment, CPDF has secured finance for 52 projects with costs of $120 million. Most of this activity has been accomplished recently with nine project proposals totaling $83 million being done during 1989.

Energy Program

The IFC's energy program for exploration and development of resources in LDCs was begun in FY1984. An example of activities in Latin America by the energy program is the $70 million loan to Oleoducto de Colombia which was part of a $321 million project to construct a crude oil pipeline. The pipeline will increase production and export of crude oil from Colombia's two major oil producing areas. The IFC loan was divided equally between the IFC and a syndication among seven commercial banks (IFC, *Annual Report*, 1990, p. 43).

Foreign Investment Advisory Service

The Foreign Investment Advisory Service (FIAS) is operated jointly by the IFC and Multilateral Investment Guarantee Agency (MIGA) to provide advice to member country governments seeking to develop policies and programs which will encourage foreign direct investment. FIAS activities have concentrated on other geographic regions of the world. It has had very few operations to date in Latin America.

Technical Assistance and Technology Service

The IFC carries out technical assistance with the help of its Technical Assistance (TA) Trust Funds Programs, financed with donations from other multilateral international development finance institutions and government agencies, and helps businesses in member countries to identify, evaluate, select, and acquire technologies with its Technology Service (TS). Examples of the IFC's activities in Latin America with technical assistance have included feasibility studies for a compressed natural gas application for commercial vehicles and a leasing company in Bolivia and project rehabilitation of a fishery/fish processing project in Uruguay. In terms of technology service, the TS conducted a search in Brazil for a company interested in manufacturing a computer developed by a Scandinavian company (IFC, *Annual Report*, 1990, pp. 45-46).

SUMMARY AND CONCLUSIONS

Historically, the IFC has made a major effort in Latin America to fulfill its objectives of private sector development. The region has received more funds from the IFC than has any other. Early IFC operations in promoting development finance companies, discussed in Chapter 5, were emphasized in Latin America. Some of the largest investments by the IFC in any project have been made to projects in this region. Its Caribbean Development and Project Facility recently established for that area is a model institution. As foreign investors' attitudes soften toward Latin America, the IFC will be able to encourage more syndications of its project loans to international banks. Latin American government attitudes will also soften toward foreign direct investment, given the global nature of business. In conclusion, the IFC's efforts in Latin America's private sector have resulted in foreign exchange savings, competitive enterprises, local private development institutions capable of assisting small and medium-size enterprises, and a more viable private sector overall.

Chapter 8

The International Finance Corporation in Asia

INTRODUCTION

The discussion in this chapter emphasizes the IFC's operations and investment activities in Asia. In addition to a general aggregative analysis of the IFC's operations in this region, selected case studies will be covered. These include the IFC's investments in Mahindra Ugine Steel Company (MUSCO) in India, the Manila Electric Company (MERALCO) in the Philippines, the Pakistan Petroleum Ltd., the Korea Stock Exchange, the Korea Fund, and others. The chapter will also include a discussion of the operations of other IFC activities in Asia including work of the FIAS, the CFS, the Capital Market Department, and Technology Services, as well as syndications/participations with international commercial banks and other financial institutions.

The IFC's investment approvals in this area, ranging from Pakistan and India to the Pacific Rim of Asia, have grown steadily. The IFC currently holds 113 investments in projects located in 13 countries of this area. The IFC also holds investments in three regional projects in Asia. The original IFC investments in these projects totaled $1,292,254,000. The book value of the IFC's current holdings in these projects is $921,029,000. See Table 8-1 for a breakdown by country of the IFC's holdings in Asia.

The IFC has concentrated on manufacturing projects in Asia but, in recent years, it has also invested in natural resource-based ventures, such as projects in agribusiness, fuels and minerals, as well as the promotion of capital markets institutions including venture capital and securities companies. IFC efforts in the privatization of

TABLE 8-1. IFC Investments in Asia (held in portfolio end of FY1990, thousands of US$)

Country	# of Projects Held	Original Total IFC Investment	Currently Held
Bangladesh	3	$ 7,789	$ 6,362
China (PRC)	5	44,261	42,490
China (Taiwan)	1	4,019	36
Fiji	3	14,792	12,145
India	28	398,469	336,532
Indonesia	13	104,408	66,151
Korea	11	162,369	87,992
Malaysia	2	6,238	6,050
Nepal	2	8,094	9,144
Pakistan	14	166,731	100,513
Philippines	12	179,729	139,703
Sri Lanka	4	16,842	5,414
Thailand	12	166,041	97,315
Regional	3	12,472	11,182
Total	113	$1,292,254	$921,029

Note. From Annual Report 1990, by IFC, 1990, Washington, D.C.: International Finance Corporation, pp. 78-91

unprofitable state-owned enterprises have been facilitated by the establishment of CFS within the IFC.

The IFC has been sufficiently successful in Asia to encourage the Asian Development Bank to increase its activity in private sector development finance. During the 1986-1988 period, the IFC invested in 70 projects in Asia (22 in 1986, 23 in 1987, and 25 in 1988, respectively) and its net loans and equity investments to these projects were $159.0 million in 1986, $192.0 million in 1987, and $288.3 million in 1988, respectively. The Asian Development Bank made 26 private sector investments during this period totaling $112.8 million. And the Asian Development Bank proposed a new private sector affiliate, the Asian Finance Corporation. This affiliate will finance private sector projects in India, Pakistan, the Philippines, and less needy Asian countries as well (Friedland, 1989).

IFC Investments 1987-1990

The IFC's Asian investment commitments in Asia rank second to its operations in Latin America and the Caribbean area (IFC, *Annual Reports*, 1987, 1988, 1989, and 1990). This is especially so for the last four fiscal years, 1987-1990. During this period, the IFC made 89 investments to projects located in Asia. IFC commitments to these projects totaled $1,411.45 million. In addition, its Capital Markets Department made 30 approvals in 1987-1990 totaling $179.53 million. Combining regular projects and capital market activities, the IFC made total commitments of $1,590.98 million to 119 separate projects during the 4-year period. The total cost of these projects, including the capital market operations, was $8,785.77 million, and $7,567.68 million excluding them.

Analysis of the Asian projects, excluding capital market operations, shows that average IFC investment and average total project cost, respectively, during the 1987-1990 period were approximately 2/3 the size of the IFC projects in Latin America. The average size of the IFC investment in each private enterprise during this period amounted to $15.9 million whereas the average total cost of each project amounted to slightly more than $85 million. The IFC investment approvals for Asia during the most recent year, FY1990, are shown in Table 8-2.

SELECTED IFC INVESTMENTS IN ASIA

The remaining sections of this chapter are devoted to a discussion of case studies involving selected IFC investments in Asia. These projects are representative of the types of investments which have

TABLE 8-2. IFC Investment Approvals — Asia (FY1990, millions of US$)

Company	Country	Activity	Gross Investment	Project Cost
Bengal Glass Works Ltd.	Bangladesh	General mfg.	2.30	6.80
CESC Ltd.	India	Electricity distribution	20.10	92.20
Herdillia Oxides and Electronics Ltd.	India	General mfg.	.32	13.40
Industrial Credit and Investment Corp. of India Ltd.	India	Equity line	25.00	25.00
Mahindra & Mahindra Ltd	India	Automobile mfg.	16.37	212.00
Mahindra Ugine Steel Co.	India	Steel/tourism	1.32	26.20
Tata Electric Companies	India	Electricity generation/ distribution	60.00	273.70
Tata Keltron Ltd.†	India	General mfg.	.13	.68
Titan Watches Ltd.†	India	General mfg.	.17	9.10
Bank Umum Nasional*	Indonesia	Agency credit line	10.00	20.00
P.T. Indo-Rama Synthetics	Indonesia	Textiles	12.00	74.00
P.T. Kayu NIC Indonesia	Indonesia	Wood products	13.10	52.10
Raja-Pendopo Petroleum Exploration Project	Indonesia	Oil exploration	3.60	32.60
Hae Un Dae Development Company Ltd.	Korea	Tourism	.50	15.80

Korea Long Term Credit Bank	Korea	Commercial/merchant banking	15.98	450.00
Twenty First Century Oleochemicals Sdn. Bhd.	Malaysia	Chemicals	8.63	20.00
Pak-Suzuki Motor Co. Ltd.	Pakistan	Automobile mfg.	15.14	92.60
Rupali Polyester Ltd.	Pakistan	Petrochemicals/textiles	24.51	89.00
Avantex Mill Corporation	Philippines	Textiles	13.74	51.00
General Milling Corp.	Philippines	Food & agribusiness	.64	14.20
Luzon Petrochemical Corp.	Philippines	Petrochemicals	105.00	500.00
Makati shangril Hotel and Resort Inc.	Philippines	Tourism	59.00	118.00
Northeast Agriculture Company Ltd.†	Thailand	Food & agribusiness	.05	.41
Shin Ho Paper	Thailand	Paper products	57.08	108.00
Siam Asahi Technoglass Co.	Thailand	General mfg.	8.06	313.00
Vinythai Company Ltd.	Thailand	Petrochemicals	<u>150.00</u>	<u>529.00</u>
		Subtotal	622.74	3,138.79
		Capital Markets approvals	<u>74.69</u>	<u>442.44</u>
		Total	**697.43**	**3,581.23**

* Project undertaken in cooperation with Capital Markets Department.

† As a rights issue below $250,000, this project is not included in the total number of approvals.

Note. From <u>Annual Report 1990</u>, by IFC, 1990, Washington, D.C.: International Finance Corporation, p. 24.

appealed to the IFC at various stages of its operations. Two companies, Mahindra Ugine Steel Company (MUSCO) and Packages Ltd., and one development finance company, Pakistan Industrial Credit and Investment Corporation Ltd. (PICIC), were IFC investments initiated in the first decade of operations. The Korea Stock Exchange and the Korea Fund, projects of the IFC's Capital Markets Department, and the project investment in Pakistan Petroleum Ltd. were financed during the IFC's middle to later stages of operations. Finally, three projects financed by the IFC during its most recent years of operations were selected. These are Manila Electric Company (MERALCO) and the Philippine Long Distance Telephone Company in the Philippines and Vinythai Company Ltd. of Thailand.

Mahindra Ugine Steel Company Ltd. (MUSCO)

India is a country with the largest population of any free-world nation. It was a former member of the British Commonwealth and has a socialist-oriented parliamentary government with states being administered by presidentially-appointed governors. The country has suffered from overpopulation and, although becoming more and more diversified in recent years, is basically an agricultural economy.

During the early years of IFC operations, the Indian economy underwent development pains and its foreign exchange reserves were quite limited. The rapid increase in industrial production programmed at that time required an increase in steel requirements of the Indian economy. From 1959 to 1962, the Indian output of ordinary steel doubled.

Thus, the Indian Government gave high priority to developing the means of production of alloy steel to complement the common steel output. Imports of alloy steel had increased and foreign exchange reserves were needed for those imports even though controls were placed on such imports. Indian and French industrial interests were encouraged to plan the construction and operation of an alloy steel plant at Khopoli, near Bombay. The plant was planned to serve the Bombay industrial area which, with the Calcutta area, was one of the leading industrial centers in India.

The new company, the Mahindra Ugine Steel Company Ltd. (MUSCO) was formed for the purpose of building and operating the plant. The local sponsor of this project was Mahindra and Mahindra Ltd., of Bombay, a conglomerate manufacturer of jeeps, trailers, agricultural machinery, and engines. A French sponsor, Société d'Electro-Chimie, d'Electro-Metallurgie et des Acieries Electriques d'Ugine (Ugine), joined the venture. This company was a principal alloy steel maker. A subsidiary company, Société IndeUgine, was formed to hold a participation in MUSCO for Ugine, along with Compagnie Financière de Suez in Paris and the Comptoir National d'Escompte de Paris.

This new plant had an annual capacity of 18,000 tons of finished alloy steel products but was expanded to 24,000 tons capacity. If alloy steel were not produced, the plant was able to produce 50,000 tons of ordinary steel. MUSCO began operations in 1966.

The financial requirements of the project were $13,650,000, half of which was financed by long-term loans. The other half was financed with an initial stock issue of common and preferred shares and suppliers' credits. The IFC made an equity investment of $300,000 contingent if an additional share issue were needed. The IFC's contribution was slightly less than one-fourth of the total project cost and consisted of a loan of $2.31 million and a subscription to shares with a value of $845,000. Including the equity standby, the IFC's total investment in this project amounted to $3,450,000 (IFC, *Annual Report*, 1963-1964, p. 23).

Indian development institutions furnished another source of funds. The Industrial Finance Corporation of India (IFCI), a government-sponsored institution, made a loan to MUSCO amounting to slightly more than $3.1 million in local currency. In addition, the Industrial Credit and Investment Corporation of India (ICICI), a privately-owned development finance company, made a local currency loan to MUSCO totaling $1,365,000. The ICICI funds were made possible as a result of foreign exchange resources loaned to ICICI by the World Bank.

Conditions imposed by the IFC on its commitment were typical at that time including 7 percent interest on the loan (Mistry, 1967). The loan was repayable in 20 semiannual installments with a semiannual 1 percent per annum commitment fee payable by MUSCO.

The IFC portion of the project cost related to the construction, equipment, and operation of, and provision of working capital for a plant with annual production of 24,000 tons of finished tool, alloy, and special steels and related products.

Under the investment agreement, the IFC subscribed to 400,000 shares of MUSCO common stock. The shares were subscribed to in the ratio of 20,000 shares of each $115,500 of disbursement under the IFC loan requested by MUSCO.

Other international financial institutions were encouraged by the IFC to participate in this project. The Continental International Finance Corporation, Edge Act subsidiary of the Continental Illinois National Bank of Chicago, participated in the IFC loan to the extent of $150,000.

The original total cost estimated for the project was exceeded by several million rupees. However, a large foreign exchange savings resulted from its operations because of the lessened requirements for special alloy steel imports. At full capacity, it was estimated that these savings would be 60 million rupees annually ("Mahindra Ugine Steel Company," 1968, p. 6).

The IFC has continued to support MUSCO's operations and holds in its portfolio investments in the company. Further IFC commitments were made for company expansions in FYs 1975 and 1979. In FY1990, the IFC was invited by MUSCO to exercise its pre-emptive rights in a partially convertible debenture issue of $14.9 million which MUSCO offered to its shareholders and employees. The IFC committed $1.32 million to MUSCO company shares at that time. At this time, MUSCO announced a joint venture with Days Inns, Inc., of the United States, to construct and operate five three-star hotels and two commercial/residential complexes as part of the company's diversification into hotels and real estate.

MUSCO remains one of India's leading alloy and specialized steel producers (IFC, *Annual Report*, 1990, p. 68). The IFC has committed a total of more than $14.3 million to MUSCO's operations and still holds nearly $2.5 million in equity in the company (IFC, *Annual Report*, 1990, p. 83). Given nearly 25 years of foreign exchange savings to India totaling 60 million rupees annually from MUSCO's operations, the role played by the IFC in bringing together Indian and French sponsors has been significant in the development of India.

Packages, Ltd.

One of the leading economic indicators in any nation is paperboard production because goods have to be packaged. This is certainly true in most LDCs and was especially so in Pakistan in the early years of the IFC's operations. Most of the packaging materials used in Pakistan before 1957 were imported. Such practice consumed scarce foreign exchange reserves. In 1955, three paper and board mills were being operated in Pakistan and the Government decided to convert some of their production into packaging materials. A new company, Packages Ltd., was formed by the efforts of two European companies, Akerlund & Rausing of Sweden and G.-Man, a northern European ink manufacturer, which joined with a Pakistani family firm, House of Wazir Ali, which had interests in manufacturing, processing, and service industries including automobiles, motor scooter and tractor assembly, cotton textiles, soap manufacturing, and insurance.

Construction of the new plant was begun in 1956 and manufacturing operations began in early 1957. Technical advice and training was furnished by the Swedish sponsors. The company's first operations furnished containers and packages for the cigarette and soap industries. It has diversified since then and is furnishing packaging materials for more than 40 industries.

The company was expanded in 1965 when an integrated pulp and paperboard mill was constructed adjacent to the facilities for converting paperboard into packages and containers. This mill has an annual capacity of 15,000 tons and the capacity of the converting operations was increased from 12,000 tons to 18,000 tons. Locally obtained raw materials — wheat straw and cotton linters — were used to make the paperboard. The cost of this expansion was estimated to be $12,680,000.

The IFC entered a joint agreement with the Pakistan Industrial Credit and Investment Corporation (PICIC), a development finance company which previously had been assisted by the IFC. PICIC made a loan to Packages to assist the company in purchasing machinery and equipment abroad. A portion of this loan came from a World Bank line of credit and part was from a Japanese Government yen loan. A public share issue of 10 million rupees was made as the result of the conversion of the company into a publicly-owned enterprise and represented a secondary offering of shares held by the sponsors. The IFC investment in the Packages expansion was equivalent to $2,310,000 on a loan and $840,000 on the subscription to shares. The Stockholms Enskilda Bank of Stockholm and The Chartered Bank of London participated in the IFC loan (IFC, *Annual Report*, 1964-1965, p. 18).

Packages Ltd. has had a fairly profitable history of operations. In its early years, a nine-year summary of operations, 1958-1966, showed that sales increased in each successive year and quadrupled during the entire period. Profit margins for the period averaged 8.7 percent (Packages Ltd., *Annual Report*, 1966; Hussain, 1967).

The IFC has continued to support Packages Ltd. After further investment commitments to Packages in FY1980 and FY1982, the IFC carried out further investments in the company in FY1987 and FY1988. During the third phase of Package's modernization, expansion and product diversification program, the IFC loaned the company $6,750,000. The project included construction and operation of a 9.4 megawatt power plant capable of supplying the entire steam and electrical requirements of the company. This project increased plant utilization, improved overall plant efficiency, and reduced operating costs. The total project cost was $12.8 million. Subsequent to this project financing, Packages made a stock offering of $1.95 million to shareholders to which IFC subscribed $170,000 for shares (IFC, *Annual Report*, 1987, p. 60).

Packages has continued to be a successful company and has met its three expansion phases on time with the assistance of the IFC. The company's operations are quite diversified and have now been significantly expanded. Pakistani management and Swedish technical advice have combined to produce good financial results.

The IFC investments in Packages appear to have been sound and the agency has again been successful in fulfilling its objectives of encouraging local and foreign financial institutions to participate in the economic development process. The IFC has joined with a local private development finance company to assist in filling a need in a developing nation. Finally, the IFC still holds in its portfolio investments totaling $6.8 million in loans and equity in Packages. Its decision to hold these investments is predicated on the fact that Packages has been a very profitable company. At year-end 1989, the company had 2,900 employees, 2,700 shareholders, sales of 1.07 billion rupees—up from 875 million rupees in 1988, total assets of 1.2 billion rupees, and its net profits were 66.9 million rupees, up from 36.1 million rupees in 1988 (Moody's, 1990).

Pakistan Industrial Credit and Investment Corporation Ltd. (PICIC)

The Pakistan Industrial Credit and Investment Corporation Ltd. (PICIC) was one of the first development finance companies (DFC) financed by the IFC under its early program of assisting privately-owned development finance institutions in LDCs. The IFC initial investment in PICIC was discussed in Chapter 5. Along with MUSCO and Packages, PICIC is representative of one of the IFC's more successful investments in its first decade of operations.

PICIC, at the time of the IFC's investment in FY1962-1963, was the principal private institution furnishing medium- and long-term financing to industrial firms in Pakistan. The company was organized in 1957 by Pakistani and foreign investors including the World Bank. PICIC had been organized with resources including a 30-year interest-free advance of 30 million rupees ($6.1 million), with a 15-year grace period, from the Pakistani Government. By early 1963, the World Bank had made loans totaling $50 million to PICIC. Sixty percent of PICIC's stock was held at the end of 1966 by Pakistani investors. The remainder was held by British (10.8 percent), German (6 percent), Japanese (7.3 percent), and American (10.9 percent) investors, as well as the IFC which held 5 percent of PICIC's shares.

In addition to the IFC investment in FY1962-1963 in which the agency subscribed to 200,000 shares for $449,400, the IFC has made three further investments in FYs1969, 1975, and 1989. These investments totaled $3.6 million. The IFC still holds PICIC shares in its portfolio with a value of $592,000 (IFC, *Annual Report*, 1990, p. 86).

IFC in Korea

Two projects assisted by the IFC in the Republic of Korea (Korea) are worthy of mention in this chapter. These are the Korea Stock Exchange and the Korea Fund. These projects were developed in the capital markets sector and are representative of the IFC's activities in this sector.

The Korea Stock Exchange

Today the Korea Stock Exchange (KSE) is one of the world's ten most active organized securities exchanges, in terms of reported volume. During the 1980s, the KSE grew (1) from 352 companies listed in 1980 to 626 listed in 1989; (2) from total combined market capitalization of listed companies in 1980 of $3,829 million to $140,946 million in 1989; (3) from trading value in 1980 of $1,867 million to $121,264 million in 1989; (4) from a KSE Composite Index of 106.9 in 1980 to 909.7 at the end of 1989 (January 1980 = 100) (IFC, *Emerging Stock Markets Factbook*, 1990, p. 96).

The KSE was established in 1956 but was unattractive for several years because of a decline in market volume and a very marginal increase in the number of companies going public with their shares. A number of government laws were enacted which improved the status of the KSE. First, the Securities and Exchange Law of 1962 was passed which provided the legal framework on which to build an efficient market (Kim, 1982, pp. 107, 110-111). Second, the Capital Promotion Act of 1968 was passed which granted a wide range of tax benefits to listed companies and provided private shareholders with preferential dividend treatment – all done to promote the stock market. And third, the Security Investment Trust Business Law of 1969 was enacted presenting the steps for precondition of the capital market – designed to encourage private investors to participate more actively in the stock market (Lee, 1989, pp. 36-37).

The Capital Markets Department of the IFC began operations in 1971. One of its earliest projects entailed an analysis of the Korean capital markets in 1974. A capital markets institution, the Korea Securities Finance Corporation (KSFC) was established with the assistance of the IFC in 1975 as a result of this study. The IFC made a $5 million loan at 8.6 percent interest to KSFC and purchased 26 percent of the shares for $581,000. This company, instrumental in promoting securities trading on the KSE, received four subsequent investment commitments from the IFC, which still holds $2 million in equity in the KSFC.

These operations were instrumental in the establishment of the KSE as one of Asia's most active stock markets. Major activity in the KSE has been measured since 1985. The market rose sharply during the late 1980s as measured by the KSE Composite Index, rising more than sevenfold during this period. The overheated market can be attributed to several factors, including a shortage of shares available for trading, the internationalization of the Korean capital market, capital market liberalization in Korea, and rapid growth of the Korean economy (Euh and Baker, 1990, p. 58). In addition, most of Korean securities trading is in the hands of Korean stock brokerage firms, such as the KSFC. Liberalization of the securities markets will increase competition, especially from abroad, in this industry in Korea and will result in more efficiency, as happened in the Korean banking sector when foreign banks began to operate in Korea. In short, red tape will be eliminated or reduced.

The IFC again has fulfilled its charter objectives through its several investment operations with KSFC and other development finance institutions as well as its advisory operations of the KSE through the IFC's Capital Markets Department. The KSE market is now considered sufficiently significant that its data is now included in the Emerging Markets Data Base, compiled by the IFC, as well as in the IFC's *Emerging Stock Markets Factbook*, both quarterly and annual editions.

The Korea Fund

Another institutional means of reducing red tape in capital market operations in Korea was formed with the assistance of the IFC. The Korea Fund, a closed-end investment company or "country fund" specializing in investments in Korean companies, was started in 1984 with help from the IFC. This was the first of 12 country funds in Korea whose total combined market value at the end of 1989 amounted to $2,014 billion. The Korea Fund's market value at year-end 1989 was $740.99 million but this includes the original as well as two subsequent Korea Funds, II and III (IFC, *Emerging Stock Markets Factbook*, 1990, p. 22).

The issue of the original Korea Fund, also discussed in Chapter 6, was co-managed by First Boston and Lehman Brothers, with the IFC in a $60 million offering. The issue was an immediate success despite concerns from both Wall Street and the Korean Government. The shares immediately began to trade at a premium to the Fund's net asset value, a situation seldom encountered by closed-end investment companies whose shares usually trade at a discount from net asset value. By 1986, a second successful offering of $40 million worth of shares in Korea Fund II was made. The country fund gave American investors the first chance to enter the Korean stock market without incurring red tape from Korean securities dealers. This fund was the first of many whose establishment has been underwritten by the IFC.

Pakistan Petroleum Ltd.

Another representative IFC operation in the middle years of its operations may be found in its 1983 investment in Pakistan Petroleum Ltd. and subsequent commitment to this company in 1985. In FY1983, the IFC organized a syndicate of 12 international financial institutions to provide more than half of the financing for Pakistan Petroleum to maintain natural gas production in the Sui Field, an area which accounted for more than 80 percent of Pakistan's natural gas production.

The Pakistan Petroleum commitment in FY1983 was one of the largest IFC investments to that time. The total project cost was $176.60 million and the IFC commitment totaled $90.21 million. Of this, the IFC syndicated $73.2 million to the international banks mentioned above. The IFC loaned Pakistan Petroleum a total of $15.45 million and subscribed to an equity position in the company of $1.56 million.

The second IFC commitment to Pakistan Petroleum was made in FY1984 and finalized in 1985. This was a project whose total cost was $73.9 million to bring into production the company's Kandhkot gas discovery with an eventual 30 million cubic-feet-per day output. This discovery helped to alleviate the nation's energy deficit, provided power for a new electric generating unit and generated approximately $38 million in net foreign exchange savings. The IFC made a loan of $14.6 million to the company and encouraged international banks to participate in a syndication for $6 million of the loan to Pakistan Petroleum Company (IFC, *Annual Report*, 1984, p. 48).

The investment fulfilled two local objectives: it saved a large amount of foreign exchange by decreasing oil imports and it assured Pakistan a reliable fuel supply (IFC, *Annual Report*, 1983, pp. 27, 41). After the subsequent IFC investment in 1985, the IFC now holds in its portfolio loans to Pakistan Petroleum totaling $13.81 million. The IFC still owns the original $1.56 million shares subscribed to in FY1983. In addition, total syndications in the IFC's loans to this company have totaled $79.2 million.

Recent IFC Investments in Asia

The IFC has made three investments in Asian projects since 1988 which are typical of its trend to expanding and diversifying operations in this region of the world. Two of these are located in the Philippines — Manila Electric Company (MERALCO) and the Philippine Long Distance Telephone Company, and the other is a chemical company in Thailand — Vinythai Chemical Company.

Manila Electric Company (MERALCO)

The Manila Electric Company (MERALCO) distributes electricity in the city and suburbs of Manila. MERALCO had total assets in 1987 of 13.7 billion pesos, up from 13.4 billion pesos in 1986. Net revenues increased from 13.45 billion pesos in 1986 to 14.84 billion pesos in 1987, while net income more than doubled from 1986 to 1987, increasing from 196.3 million pesos to 500.1 million pesos. The company's return on equity rose from 3.8 percent in 1986 to 9.0 percent in 1987. Thus, the company has been very profitable in recent years (*Asia 1989/1990 Measures and Magnitudes*, 1989, p. 315). In FY1988, it announced plans to expand and upgrade its primary and secondary distribution systems. The project was designed to improve the quality of service to Manila customers and to reduce system losses.

The IFC recognized that the Philippines had a growth rate of 5.7 percent in 1987 after several years of stagnant economic performance. An investment in an electric utility also enabled the IFC to further diversify its sectoral investments. Thus, the IFC made a loan of $30.21 million to the MERALCO improvement project whose total cost was $313 million (IFC, *Annual Report*, 1988, p. 68). The IFC loan commitment was increased subsequently to $36.926 million. Total syndications in these loans have amounted to $2.958 million and the IFC, after sales of its investment and repayments, still holds a total $25.9 million loan position in its portfolio (IFC, *Annual Report*, 1990, p. 87).

Philippine Long Distance Telephone Company (PLDT)

Philippine Long Distance Telephone Company offers the largest telecommunications services in the Philippines and also controls the telephone network. Its total assets rose from 18.97 billion pesos in 1986 to 21.26 billion pesos in 1987. Net sales were up from 6.059 million pesos in 1986 to 6.59 million pesos in 1987, although net income fell from 1.896 million pesos in 1986 to 1.36 million pesos in 1987. Its return on equity fell from 36.3 percent in 1986 to 20.7 percent in 1987, still high by any standards (*Asia 1989/90 Measures and Magnitudes*, 1989, pp. 320-321). Thus, the company has been relatively successful in recent years.

The IFC has made five investment commitments to the Philippine Long Distance Telephone Company (PLDT), the first carried out in 1969. The IFC made two recent investments in PLDT in 1988 and 1989. During FY1988, the company undertook an expenditure program whose total cost was $95.8 million to add a 10,000-line digital switching system for Metro Manila and to upgrade and expand certain rural exchanges and networks. The IFC made a loan of $24 million to PLDT to assist this improvement program.

During FY1989, PLDT began a fifth expansion program with plans to add 130,000 new telephone lines throughout the Philippines. This project's total cost was estimated to be $400 million, one of the largest ever assisted by the IFC which made a $70 million loan to the company. Other international financial institutions were encouraged to participate in $40 million of the IFC financing making this the first syndication by the IFC of a Philippines company loan since 1983. Syndications in that country had been difficult since the country's debt moratorium made new commercial financing, especially from abroad, very difficult (IFC, *Annual Report*, 1989, pp. 28, 72).

The assistance given the various PLDT expansion programs by the IFC since 1969 have resulted in a massive improvement of telecommunications in the Philippines. The IFC has committed a total of $88.53 million during these investments while encouraging international banks to participate in $40 million of these loans and continues to hold $84 million of the loans in its portfolio.

Vinythai Company Ltd.

During FY1990, the IFC participated in a project aimed at constructing and operating facilities near Thailand's petrochemical complex at Map Ta Phut. This plant, built by Vinythai Company Ltd., a diversified chemical producer, will produce 135,000 tons of polyvinyl chloride and 140,000 tons of vinyl chloride monomer annually. Ethylene, to be used in the manufacturing process, will be drawn from the petrochemical complex. The total project cost was estimated to be $529 million. The IFC made a loan of $150 million to Vinythai with $100 million of this loan syndicated to international banks. The cost of this project represents one of the highest of any project financed by the IFC. It is designed to save foreign exchange for the country as well as increase employment.

SYNDICATIONS, ADVISORY, AND MISCELLANEOUS IFC OPERATIONS IN ASIA

In the concluding sections of this chapter, the discussion will turn to the non-investment roles performed by the IFC. These operations, most developed during the 1980s, however, do have as their principal goal the encouragement of foreign investment in the private sector of member country LDCs.

Syndications

The syndication of IFC loans has been a tool used by the IFC since its earliest investments to encourage other international financial institutions from the private sector to participate in its investments. The achievement of this activity has facilitated the IFC's fulfillment of one of its major objectives: the encouragement of financial institutions in industrialized countries to participate in the economic development process.

Syndication has played an important role with most of the projects discussed in this chapter. For example, international banks participated in $100 million of the loan made by the IFC to Vinythai Ltd., the Thai chemical producer, whose project was to produce, among other products, polyvinyl chloride. International banks also syndicated $40 million of the IFC loan to the expansion project of the Philippine Long Distance Telephone Company in the Philippines. More than $79 million of loans from the IFC to the Pakistan Petroleum Company was syndicated. In total, international financial institutions have participated in a total of $384.4 million of IFC loans to private companies in Asia.

Corporate Finance Services

The Corporate Finance Services Department (CFS) began operations during FY1990 (IFC, *Annual Report*, 1990, p. 36). It concentrates on fee-based advisory services concerned with financial restructuring for companies and privatization of state-owned enterprise. During its first year of operations, CFS has been active in the region of Asia. First, CFS assisted with the financial restructuring of Philippine Associated Smelting and Refining Corporation (PASAR), a government-owned enterprise. PASAR needed to develop a viable financial structure through a debt reduction program. This restructuring program may also result in the privatization of the company because of the reduction of the government's majority shareholding. Second, CFS advised the Philippine Airlines (PAL) in a restructuring and privatization program. The recommendations made by CFS were accepted by PAL and the program will be implemented. Third, CFS consulted with the Government of Pakistan about privatization of a number of Pakistani state-owned companies. Fourth, CFS advised the Government of Nepal in the formulation of a privatization policy. CFS also carried on discussions with companies and governments in India, Malaysia, and Thailand about a variety of issues.

Energy Program

The IFC's Energy Program (EP), begun in FY1984, had one project in Asia during FY1990 which is representative of its operations in this area. The IFC approved an equity investment in Raja-Pendopo Petroleum Exploration Project in South Sumatra, Indonesia, through the efforts of the EP. The IFC equity commitment was for $3.6 million as part of a $32.6 million project.

Foreign Investment Advisory Service (FIAS)

The Foreign Investment Advisory Service (FIAS), in its role of advising governments in ways to encourage foreign direct investment, has been fairly active in Asia during the past few years. During FY1990, FIAS identified investment policy issues in Bangladesh and made recommendations to that government which could lead to the creation of investment institutions. It reviewed investment incentives in the ASEAN countries and helped the Philippines to improve its foreign investment data base (IFC, *Annual Report*, 1990, p. 44).

Technical Assistance and Technology Services

IFC was active in six Asian countries in its Technical Assistance (TA) programs in FY1990 (IFC, *Annual Report*, 1990, pp. 45-46). In Bangladesh, TA carried out a sector study dealing with the fabrication and export of leather goods from that country. In Thailand, TA performed a project identification study which found that production of raw silk was feasible, performed a feasibility study to determine if silk could be produced there, and did the first phase of a multi-phase study to identify further investment opportunities. In Malaysia and Pakistan, TA performed the second phase of such a study. In Indonesia, TA performed the third phase of the investment opportunity identification study, performed feasibility studies on projects dealing with soft drinks and porcelain/ceramic tableware, and set up a pilot plant for growing paddy straw mushrooms. TA also performed project rehabilitation in the Philippines on a nickel mining project. TS prepared a study for an agribusiness firm in India which compared the technologies and business potential of by-products produced by biotechnological processes which might be underutilized or treated as waste.

SUMMARY AND CONCLUSIONS

The IFC has shown its versatility in the projects assisted in Asia. Among the geographic regions, Asia has received the second largest amount of IFC investments. Investments by the IFC have been well-diversified in various industrial sectors and have developed financial institutions and markets in the area. The investments in the Philippine Long Distance Telephone Company and Vinythai Chemical Company were made to some of the highest cost projects yet financed by the IFC. Syndications were implemented in all of the companies covered in this chapter. The first country fund co-managed by the IFC was the Korea Fund and the Korea Stock Exchange was supported by the IFC through advice given by the Capital Markets Department.

The manufacturing and service companies discussed in this chapter benefited the host economies in a number of ways. Foreign exchange savings were made from the Vinythai, MUSCO, Packages Ltd., and Pakistan Petroleum projects. These operations also added employment in Thailand, India, and Pakistan and raised the standard of living in these countries.

These projects, along with the PICIC development finance activities, the introduction of Korean securities to the world's investors by means of the Korea Fund, and the significance of an improved Korea Stock Exchange resulting from IFC assistance, are representative of the hundreds of projects to which the IFC has committed funds during its history. If only the past four years of IFC operations are considered, projects with a total cost of $8.8 billion have been established or expanded with IFC help. The increased market value of these projects, difficult to measure, has pushed the capital markets of many of these emerging Asian nations to a par with many of the markets in the industrialized nations. It is doubtful that such growth could have happened without the catalytic efforts of the IFC in these projects.

Chapter 9

The International Finance Corporation in the Middle East

INTRODUCTION

The Middle East has been a geographic region in which the IFC has been relatively inactive. In fact, the IFC combines Europe and the Middle East in its regional operations. However, with the Persian Gulf crisis created by the annexation of Kuwait by Iraqi invasion and the armed attack on Iraq by the Allied forces, not to mention the growing geopolitical and strategic importance of this area, the IFC's activities take on added importance, especially with the rising aspirations of the nations of this area and growing emphasis on the private sector in the Middle East.

Thus, the discussion in this chapter moves to the IFC's operations in the Middle East. This region includes the major non-African Arab countries in the area east of the Mediterranean Sea to the Persian Gulf area with Iran and Afghanistan bordering the region on the east. After a brief general aggregative analysis of IFC operations in this area, specific case investments by the IFC will be covered. These cases will include the Dusa Endurstriyel Iplik Sanayi ve Ticaret A.S., the Turkiye Sinai Kalkinma Bankasi A.S., and Conrad International Hotel, all in Turkey; and the Sherkate Sahami Kahkashan Company and the Iran Pulp and Paper Mill, both located in Iran. After the discussion of these and other cases, the work of the IFC's new departments will be covered. These departments include CFS, FIAS, and Technology Services.

The IFC's portfolio currently contains 36 investments located in five Middle East countries. The original IFC investments in these projects totaled $457,555,000 and the IFC's current holdings on a book value basis is $365,848,000. A breakdown by country of these investments is shown in Table 9-1.

IFC Investments 1987-1990

The IFC has recently become more active in the Middle East than has been the case in earlier years. During the FYs1987-1990, the IFC made 32 investments in projects in the region (IFC, *Annual Reports*, 1987, 1988, 1989, and 1990). Commitments to these projects totaled $741.48 million. In addition, the IFC made six capital markets investments totaling $138.25 million. Thus, the IFC's total commitments to 38 projects in the Middle East amounted to $879.73 million. The total cost of these projects was estimated to be $1,376.08 million, including the Capital Market approvals, and $1,093.98 million excluding these operations.

Analysis of the IFC investments in the Middle East shows that

TABLE 9-1. IFC Investments in the Middle East (held in portfolio end of FY1990, thousands of US$)

Country	# of Projects Held	Original Total IFC Investment	Currently Held
Cyprus	1	$ 2,058	$ 274
Jordan	3	44,270	7,166
Oman	1	2,029	1,014
Turkey	27	389,046	347,062
Yemen Arab Republic	4	20,152	10,332
Total	36	$457,555	$365,848

Note: From <u>Annual Report 1990</u>, by IFC, 1990, Washington D.C.: International Finance Corporation, pp. 78-91.

average investments by the IFC in the area are similar to those in other regions of the world. However, the average total cost of the projects financed is dramatically smaller. The average size of the IFC investments during the 1987-1990 period, excluding capital market operations, amounted to $23.2 million. However, the average total cost of each project was $34.2 million, roughly one-fourth of the average project size for Latin American projects. Thus, projects in this area are much smaller despite the fact that, although the area is populated primarily by Moslems, the countries have economies based on private enterprise. At any rate, operations by the IFC in the Middle East are much less active than in Latin America, Asia, or Africa. IFC activity in the Middle East for the FYs1987-1990 are shown in Table 9-2.

An analysis of the IFC's portfolio shows that investments in only four countries of the region are still held by the agency. These are Jordan, Oman, Turkey, and Yemen Arab Republic. Most of these investments were made in the 1980s, particularly the latter part of the decade. The earliest investment made in these countries was a 1964 commitment to a development bank in Turkey. The investments made in Iran by the IFC are no longer held in its portfolio.

SELECTED IFC INVESTMENTS IN THE MIDDLE EAST

Five cases of IFC-financed projects have been selected for analysis in the remainder of this chapter. As in previous chapters, the cases covered here are representative of IFC projects in this area. Three are manufacturing companies, one is a banking firm, and one is a hotel. The manufacturing firms are Dusa Endustriyel Iplik Sanayi ve Ticaret A.S. of Turkey and the Iranian firms, Iran Pulp and Paper Mill and Sherkate Sahami Kahkashan Company. The hotel is the Conrad International in Turkey. A fifth IFC-assisted project, Turkiye Sinai Kalkinma Bankasi, A.S., is included as an example of a development finance company whose first IFC assistance was given in 1964, the first of ten IFC commitments to the firm.

TABLE 9-2. IFC Investment Approvals — Middle East (FY1990, millions of US$)

Company	Country	Activity	Gross Investment	Project Cost
Leptos Calypos Bay				
Hotels Ltd.	Jordan	Pharmaceuticals	2.00	5.32
Anadolu Cam Sanayii A.S.	Turkey	Glass mfg.	.10	1.56
Conrad International	Turkey	Tourism	49.00	93.00
Kamelya Turism Islemecilik				
and Sol Hotels	Turkey	Tourism	11.84	43.00
Kepez Electric Company	Turkey	Power generation	25.00	67.60
Kiris Otelcilik ve				
Turizm A.S.	Turkey	Tourism	5.26	20.30
Koy-Tur	Turkey	Poultry production	12.60	25.90
Mersin Enternasyonal				
Otelcilik A.S.	Turkey	Tourism	12.50	25.00
Nasas Aluminyam Sanayii ve				
Ticaret A.S.†	Turkey	Non-ferrous metals	.05	14.67
Silkar Turism Yatirim ve				
Isletmeleri A.S.	Turkey	Tourism	22.64	38.50
Simplot ve Besikcoiglu				
A.S.	Turkey	Agribusiness/		
		food processing	<u>9.50</u>	<u>47.33</u>
		Subtotal	150.49	382.18

Capital Markets Approval	10.23	61.30
Total	160.72	443.48

* Project undertaken in cooperation with the Capital Markets Department

† As a rights issure under $250,000, this project is not included in the total number of approvals.

Note: From Annual Report 1990, by IFC, 1990, Washington, D.C.: International Finance Corporation, p. 27.

IFC Operations in Turkey

Turkish companies and banks have been recipients of several IFC commitments during the past 25 years or so. Most of the IFC's financing in the Middle East has been aimed at Turkish firms. One of Turkey's most severe problems in recent years has been its high inflation rate. The inflation rate there in 1988 was 75 percent and fell slightly to 69 percent in 1989. It remained relatively high in 1990. The private sector in Turkey has had great difficulty in obtaining long-term financing because of the high rate of inflation. Because Turkey may become a future member of the European Community and is now a member of the North Atlantic Treaty Organization, it is recognized as a very strategic location, especially with its proximity to Iraq and the U.S.S.R. Thus, foreign direct investment in Turkey has increased in recent years. As a result, the IFC has concentrated on its investments in the Middle East to Turkish firms.

Dusa Endustriyel Iplik Sanayi ve Ticaret A.S.

One of the firms supported by an IFC commitment is the Dusa Endustriyel Iplik Sanayi ve Ticaret A.S. (Dusa) (IFC, *Annual Report*, 1988, pp. 30, 68). This company produces nylon and is part of the Sabanci Group, a Turkish conglomerate. The project was financed in FY1988 by the IFC and is a 50-50 joint venture between the Haci Omer Sabanci Group and E.I. duPont Company of the United States to become the first Turkish firm to manufacture "Nylon 6.6" yarn. Of the yarn produced, two-thirds will be consumed domestically by the Turkish tire industry while the remainder will be exported. Thus, the project, in addition to furnishing employment to Turkish people, will save as well as produce foreign exchange.

The project is one of the larger projects financed by the IFC in the Middle East. The total project cost was $66.6 million. The IFC made a $25 million loan to Dusa and syndicated $8 million of this loan to international banks.

Conrad International

During the second half of the IFC's history, the agency began to diversify away from heavy industrial projects such as steel, fertilizer, cement, and petrochemicals, and into service areas such as tourism, utilities, and financial institutions. The FY1990 commitment to Conrad International to construct a 667-room international deluxe hotel in Istanbul is representative of the IFC strategy to diversify into the service sector (IFC, *Annual Report*, 1990, p. 75).

The project is a relatively large one for the Middle East area. Total cost was estimated to be $93 million. The IFC made a $49 million commitment to the project, representing more than 50 percent of the cost. Only $22 million of the investment was taken directly by the IFC. This consisted of a loan of $18 million and a subscription to equity shares amounting to $4 million. An additional $24 million of loans by the IFC was syndicated to international banks and the IFC also committed to furnish a $3 million standby facility. The project will be completed in the next few years; thus, little information is available about it.

Turkiye Sinai Kalkinma Bankasi A.S. (Bankasi)

One of the earliest commitments by the IFC to a firm in the Middle East was made to Turkiye Sinai Kalkinma Bankasi A.S. (Bankasi) in 1964. Bankasi is a development finance company and received IFC commitments in FYs1967, 1969, 1972, 1973, 1975,

1976, 1977, 1980, and 1983 (IFC, *Annual Report*, 1989, p. 86). Its establishment was assisted by the IFC.

During the 1980s, the IFC reduced its activity in Bankasi but still made two investments in the early part of the decade. The first included a $610,000 equity position in a project whose total cost was $20.47 million (IFC, *Annual Report*, 1982, p. 42). The second IFC investment in Bankasi in the 1980s involved the provision of $150 million in guarantees for bonding Turkish overseas contractors through the Turkish Overseas Construction Sector. This facility was expected to obtain $1 billion in contracts and to create 20,000 jobs for Turkish workers while generating $250 million in foreign exchange. The entire guarantee was taken up by the IFC commitment with a $150 million loan, the IFC keeping $25 million of the loan and syndicating the remainder to international banks (IFC, *Annual Report*, 1984, p. 50).

During the long relationship between the IFC and Bankasi, the IFC has committed $19.7 million to the DFC while arranging syndications of its loans totaling $45 million. The IFC retains a $2.7 million equity holding in Bankasi.

IFC Operations in Iran

The IFC made investments to Iranian companies in its 15 years of operations but has made no investments there since the revolution in the late 1970s and holds no Iranian investments in its portfolio. The two investments discussed in this section, however, are representative of the earlier IFC commitments in Iran.

Sherkate Sahami Kahkashan Company

In the early years of the IFC's operations, Iran's economy was centered around oil production and refining, with 80 percent of the population engaging in agricultural activities. Some government-induced investment had been aimed at development of cement manufacture, textiles, chemicals, sugar, and tobacco. However, except for the oil industry, most private industry at that time consisted of small, bazaar-type firms.

One of the imports in demand at that time was quality tiles. These could not be produced in Iran, so foreign exchange reserves had to

be used for the import of this commodity. The building boom in
Iran created a market for a large supply of quality tiles. As a result,
the Sherkate Sahami Kahkashan Company was organized by local
businessmen in 1956 (Garner, 1960). The company obtained help
from English and German firms for the design and equipment of the
firm. A British consulting firm assisted in the manufacture of quality tiles using local Iranian clays. The founding sponsors invested
their own funds totaling $500,000 into the project and obtained a
loan from a local bank. However, the funds were insufficient to
equip the plant.

At this point, the sponsors applied for assistance from the IFC.
After an analysis of the project, the IFC invested $300,000 neces-
sary to complete the project, which immediately became successful
producing 5,000 floor tiles and 10,000 wall tiles of high quality on
a daily basis. The enterprise employed 120 people when it began
operations, most of whom were unskilled laborers. The project
saved Iran $300,000 in foreign exchange in its first two years of
operations, equal to the amount of the IFC investment.

Iran Pulp and Paper Mill

The IFC investment commitment to the Iran Pulp and Paper Mill,
an Iranian company, was made in FY1972 (IFC, *Press Release*,
February 10, 1972). The project was the largest in Iran supported
by the IFC to that time. It was a $62 million expansion of Iran's first
integrated pulp and paper mill. The project allowed greater use of
local raw materials in substituting imports of paper used to produce
books for Iran's educational system. The expansion, completed in
1975, tripled capacity from 30,000 tons to 105,000 tons by the
installation of more pulping and bleaching equipment, two new paper machines, and a chemical recovery system.

The Pars Paper Company, the Iranian sponsor of the project and
principal partner, was wholly owned by Iranian shareholders, although a minority of the shares were held by government institutions. It was the most widely-owned private company in Iran. The
Pars Paper Company and the Industrial Mining and Development
Bank of Iran (IMDBI) were partners in the new paper mill.

The IFC portion of the investment furnished the foreign exchange to enable the project to maintain adequate debt servicing and debt/ equity ratios. The IFC committed $12 million with a long-term loan, subscribed to $2 million in equity in the new venture, and made a contingent commitment, or standby, of $200,000. Two British banks, National and Grindlays Finance and Development Corporation Ltd. and Williams and Glyn's Bank Ltd. shared in the IFC loan. Other portions of the project financing were furnished by a group of local banks headed by IMDBI along with suppliers' credits which totaled $22 million. The company made a share issue which increased the company's shares by $10.9 million in addition to the $2 million investment by the IFC. Cash generated by the partners furnished the remaining $3.5 million of the $62 million project.

The effects of this project were numerous. First, 450 new jobs were created for the company. The completed mill became the only one of its kind in Iran. At full capacity, the plant produced paper competitive with that imported from Europe and, thus, saved foreign exchange estimated at $13.3 million annually. The foreign exchange savings was partially a result of the use of locally-available bagasse and other domestic raw material used to produce the paper. The forecast increase in the demand for paper for educational purposes in Iran at that time was satisfied by the plant's production.

The Iran Pulp and Paper Mill investment by the IFC represented the fourth project in Iran to be assisted by the IFC. One investment of $300,000 in a tile plant was discussed in the previous section. A second investment of $3.9 million was made to a manufacturer of steel products. The third IFC-supported project in Iran was $4.5 million for nylon production. Since the Iranian revolution, the IFC has made no further investments in Iran and, at the present time, holds no Iranian investments in its portfolio.

SYNDICATIONS, ADVISORY, AND MISCELLANEOUS IFC OPERATIONS IN THE MIDDLE EAST

The IFC established several new services to support its investment activities during the 1980s. These were covered in Chapter 6. In this section, a few selected cases will be discussed of the IFC's

Middle East operations in these new activities. Some discussion will be made about the IFC's syndications of its loans to Middle East projects.

Syndications

As stated earlier, the IFC's overall activities have been relatively modest in the Middle East. Most of its investment activities have been centered in Turkey. Of the investments discussed in earlier sections of this chapter, the IFC has syndicated loans totaling more than $77 million, with $45 million of the loans to Bankasi in Turkey having been shared with international financial institutions, $24 million of the loan to Conrad International in Turkey being syndicated, and $8 million of the Dusa investment shared with other banks. Of the investments in the Middle East still held in the IFC's portfolio, more than $271 million have been syndicated. Of these, more than $221 million involved Turkish firms assisted by the IFC. Among the largest most recent syndications of IFC loans to Turkish firms have been those to two Turkish banks, in FY1988 – a $45 million backstop facility for a Euro-commercial paper program of the Interbank-Uluslararasi Endustri ve Ticaret Bankasi A.S. (IFC, *Annual Report*, 1988, p. 69) and in FY1989 – a $47.5 million syndication for a similar purpose for the Turk Dis Ticaret Bankasi A.S. (Disbank) (IFC, *Annual Report*, 1989, p. 74).

Corporate Finance Services

The Corporate Finance Services Department (CFS) began operations in FY1990, primarily to carry out advisory services dealing with privatization of state-owned companies and financial restructuring of firms on a fee basis. No activities by CFS have been consummated in the Middle East although discussions concerning these activities have been held with Turkish government officials about the possible privatization of an integrated government-owned textile mill.

Energy Program

Again this is an area in which the IFC has not been very active, geographically speaking. In FY1986, the IFC made a $9 million investment to Yemen Hunt Oil Company in the Yemen Arab Republic for energy expansion purposes. After selling off most of the loan made, the IFC still holds $1.125 million of the loan in its portfolio.

Foreign Investment Advisory Service

The Foreign Investment Advisory Service (FIAS) operates jointly with the World Bank's Multilateral Investment Guarantee Agency (MIGA) to advise member governments about means to encourage foreign direct investment. The FIAS has done very little in the Middle East, concentrating instead on Africa and East Europe.

Technical Assistance and Technology Service

The IFC utilizes its Technical Assistance (TA) Trust Funds Programs to give technical assistance to firms in member LDCs and its Technology Service (TS) to help firms identify, evaluate, select, and acquire technologies. Recent activity by TA or TS was carried out in Turkey. The first phase of a multi-phase study to identify investment opportunities has been initiated there.

SUMMARY AND CONCLUSIONS

The IFC's activities in the Middle East have not been as impressive as those in Latin America, Asia, or, currently, Africa. Although its average investments are on a par with those in other regions, the average total cost of the projects financed by the IFC in this area is much lower — only one-fourth the size of those in Latin America during the last four years. And most of the IFC's investments have been in Turkish companies. It holds investments in its portfolios from only four countries in the area.

A number of reasons may be cited for the lower level of operations by the IFC in the Middle East. In Turkey where the IFC has been quite active, high inflation has kept foreign investors from entering Turkey. With local financial problems encountered by domestic firms, the IFC has had few good proposals from private enterprise in Turkey. The Iranian Revolution in 1979 followed by the Iran-Iraq War has created political risk in the area. The armed conflict in the area as a result of the Israeli-Arab wars has had a negative effect on foreign investment and private enterprise. The IFC was active in supporting Iranian firms in its formative years. However, no IFC investments were made to Iranian firms in the 1980s nor does the IFC hold any Iranian investments in its portfolio.

Another problem with foreign direct investment in the area may stem from the Islamic attitude and requirements toward investment income, particularly interest on loans, as a result of the many Arab countries in the area. With the Persian Gulf Crisis of 1990 and the future uncertainty of this situation, the IFC may continue to avoid the area and move its emphasis to other regions, although the agency does attempt to keep a geographical balance in its operations.

Chapter 10

The International Finance Corporation in Africa

INTRODUCTION

The African continent, especially the area south of the Sahara, is one of the lowest income areas among the regions whose countries are members of the IFC. This area has seemingly been ignored by foreign investors and a number of factors can be identified as reasons for this. Political risk has been high in Africa, particularly sub-Saharan Africa. Warfare and civil strife have been rampant in some African nations during the past three decades. This has been true in Chad, Ethiopia, Liberia, Nigeria, Sudan, and Uganda, as well as Southwest Africa. Unemployment is quite high, especially in the urban areas where it is 20-30 percent or more. Inflation is high and expected to increase further in many countries. The higher price of oil because of the Persian Gulf crisis of 1990 has increased the cost of living in most African nations which do not produce oil. Per capita income in African nations is among the lowest worldwide, about $330 for Africa's 475 million inhabitants.

African local entrepreneurs have an uncertain environment in which to operate. Contributors to this adverse environment include a multiplicity of regulations implemented by a variety of public agencies, commissions, licensing agencies, and company laws. In addition, sub-Saharan Africa has an undeveloped financial infrastructure of capital markets, intermediation, financial instruments and other tools which bring savers and investors together (Pinckney, 1989, pp. 5-7; Marsden and Bèlót, 1988, pp. 21-32).

As a result of these problems, total investment in Africa declined in the 1980s to a level which is inadequate to finance economic growth. Private investment in total is no more than 5 percent of gross domestic product while foreign private investment is only 0.5

percent. This level of foreign investment is only one-third of the average for all LDCs (Ryrie, 1989, p. 1).

Another factor found in African nations which makes development difficult is low productivity. The lack of private investment is a factor which causes productivity to remain low. Private investment, about 5 percent of GDP or $7-8 billion annually, was halved in the 1980s. Foreign direct investment is only about 0.1 percent of private investment. The stock of foreign investment in Africa has been estimated to be about $10 billion (Ryrie, 1989, p. 2). This is equivalent to only $2 per capita.

In addition to these problems, Africa has the highest population growth rate in the world. The current African population is estimated to double in the next 20 years to about one billion people. Thus, some 200 million new jobs will need to be created in Africa during this period to absorb the new population coming into the work force.

In order to alleviate these conditions, the IFC has recently made commitments to expand development operations in the sub-Saharan Africa region. This was especially true in FY1990 when the IFC committed investment funds to 22 African projects including six credit line extensions in cooperation with the IFC's Capital Markets Department. One other Capital Market operation was carried out in Malawi. These investment operations represented a 37 percent increase over FY1989 in the IFC's investments in Africa ("IFC Brightens Battered Africa," 1990, p. 11).

Africa has always been a major area of the IFC's focus of operations. Currently, the IFC holds 145 project investments in its portfolio. The original investment by the IFC in these projects totaled $1,185,360,000. The current book value of these investments, after sales and completion of some of the projects, is $819,060,000. See Table 10-1 for a country breakdown of these holdings.

Three aspects of the IFC's operations in Africa will be covered in this chapter. First, a general aggregative analysis of the IFC's presence in Africa will be discussed. Second, selected case studies of IFC investments in Africa will be presented. These will include Arewa Textiles Ltd. of Nigeria, Alexandria National Steel Company of Egypt, and Industries Chimiques du Sénégal, S.A. A discussion of activities by some of the newly-formed IFC operations in

TABLE 10-1. IFC Investments in Africa (held in portfolio end of FY1990, thousands of US$)

Country	# of Projects Held	Original Total IFC Investment	Currently Held
Botswana	2	$ 1,030	$ 1,030
Burundi	1	5,878	1,108
Cameroon	9	26,140	16,046
Congo	2	4,268	5,500
Ivory Coast	6	19,726	19,014
Egypt	12	165,647	57,229
Ethiopia	1	7,800	7,800
Gabon	4	95,671	91,386
Gambia	1	2,823	4,623
Ghana	6	89,575	92,475
Guinea	3	23,335	15,830
Guinea-Bissau	1	5,850	5,850
Kenya	11	81,901	44,206
Liberia	2	9,202	7,356
Madagascar	4	33,350	19,613
Malawi	6	30,438	14,154
Mauritius	3	12,698	12,406
Morocco	7	163,766	136,101
Mozambique	2	10,250	7,237
Niger	1	2,267	2,404
Nigeria	6	58,785	37,206

TABLE 10-1 (continued)

Country	# of Projects Held	Original Total IFC Investment	Currently Held
Rwanda	1	197	197
Sénégal	4	45,265	21,933
Seychelles	1	9,132	10,762
Sierra Leone	1	2,050	2,050
Somalia	2	1,351	1,172
Sudan	2	18,062	1,540
Swaziland	5	28,127	15,191
Tanzania	3	8,120	5,242
Togo	3	3,764	3,948
Tunisia	11	35,967	22,195
Uganda	4	12,306	11,954
Zaire	4	38,271	36,005
Zambia	6	77,034	54,438
Zimbabwe	6	50,141	31,914
Regional	2	5,173	2,035
Total	145	$1,185,360	$819,060

Note: From Annual Report 1990, by IFC, 1990, Washington, D.C.: International Finance Corporation, pp. 78-91.

Africa will conclude the chapter. These operations include those of the FIAS, CFS, the African Management Services Company, and the Africa Project Development Facility (APDF), as well as partici- pations and syndications of the IFC's investments with other inter- national financial institutions.

IFC Investments 1987-1990

During the last four years of the IFC's operations, 1987-1990, the agency has invested in a relatively stable number of projects each year (IFC, *Annual Reports*, 1987, 1988, 1989, and 1990). However, the amount of funds committed by the IFC has grown by nearly three-fold from 1987's commitments to those of 1990. During this period, 82 projects have been financed by the IFC along with seven additional Capital Markets Department operations in Africa. IFC commitments to the 82 projects totaled $890.81 million. The seven Capital Markets investments totaled $12.66 million, a very small amount relative to such IFC commitments in other geographical regions, thus reflecting the fact that the national financial systems in Africa are not well developed and, thus, not conducive to capital markets operations. Total IFC funding for the 89 projects was $903.47 million. The total cost of these projects was estimated to be $2,872.98 million, including the Capital Market approvals, and $2,847.66 million excluding these operations.

Analysis of the African projects approved by the IFC shows that these projects have been relatively large when compared with earlier IFC operations elsewhere. For example, the average size of the IFC investment in each private enterprise during the 1987-1990 period, excluding capital markets operations, was $10.9 million and the average total cost of these 82 projects amounted to $34.7 million, both figures representing relatively low average amounts given IFC investments in other regions. The IFC investment approvals for Africa for the most recent year, FY1990, are shown in Table 10-2.

SELECTED IFC INVESTMENTS IN AFRICA

The remainder of this chapter contains a discussion of selected cases of IFC investments in Africa. The companies covered in these sections are representative of the private sector enterprises appealing to the IFC in this geographic region. Six IFC investments will be covered. These include Kilombero Sugar Company Ltd. of Tanzania and Cotton Company of Ethiopia, both companies which the IFC assisted either when they were established as in the case of

TABLE 10-2. IFC Investment Approvals—Africa (FY1990, millions of US$)

Company	Country	Gross Activity	Project Investment	Cost
Société Industrielle Laitière du Cameroun	Cameroon	Food and food processing	.136	4.10
Société des Industries Alimentarires et des Produits Laitiers de Côte d'Ivoire	Ivory Coast	Food and food processing	2.09	4.90
Pelican Seafood (Gambia) Ltd.	The Gambia	Fisheries	1.65	2.50
Ashanti Goldfields Corp.	Ghana	Mining	70.00	93.00
Ghanaian-Australian Goldfields Ltd.	Ghana	Mining	3.00	13.50
Anetibene Petroleum Exploration Program	Guinea-Bissau	Oil exploration	5.85	39.00
Clearwater Fishing Project	Guinea-Bissau	Fishing	.20	1.15
Saxon Properties Ltd.	Mauritius	Tourism	3.59	14.70
Textile Industries Ltd.	Mauritius	Textiles	3.10	7.60
Crédit Immobilier et Hôtelier	Morocco	Tourism	92.12	200.00
Société Ennasr de Péche	Morocco	Fishing	4.83	13.00
Afcott Nigeria Ltd	Nigeria	Agribusiness	4.50	17.30
Tiger Batter Co., Ltd	Nigeria	Dry-cell batteries	1.70	1.70

Togotex	Togo	Textiles	1.61	22.70
Barclays Bank of Zimbabwe Ltd. *	Zimbabwe	Credit line	20.11	20.11
Mashonaland Holdings Ltd.	Zimbabwe	Wire drawing	4.44	6.54
Merchant Bank of Central Africa Ltd. *	Zimbabwe	Credit line	25.21	25.21
RAL Merchant Bank Ltd. *	Zimbabwe	Merchant bank/ credit line	17.85	19.00
RAL Merchant Bank Ltd. *	Zimbabwe	Credit line	30.21	30.21
Sotfin Ltd. *	Zimbabwe	Credit line	7.50	7.50
Standard Chartered Merchant Bank Ltd. *	Zimbabwe	Credit line	30.21	30.21
Syfrets Merchant Bank Ltd. Zimbabwe *	Zimbabwe	Credit line	25.21	25.21
		Subtotal	356.34	599.14
		Capital Markets Approvals	.11	1.08
		AEF Totals **	5.61	19.95
		Total	362.06	620.17

* Project undertaken in cooperation with the Capital Markets Department.

** See Table 10-3

Note: From <u>Annual Report 1990</u>, by IFC, 1990, Washington, D.C.: International Finance Corporation, pp. 20.

Kilombero or when an initial expansion was needed, as in the case of Cotton Company. Arewa Textiles Ltd. of Nigeria is included as a company whose establishment was assisted by the IFC and to which the IFC still commits investment funds. The Alexandria National Steel Company of Egypt will be covered and is an IFC investment which represents one of the largest projects assisted by the IFC. Industries Chimiques du Sénégal, S.A., is a project just recently financed by the IFC, as was the Phoenix Resources Company project in Egypt. Investments by the IFC in African development finance companies (DFCs) were covered in Chapter 5.

Other IFC activities will be covered in this chapter. These include the IFC's new operations in syndications, as well as relatively new functions such as Corporate Finance Services dealing with financial restructuring and privatization, the Foreign Investment Advisory Service, energy and technology, and the new African departments at the IFC: Africa Project Development Facility, the African Management Services Company, and the Africa Enterprise Fund.

Kilombero Sugar Company, Ltd.

Kilombero Sugar Company, Ltd. (KSC) is located in Tanzania (Baker, 1968, pp. 127-133). The country was formed by a merger of Tanganyika and Zanzibar in 1964. Tanganyika gained independence in 1961 and became a republic a year later. The country is a nation with an area of more than 360,000 square miles and its population is composed of Asians, Arabs, and Europeans, in addition to Africans.

The political and economic environment of Tanzania is not conducive to the encouragement of foreign investment. The government is classified as very socialist. The economy is primarily agricultural with much of agricultural output being for subsistence. Tourism also furnishes foreign exchange earnings. An informal customs union including Kenya and Uganda had linked the economies of the late 1950s and early 1960s. However, the civil strife in Uganda and political animosities between Tanzania and Kenya resulted in the failure to formalize this arrangement and to the closing of the border for commerce between Kenya and Tanzania during the early 1980s. The country has remained a relatively underdeveloped area.

Prior to 1960, the country had been an importer of sugar for several years. Scarce foreign exchange had been needed for the importation of sugar. A project was implemented which developed Kilombero Valley in Tanzania. One of the first industrial enterprises proposed for that project was a new manufacturing company, KSC, which grew and milled sugarcane and produced sugar for the domestic market. The company was designed and organized to distribute sugar more effectively than the import business so that local consumption was increased and foreign exchange reserves were saved. Total cost of the project was $8 million, a small amount for an IFC-financed project today, but about average for the early years of the IFC.

KSC acquired a land concession from the government on the Great Ruaha River in the Kilombero Valley. Some 7,000 acres were cleared for sugarcane and a sugar mill with a capacity of 20,000 tons was built. Production began in 1962 after the mill was expanded to 30,000 tons.

The IFC made its first investment in Africa in committing funds to the KSC project. A total of $6.4 million was committed by the IFC in conjunction with three financial institutions in The Netherlands, the Colonial Development Corporation (CDC), The Netherlands Overseas Finance Company (NOFC), and Vereenigde Klattensche Cultuur Maatschappij (VKCM). The remainder of the project cost consisted of an issue of $2 million of convertible preferred shares issued by KSC and subscribed by the Standard Bank of South Africa and the CDC, and a supplier's credit of £210,000. The convertible preferred stock was offered for sale to Africans and other Tanzanian residents. The IFC's total commitment was the equivalent of $2,800,000.

The project financing was structured as follows:

1. £1,150,000 in debentures carrying 7 percent interest, which matured between 1967 and 1973. These included $1.4 million and £250,000 subscribed by the IFC, £300,000 subscribed by the CDC, and Fl. 1,060,000 subscribed by NOFC;

2. £500,000 convertible income notes which matured between 1973 and 1975, subscribed in equal amounts by the IFC and the CDC, and carrying a return contingent on earnings but no interest;
3. £650,000 ordinary share capital — £250,000 subscribed by the CDC, £270,000 by NOFC, and £130,000 by VKCM;
4. The IFC, the CDC, and NOFC received ordinary shares or options as a commission for subscribing to the debentures.

The operations of KSC were managed by VKCM. The company employed 4,000 and the project included housing for workers as well as medical and welfare facilities for KSC personnel.

Production began in 1962-1963 and the plant produced 11,000 tons of sugar. However, the company incurred a net loss of more than £250,000 ($700,000 at the exchange rate in effect at that time). Planned production for the second season was set at 21,000 tons but operations realized only 12,700 tons because of an unforeseen shortage of mature cane. Further losses resulted and the need for additional funds became apparent.

Three principal shareowners initiated an investigation and determined that KSC's potential was great and, thus, an expansion to 31,500 tons capacity was planned after recommendations were made concerning changes in management, organization, and agriculture practices.

In 1964, the capital structure of the company was reorganized by KFC, CDC, and NOFC. New funds were provided and new management and technical expertise were injected into KSC.

The new financial arrangements were made as follows:

1. The convertible income notes held by the IFC, the CDC, and NOFC were converted into ordinary shares;
2. The convertible cumulative preferred stock, except for that held by Tanzanians, was converted into ordinary shares;
3. The debentures were converted into income notes with extended maturities and accrued and unpaid interest was cancelled;

4. An initial investment was made by the three investment institutions in senior debentures totaling £1,500,000 ($4.2 million) to replenish working capital and to provide for expansion.

The IFC share in the new financial structure consisted of £690,000 in debentures ($1,931,172), £750,000 in income notes, and £325,000 in ordinary shares including £75,000 at no cost. The total new infusion of capital, $4.2 million, brought total investment in the KSC project to $13.9 million. The new IFC commitment totaled $1,931,172, bringing the IFC's total commitments in KSC to $4,731,172.

Losses continued to occur at KSC. Through the 1965-1966 fiscal year, KSC had accumulated losses of $21,640,000 although 1965-1966 operations resulted in a profit of nearly $3 million. Production of refined sugar in 1965-1966 totaled 24,813 tons compared with 20,497 tons in 1964-1965.

One of the problems in 1965-1966 which affected KSC's operations was the adverse weather which reduced sucrose content in the sugarcane. Yellow wilt disease, found nowhere else in the world, also reduced yield. In addition, the company had to increase salaries and wages, and cost of goods and taxes also increased. Thus, the outlook for 1966-1967 had been considered bleak. However, KSC produced 31,500 tons of sugar and, as a result, Tanzania became self-sufficient in sugar.

Although the Kilombero Valley continued to be developed, adverse weather created problems for KSC in the remainder of the 1960s and the political climate in Tanzania caused long-term problems for the company. The IFC has disposed of its investment in KSC and continues to hold investments in only three companies in Tanzania. These are relatively small investments, all are loans, and only one of them was made recently. Although the first IFC investment in Africa was made in this country, the IFC has considered few investments there since these early investments, primarily as a result of the poor private sector climate stemming from local government policies.

Cotton Company of Ethiopia

The IFC commitment to Cotton Company of Ethiopia in 1964 represented one of the projects during that year in which Japanese technical interests in the textile business were brought together with African entrepreneurs to develop this industry in Africa (Baker, 1968, pp. 136-137). Another project of this type was Arewa Textiles in Nigeria, to be discussed in the following section.

Ethiopia, predominately an agricultural nation in 1964, had to import large amounts of finished textiles, thus losing large amounts of foreign exchange. The Cotton Company of Ethiopia, S.C., a leading producer of textiles, had a small mill located at Dire Dawa. In 1963, a majority interest in the company had been acquired by two large Japanese companies, Fuji Spinning Company and Marubeni-Iida Company.

During 1964, Cotton Company initiated a $5,410,000 expansion program including modernization of the Dire Dawa plant, expansion of its finishing facilities, and construction of a new plant adjacent to its existing plant. The new plant was equipped with 12,000 spindles and 400 looms and was designed to satisfy rising demand in Ethiopia for higher quality textiles as well as to meet competition from local producers and imports.

The project was approved by the IFC which invested $2,507,557 in the project including a $1.5 million loan and the purchase of Cotton Company shares totaling $1,007,557. The two Japanese companies invested $1,650,000 and the Export-Import Bank of Japan made a loan for the remaining portion of the project's financial cost to cover some purchases of machinery and equipment.

The IFC syndicated part of its loan, $430,000, to other international financial institutions. These were Bamerical International Financial Corporation, an Edge Act subsidiary of Bank of America, and the Irving Trust Company of New York.

The Japanese companies also furnished managerial and technical assistance to the project. A training program was initiated in both Ethiopia and Japan for Cotton Company staff. Two Ethiopian technicians were trained in Japan each year by the Fuji Management Group.

The new plant at Dire Dawa did not go on stream until late 1966 but by Spring 1967, the increased capacity resulted in several benefits to the company. Increased productivity and efficiency resulted in a higher quality product. Net profits from operations increased. Finished goods inventories, which had always been high in the past, were reduced by more than 50 percent in the first year of operations. Foreign exchange reserves were saved by using locally grown cotton and by domestic sales of finished products. Again these benefits to the local economy were fulfillment of the IFC's objectives in its operations.

The IFC has been very inactive in Ethiopia in recent years. The Cotton Company investment has been eliminated and only one Ethiopian investment is now held in the IFC portfolio. This is a recent equity commitment to an energy project made in FY1989. The political environment in Ethiopia and its adverse effects on the private sector in that country has discouraged foreign investment. Thus, the IFC has had difficulty in approving Ethiopian projects in which both local and foreign investment must play a major role.

Arewa Textiles Ltd.

Arewa Textiles Ltd. is another African textiles project initially assisted by the IFC in the 1960s in which Japanese investors supplied technical assistance (Baker, 1968, pp. 140-142). The company, although it has had its share of problems, remains successful and continues to be assisted by the IFC.

Nigeria, located in West Africa, is an oil exporting developing nation whose major ethnic groups, or tribes, are the Yoruba and Ibo in the south and the Hausa and the Arab-like Fulani in the north. Health standards have generally been relatively low and tropical diseases are prevalent.

Nigeria has had a history since 1965 of civil strife and violent turmoil. Elections in 1965 led to bloody reprisals and a military coup in early 1966. Top government officials were assassinated and part of the country revolted during 1967 to form the new government of Biafra. Civil war followed.

One of Nigeria's major agricultural products for export has been cotton. Before 1964, Nigeria also imported large amounts of cotton cloth and other textiles. Thus, an integrated textile industry had a built-in base for development at that time. In early 1964, the IFC joined with a group of ten leading Japanese cotton textile firms and two Nigerian development institutions to finance the construction of an integrated cotton textile mill at Kaduna, in the northern region, by Arewa Textiles Ltd., a new company.

The Japanese group, the Overseas Spinning Investment Company Ltd. (OSIC), was established for the purpose of investing in textile projects outside Japan and providing them with managerial and technical advice. The two Nigerian institutions were the Northern Nigeria Development Corporation and Northern Nigeria Investments Ltd.

The total cost of the project was $4.48 million. The two Nigerian financing institutions contributed long-term financing of $980,000. Of the total 1.6 million Nigerian pounds (£N) cost of the investment, OSIC contributed £N420,000 in shares, or 60 percent of Arewa's equity, and £N480,000 for machinery credits. OSIC also agreed to recruit the Japanese for management and technical assistance.

The IFC contributed the remainder of the capital, $770,078 consisting of capital shares, £ sterling loans, and standby credits in local currency in the event of cost overruns. In addition, Barclays Overseas Development Corporation Ltd., London, a subsidiary of Barclays D.C.O., Handelsfinanz A.G., Zurich, and the Kuwait Investment Company agreed to participate in the IFC's loans. In order to encourage local investment, the IFC and the Nigerian institutions reserved 10 percent of their holdings for sale to Nigerian investors.

The Arewa investment is unusual for a number of reasons. It was the IFC's first commitment in Nigeria and the first in which it cooperated with Japanese industrial interests. Such cooperative effort led to the Japanese investments in Cotton Company of Ethiopia. OSIC overcame all the problems inherent in an African tribal situation in training the Hausa, the principal employees of the company. The Japanese utilized the latest managerial and technical skills, including marketing research, and thereby achieved a three-shift operation within 3 to 4 months. This was accomplished despite the fact that the Japanese involved in the project spoke no Hausa and the Hausa spoke no Japanese. The Japanese had extensive textile marketing experience in West Africa but no previous operating experience (Rosen, 1967, pp. 156-157).

The company went on stream in late 1965, a full year ahead of schedule, and reported a profit after the first year of operations. By 1967, Arewa had exceeded original production targets by 20 percent and was able to produce 12 million yards of cloth annually. The company tripled this output to 36 million yards in 1968 with an additional $5 million expansion project to which the IFC contributed $831,324 in additional share and loan capital.

With this mill, Nigeria satisfied half its needs for cotton fabric. Arewa consumed 9 percent of the Nigerian cotton crop after the 1968 expansion and employed more than 1,650 Nigerians. In addition, Arewa declared its first dividend in fiscal 1967, very early for a new company.

The company was able to accomplish its objectives in much less time than originally planned despite the Nigerian civil war. Without the cooperation of the Nigerian government, the IFC's assistance, and the Japanese technical expertise, the early successful results of the Arewa project probably could not have been achieved.

However, the company became one of the first projects to default on loan payments to the IFC as a result of the war. As the war dragged on, more and more Arewa employees were drafted into the military by the government to fight the war. Although the war was fought mostly in the Ibo section of the country, Hausa and Yoruba employees of Arewa were sent to fight. Thus, production schedules were not kept and the company was unable to pay some interest on the IFC loan.

The earlier problems were worked out with the assistance of the IFC and another IFC project approval was made in FY1970. Just recently, in FY1989, the IFC approved a $6 million commitment to Arewa for a $12 million project to modernize and rehabilitate existing equipment to reduce operating costs while the company maintains quality. The IFC investment included a $5.88 million loan and a purchase of Arewa shares amounting to $120,000 (IFC, *Annual Report*, 1989, p. 72). These funds were not distributed as of the end of FY1990 but the IFC continues to hold Arewa investments in its portfolio totaling $442,000 and has syndicated to international

banks a total of $728,000 of its loans made over the years to Arewa
(IFC, *Annual Report*, 1990, p. 86).

Alexandria National Steel Company

One of the largest projects ever invested in by the IFC is the
Alexandria National Steel Company of Egypt. This project whose
total cost was $800 million was made for the construction of a rein-
forcing bar plant with annual capacity of 750,000 metric tons. This
investment substantially reduced reinforcing bar imports and saved
foreign exchange while helping to develop the housing industry.
The reinforcing bars were used in local building construction (IFC,
Annual Report, 1983, p. 39).

The Alexandria project was a joint venture which included several Egyptian industrial and financial organizations and a consortium of Japanese companies which had major managerial responsibility for the project. The project was the largest joint venture
company in Egypt and was a prime example of the Egyptian Government's new policy to establish joint ventures in the private sector
(IFC, *Annual Report*, 1983, p. 24).

The IFC portion of the project financing included debt and equity. The IFC made a loan amounting to $95.2 million to the project
and subscribed to $7.2 million in shares in the company. A total of
$64 million of the original IFC loan was syndicated to international
banks. Since the commitment, the remainder of the IFC loan has
been sold and only the equity investment remains in the IFC portfolio.

Industries Chimiques du Sénégal

The Industries Chimiques du Sénégal is the largest phosphate-
based fertilizer producer in West Africa. In FY1988, the company
was financially restructured with the assistance of the IFC in an
attempt to make the company profitable (IFC, *Annual Report*,
1988, p. 21). The IFC made a loan of $12 million and an equity
investment of $140,000. The total cost of the restructuring was
$136.5 million. This investment was the second IFC commitment
to Industries Chimiques. The first approval was made in 1982 and

totaled about $25 million. More than $23 million of the IFC loans made to this company have been sold to other financial institutions.

Phoenix Resources Company of Egypt

The IFC committed $500 million to its energy program for the 1985-1989 period for energy exploration and development ("World Bank Affiliate Plans $500 Million for Energy," 1984). IFC research had indicated that the exploration absorption capacity of LDCs was $3.5 billion annually, with capital expenditures for successful ventures ranging from $12 billion to $18 billion. The $500 million of planned energy investments will be in coal, geothermal, and alternative energy projects, in addition to oil and gas financing.

One representative energy project was the IFC investment during FY1988 in Phoenix Resources Company of Egypt. The Phoenix project is located in the Western Desert of Egypt and is an oil development project with total costs of $97.5 million. The project is designed to bring oil from its concession area into production (IFC, *Annual Report*, 1988, p. 30).

Phoenix holds a 50 percent interest in the Khalda Concession of Egypt's Western Desert. The IFC made a $20 million loan to the project to help finance the company's share of the expenditures required to explore and develop the concession (IFC, *Annual Report*, 1988, p. 64).

SYNDICATIONS, ADVISORY, AND MISCELLANEOUS IFC OPERATIONS IN AFRICA

The IFC initiated new operations during the 1980s to support its investment activities. These were discussed in detail in Chapter 6. A few selected cases of IFC operations in these new areas will be discussed in the following sections. But first, the syndication activities of the IFC in Africa will be analyzed.

Syndications

The IFC has had some difficulty syndicating its African loans for the reasons mentioned at the beginning of this chapter. However, international banks have participated in IFC loans from time to time. International banks have participated in five of the cases discussed earlier in this chapter, either at the time of the initial commitment or later in the purchase of part of a loan from the IFC.

In recent years, the IFC has been more successful in syndicating its African loans. For example, in FY1990, a total of $150 million of commercial bank financing was encouraged by the IFC in participations in its loans. The IFC syndicated a $35 million loan as part of the $93 million financing for the expansion of the Sansu gold mine complex of the Ashanti Gold Fields in Ghana. A second successful African investment syndication was that of $52 million, part of an IFC loan of $92 million, to Crédit Immobilier et Hôtelier, a Moroccan financial institution, to finance foreign exchange earning tourism projects. And the IFC, with the cooperation of Banque Nationale de Paris (BNP), syndicated a $65 million loan to financial institutions in Zimbabwe to enable them to make loans to new export industries.

During FY1989, the IFC arranged the largest syndication for an African project for $110 million of loans made to Shell Gabon. Nineteen international banks were involved. The IFC in that year also syndicated a $43 million loan with a group of European banks for the Canadian Bogosu Resources gold project in Ghana. As the IFC increases its African operations and as the problems discussed in the beginning of this chapter are alleviated, more foreign investment will be made in Africa. Such will encourage more international bank syndications.

Corporate Finance Services

The Corporate Finance Services Department (CFS) of the IFC concentrates its activities on corporate restructurings and privatizations. Very few of these activities have been done in Africa. Some advisory services have been done in Africa including study of the feasibility of restructuring of Gambia Marine Products, a fish processing company in The Gambia, revision of the financial plan of Zambia Hotel Properties Ltd. in Zambia, and identification of possible joint venture partners for Nigeria National Petroleum Corporation.

It has been argued that public enterprises in Africa have performed badly in the past (Nellis, 1989). Privatization of many of these firms will help alleviate some of the problems discussed in the introduction to this chapter, especially those public enterprises which do not perform well. CFS is designed to advise and assist privatization projects and should be quite beneficial for the future of African business.

Africa Project Development Facility

The Africa Project Development Facility (APDF) was established by the IFC in 1986 as a United Nations Development Programme (UNDP) project to identify promising African entrepreneurs and to assist them in the preparation of viable projects involving start-ups, expansions, privatizations, or modernization. APDF has funded 53 projects in 17 African countries since its inception through the end of its FY1989 (IFC, *The Africa Project Development Facility*, 1989). The facility's objectives and operations were discussed in detail in Chapter 6.

APDF projects in Sudan and Zambia are representative of its operations. The sponsor of Mistika Engineering Company in the Sudan made plans to set up an engineering workshop for comprehensive maintenance of diesel engines. Project costs will be $1 million. Two local banks have approved medium-term loans for the project and a loan from a local development institution was pending at the end of the IFC's FY1990. The APDF assisted in raising the $600,000 of necessary financing.

In Zambia, Siaza Industrial Ltd. established a continuous casting facility costing $500,000 to produce copper alloy billets for export to European clients, the latter identified by APDF. Equity contributed by the sponsor will finance 49 percent of the project while the Development Bank of Zambia provided a loan.

African Management Services Company (AMSCo)

The IFC established the African Management Services Company (AMSCo) in 1989 to address the shortage of well-trained and experienced managers in Africa. This enterprise was also discussed in detail in Chapter 6.

During FY1990, the IFC recruited staff for AMSCo and traveled throughout Africa publicizing its program. The program has had much demand but will not be self-sustaining before FY1992. Its first project involves assistance to a Senegalese dairy operation to improve its management.

Africa Enterprise Fund

The IFC established the Africa Enterprise Fund (AEF) in FY1989 to finance projects in Africa which are too small to obtain direct financial support from the IFC. The AEF was established to operate for a 3-year trial period and expects to invest $60 million in small and medium-size ventures in sub-Saharan African countries which are members of the IFC during this period.

The AEF has had much demand for its services in its early period of operations. More than 400 proposals have been received from entrepreneurs in 34 African nations. By the end of FY1990, AEF had approved 14 investment projects located in eight countries for a total of $7 million of investments. See Table 10-3 for coverage of AEF's investment approvals for FY1990.

Energy Program

The Energy Program (EP) was begun by the IFC in FY1984 for exploration and development of energy resources in LDCs. In FY1990, one EP project in Africa involved an IFC investment of $5.85 million in a $39 million project in Guinea-Bissau for seismic and geological studies and an exploration well as part of the Anetibene Petroleum Exploration Program. The Phoenix Resources Company of Egypt, discussed previously, was an energy development project assisted by the IFC.

Foreign Investment Advisory Service

The Foreign Investment Advisory Service (FIAS) is operated jointly by the IFC and Multilateral Investment Guarantee Agency (MIGA), a World Bank affiliate, to provide advice to member country governments that seek to develop policies and programs designed to encourage foreign direct investment.

FIAS operations involving Africa have been quite sparse. However, during FY1990, FIAS did sponsor a conference on the promo-

TABLE 10-3. Africa Enterprise Fund—FY1990 Investment Approvals (millions of US$)

Company	Country	Gross Activity	Project Investment	Cost
Northern Textiles	Botswana	Textiles	.38	1.82
Omnium de Transformations				
Alementaires, S.A.	Ivory Coast	Oils and fats	.83	1.80
Tribois S.A.	Ivory Coast	Wood processing	.54	1.30
Alugan Co. Ltd.	Ghana	Aluminum fabrication	.28	.70
Dimples Inn	Ghana	Hotel	.24	.60
Plastic Laminates Ltd.	Ghana	Plastic products	.60	2.50
Upper Qeme Holdings Ltd.	Lesotho	Concrete blocks	.12	.31
Financière d'investissement		Venture capital		
ARO	Madagascar	company	.40	2.60
General Haulage Ltd.	Mauritius	Trucking	.14	.32
Intermatch Nigeria Ltd.	Nigeria	Paper products	.96	3.10
Mat Tools and Forging Ltd.	Zimbabwe	Tool and die mfg.	.75	3.80
Retrofit Ltd.	Zimbabwe	Electrical		
	contracting		.37	1.10
		Total	**5.61**	**19.95**

Note: From <u>Annual Report 1990</u>, by IFC, 1990, Washington, D.C.: International Finance Corporation, pp. 21.

tion of foreign investment in sub-Saharan Africa which attracted more than 40 speakers and 200 participants (IFC, *Annual Report*, 1990, p. 44). The conference proceedings will become a classic in the literature of development of Africa, and may lead to significant improvements in the level of foreign investment in the continent.

SPURT

Another proposal developed by FIAS is a scheme in which a financial mechanism was designed to overcome the small market size barrier inherent in most projects in Africa that creates obstacles to intra-regional trade and investment. This proposal is for a mechanism entitled SPURT or Scheme to Promote Unlimited Regional Trade (Hartigan, 1989a). SPURT addresses not only the small market size barrier but also the lack of complementarity between many neighboring countries' industries, the low capacity utilization and inefficiency in most African countries' industry, the lack of adequate foreign exchange, and the administrative and policy barriers to cross-border trade and investment within regional groupings.

The SPURT proposal addresses these problems by (Hartigan, 1989a, pp. 5-7):

1. extending the availability and time-frame of availability of hard currency and hard currency backing for intra-regional trade and investment;
2. making possible the realization of the trade expansion and investment growth benefits of floating exchange rates;
3. giving the private sector the opportunity and incentive to generate reciprocal trade flows and supportive cross border investments;
4. enabling countries within a regional grouping that are willing to enter into such a scheme to do so, without adversely affecting other members and still leaving the door open to new entrants;
5. accomplishing all of the above within a long-term framework of modest policy reform and market-based financial discipline; and
6. enabling institutions such as the IFC to support only the investment-related part of the scheme.

It has been the SPURT proposal and other ideas which suggest that FIAS is not the traditional self-liquidating project. Mr. P.C. Damiba, Regional Director for Africa at the United Nations Development Programme advocated, at the 1989 FIAS Conference on Investment in sub-Saharan Africa, that it be built into the policy analysis of African nations and into the policy review and monitoring systems in both public and private institutions there.

Technical Assistance and Technology Service

The IFC implements technical assistance with its Technical Assistance (TA) Trust Funds Programs, financed by donations from other international development finance agencies and identifies, evaluates, selects, and acquires technologies for businesses in LDCs with its Technology Service (TS) (IFC, *Annual Report*, 1990, pp. 45-46).

TA and TS operations in Africa have begun to increase commensurate with the IFC's expanded investment commitments there. For example, one TA project in Africa involves the development of a small biotechnology project which transfers U.S. know-how to Cameroon to provide medical test kits for household use.

In terms of TS operations, the IFC has identified a project dealing with poplin fabric production in Tunisia, linked partners in an Africa/European Community integrated trucking operation in Morocco and done feasibility studies for an integrated poultry project in Cameroon and a venture capital fund in Zimbabwe.

SUMMARY AND CONCLUSIONS

Foreign investment in Africa is roughly one-third what it is on average in other developing regions. The basic reasons for the paucity of interest in African investment are civil strife leading to an unstable political and economic climate, shortage of currency, and strong government regulations and red tape. In addition, local markets and productivity have declined. The cost of doing business in African nations has risen dramatically in recent decades. The combination of these factors makes the environment for foreign investment and development of the private sector in African nations difficult and the investment climate unattractive.

The IFC has increased its operations in Africa during the last few years. This is confirmed by the fact that its average investment commitment is increasing annually as is the average size of the total costs of the projects in which the IFC is involved. It has also established the Africa Project Development Facility and the African Management Services Company. These ventures will enhance the IFC's operations in Africa by identifying projects worthy of IFC support and enhancing the managerial cadre of these and other African companies. The 1989 FIAS Conference on Foreign Investment in sub-Saharan Africa has identified and analyzed many problem areas in Africa and made recommendations to alleviate these problems.

As financial restructuring and privatization efforts increase in Africa, and as African governments increase their support of the private sector in their countries, more foreign direct investment will be made in Africa. The World Bank has increased its emphasis there as has the African Development Bank. As other bilateral aid agencies in the industrialized nations provide more economic development assistance to African nations, the economic environment will become healthier there. Foreign investment will be welcome. And the IFC will become a more beneficial catalyst in the process.

Chapter 11

The International Finance Corporation in Europe

INTRODUCTION

Another area of current significance to the IFC is Europe, especially Eastern Europe. In the beginning years of IFC operations, investment commitments were made to projects located in what today are considered to be industrialized countries. These included Australia, Finland, Greece, and Spain. At present, the IFC does not invest in these countries and holds only two investments in its portfolio totaling $923,000 in projects located in them.

IFC activities covered in this chapter include early investments by the IFC in Europe which came under the guise of reconstruction of war-torn Europe. However, the major focus will be on the IFC's current operations in Eastern Europe as a result of the political changes in this region and subsequent moves by many of the nations in Eastern Europe from state-controlled economies to nations based on market sector principles. Again a general aggregative analysis of the IFC's operations in this area will be discussed. This will be followed by coverage of selected case studies of the IFC's investments in Europe. These will include General Cement Company of Greece and Fábrica Española Magnetos, S.A., of Spain — two of the IFC's earliest investments in Europe, and current activities in Eastern Europe — Hungary, Poland, and Yugoslavia. Finally, a discussion of the activities of some of the new IFC operations in these areas will be discussed. These activities will include those of FIAS, CFS — especially in the area of privatization, and Technology Services.

The current IFC portfolio shows that most of the agency's recent operations in this area have been in Eastern Europe. The IFC holds investments in 34 projects located in six countries. The original investments in these projects by the IFC totaled $591,880,000. Currently, the IFC still holds book value totaling $466,013,000 in these projects. See Table 11-1 for a country breakdown of these investments.

IFC Investments 1987-1990

IFC operations in the most recent years of 1987-1990 have been analyzed in preceding chapters to give some idea of the trend in project commitments by the IFC (IFC, *Annual Reports*, 1987, 1988, 1989, and 1990). The analysis shows that project approvals, although active, have been relatively fewer than in other regions. The emphasis has been on Eastern Europe. It appears that this region will be the focus in the coming years for the IFC's operations.

During FYs1987-1990, the IFC made 22 investments in indus-

TABLE 11-1. IFC Investments in Europe (held in portfolio end of FY1990, thousands of US$)

Country	# of Projects Held	Original Total IFC Investment	Currently Held
Greece	1	$ 4,922	$ 577
Hungary	8	58,597	60,589
Poland	2	45,099	47,487
Portugal	5	34,545	23,299
Spain	1	877	346
Yugoslavia	17	447,840	333,715
Total	34	$591,880	$466,013

Note: From <u>Annual Report 1990</u>, by IFC, 1990, Washington D.C.: International Finance Corporation, pp. 78-91.

trial projects in Europe, including Eastern Europe. Commitments to these projects totaled $252.18 million. In addition, the IFC made seven capital markets investments totaling $51.25 million. Thus, the IFC's total commitments to 29 projects in Europe amounted to $303.43 million, making the IFC's total investments in this region for the most recent four fiscal years the smallest for any region. The major reason for the relative inactivity in this area is, of course, that most of the countries in Europe are industrialized and have incomes above the level which would make them eligible for an IFC project approval. Only Eastern Europe, with its development problems stemming from socialism and state-controlled enterprise, presents a need for the type of private sector development in which the IFC specializes.

Analysis of the IFC investments in Europe shows that the average investment commitment is relatively much smaller than for projects in other regions. Excluding capital market operations, the average size of the IFC investment in European projects for FYs1987-1990 amounted to $11.46 million, about half the average size of IFC investments in Latin America and the Middle East, 25 percent smaller than for those investments in Asia, but larger than the average investment by the IFC in Africa. The average total cost of each European project, excluding capital market operations, was $35.64 million, similar to project size in the IFC's Middle East operations, but far smaller than the average size of $85 million in Asia or of $126.6 million in Latin America, respectively.

As mentioned earlier, the IFC still holds only two investments in the industrialized nations of Europe in its portfolio. It does have a large number of holdings in Hungary, Poland, and Yugoslavia. Most of these commitments were made in the 1980s, although some of the Yugoslavian investments by the IFC were made as far back as 1972 and 1973. The IFC investment approvals for Europe during the most recent year, FY1990, are shown in Table 11-2.

SELECTED IFC INVESTMENTS IN EUROPE

The IFC investment case studies presented in this chapter will focus on two areas: early investments in what are now considered high income countries and investments in Eastern Europe: Hungary, Poland, and Yugoslavia. Two cases were selected to represent

TABLE 11-2. IFC Investment Approvals – Europe (FY1990, millions of US$)

Company	Country	Activity	Gross Investment	Project Cost
Leptos Calypos Bay Hotels Ltd.	Cyprus	Tourism	8.20	30.00
Bristol Hotel	Poland	Tourism	10.22	36.20
Export Development Bank*	Poland	Credit line/ quasi-equity facility	29.60	60.00
AL HIKMA Farmacêutica	Portugal	Pharmaceuticals	2.00	6.00
Banco Português de Investimento	Portugal	Development finance	2.03	72.35
Sociedade de Capital de Risco S.A.†	Portugal	Development finance	.02	2.10
União Industrial Textil e Quimica S.A.	Portugal	Chemicals/ petrochemicals	6.63	16.11
Salonit Anhovo	Yugoslavia	Pipe mfg.	6.82	16.70
		Subtotal	65.52	239.46
	Capital Markets approvals		47.10	200.50
		Total	112.62	439.96

* Project undertaken in cooperation with the Capital Markets Department.

† As a rights issue under $250,000, this project is not included in the total number of approvals.

Note: From Annual Report 1990, by IFC, 1990, Washington D.C.: International Finance Corporation, pp. 27.

the IFC's earliest operations. These are General Cement Company, S.A., of Greece and Fábrica Española Magnetos, S.A., (FEMSA) of Spain. Several Eastern European operations will be discussed including Agroferm Lysine and First Hungary Fund Ltd.; Hortex, Export Development Bank (EDB), and Bristol Hotel of Warsaw, all in Poland; and INA-Naftaplin in Yugoslavia.

In addition, operations of the new IFC departments in this area will be discussed. These include syndications, work of the Corporate Finance Services in restructuring and privatization, the Foreign Investment Advisory Service, the energy program, and technical assistance and technology service.

General Cement Company, S.A., of Greece

In 1966, the IFC approved an investment commitment in General Cement Company, S.A., of Greece (Baker, 1968, pp. 149-154). This investment was typical of commitments by the IFC in its early operations. Many of its investments were in heavy industrial projects such as steel, fertilizers, sugar, and cement. At the time, Greece was one of the few developing nations in Western Europe. It is now, of course, a nation preparing in stages to be a member of the European Community. The country, bordered on the north by Albania, Yugoslavia, and Bulgaria, on the east by the Aegean Sea and Turkey, on the south by the Mediterranean Sea, and on the west by the Ionian Sea, had an economy whose principal enterprise was agriculture. Forestry and mining were also important. Industry accounted for only 29 percent of national income in 1965.

The industrialization and growth of the Greek economy had created a rising demand for cement. The few large cement producers had been hard-pressed to keep up with the demand and during the preceding years had found it necessary to initiate modernization and expansion programs. Two cement companies, General Cement Company and Titan Cement Company, had each produced about 40 percent of the Greek cement demand.

The IFC invested in both companies but its investment in General Cement was larger and exceeded the size of the IFC's average commitment to that time. The General Cement investment was also unusual in that the IFC took no equity position in the company. A loan, without an equity position, was made to General Cement

Company by the IFC making this investment one of the few such investments by the agency.

During early 1966, the IFC, along with National Investment Bank for Industrial Development, S.A., (NIBID), participated in an expansion program planned by General Cement which totaled $11.7 million. General, at the time, was owned by more than 500 shareowners and these shares were traded on the Athens Stock Exchange. Major interests in the company were owned by a leading Greek industrial enterprise, the Tsatsos Group, and by the National Bank of Greece, the largest privately-owned bank in Greece at that time.

General planned a 40 percent increase in the annual capacity of its two existing factories to 2.1 million tons. In addition, General outlined a proposal for improving the company's technical efficiency and marketing operations.

The increase in capacity was the result of a new cement unit installed at the company's Volos facility located in central Greece. The capacity of this addition was programmed to be 500,000 tons per year. Also, a new cement mill was planned for the Piraeus plant, near Athens. The location of these plants reduced the transportation cost because of their more central location and proximity to the company's markets.

The marketing operations were strengthened by the establishment of four new distribution centers, located regionally in Greece and all having access to water transportation. Such a center had been opened in 1964 in Salonika.

The IFC investment commitment was a 12-year loan of $3.5 million, guaranteed by the National Bank of Greece. NIBID joined with the IFC in the project by subscribing to $2 million of debentures issued by General Cement. The IFC and NIBID had previously jointly assisted in the financing of an expansion in the Titan Cement Company, the other large cement producer in Greece. In 1965, the IFC had subscribed to shares in NIBID.

The remainder of the financing, approximately $6.2 million, was contributed by existing shareowners, French and German equipment suppliers, and by the U.S. Export-Import Bank. The latter institution made a $2.5 million loan to General Cement. A new share issue resulted in subscriptions for nearly $1.8 million and the remainder came from suppliers' credits offered by the French and German companies.

The IFC syndicated a portion of its General Cement loan to six American and foreign financial institutions. The participation amounted to $975,000 and the institutions included Detroit Bank and Trust, First National Bank of Chicago, Continental Illinois National Bank and Trust Company, Svenska Handelsbanken, Kuwait Investment Company, and Société Financière de Transports et d'Entreprises Industrielles (SOFINA) of Brussels. The IFC no longer holds any part of its investment in General Cement Company.

The General project was completed during 1966 and resulted in a greater delivery capacity for the company with the addition of the distribution centers. This decentralized organization of facilities enabled General to increase its deliveries of bulk cement. Bulk cement deliveries constituted 40 percent or more of total deliveries in most developed countries but they represented a small proportion of Greek cement deliveries. The increase in General's total deliveries in 1966 was 6 percent more than those of 1965.

One advantage which accrued to the Greek economy from the General expansion program stemmed from the additional supply of cement. Cement is the principal construction material in Greece and the increasing construction activity at that time greatly increased demand for cement. In the period 1950 to 1965, the average annual use of cement rose at a rate of 15 percent. General Cement Company had to expand and modernize its plant and equipment during that period, expanding production by ninefold. The expansion helped the construction industry in Greece, utilized local raw materials, and conserved needed foreign exchange reserves by reducing import demand for cement.

Another rather unusual factor in the IFC commitments, to assist the expansion of the Greek cement industry was the willingness on the part of the IFC to invest in competitive companies, General and Titan Cement Companies. The underlying reasoning for such an investment practice was that the competition emanating from those two giants in the Greek cement industry would result in lower costs of production, better distribution policies, increased sales, and greater benefit to the entire economy — in that case, Greece. These reasons were confirmed by the positive results from the policy.

Fábrica Española Magnetos, S.A., (FEMSA) of Spain

Another major investment by the IFC in its early years was made to Fábrica Española Magnetos, S.A., (FEMSA) of Spain, an automotive electrical equipment manufacturer. Spain is now a full-fledged member of the European Community and, as an industrialized nation, is no longer eligible for investments by the IFC. However, Spain experienced rapid economic expansion in the 1960s with the assistance of American foreign aid and a healthy tourism sector. Principal industries in the 1960s were cement, chemicals, food processing, iron and steel, shipbuilding, and textiles. The Fiat investment in SEAT Automobile Company of Spain was a catalytic factor to much of the economic development of Spain. The World Bank had been active in Spain during the first decade of the IFC's operations. Three loans from the Bank totaling $138 million had been made in Spanish social overhead capital projects.

FEMSA, formed in 1940, was a closely-held company at the time of the first IFC commitment. During the 1940s, the company had begun production of electrical equipment for farm machinery, electrical systems for vehicles, pumping systems, and other electrical equipment. Such parts for motorcycles was begun in 1948 and, after 1953, the motor vehicle industry in Europe in general and in Spain in particular incurred rapid growth.

By 1962, the company had 1,800 employees and increased demand for motor vehicles and engines in Spain caused FEMSA management to consider a facilities expansion. Past expansions had been financed with retained earnings but in 1962, the company was short on capital and its shares were not very marketable. Sources of long-term debt could not be found.

The IFC agreed to commit $3 million of equity and loan capital to the expansion project. The loan of $2.5 million was for 7 years. The IFC purchased about $500,000 in common shares of FEMSA, or about 13 percent of the company. This share investment was the first by the IFC since its charter had been amended to permit direct investments in company shares. The project approval also represented the first IFC investment in Spain.

The funds advanced permitted FEMSA to expand a number of facilities of the company. It expanded its plant in Madrid, constructed a new factory near Treto in Santander, and expanded its commercial and technical assistance facilities in Barcelona. The share issue was the first step toward broadening the FEMSA ownership.

Part of the IFC loan was syndicated in keeping with Charter objectives. Bankers International Financing Company, Inc., of New York, purchased 10 percent of the IFC loan and 10 percent of the shares held by the IFC, a total of $300,000. Dresdner Bank, one of the three largest German banks, purchased a total of $148,500 of the IFC loan.

A subsequent expansion program was approved by company management as a result of increased demand for its products. The first IFC-assisted expansion had doubled capacity and had been completed on time at a total cost of $3.7 million. The new expansion was begun in 1964 and required investment in FEMSA's Madrid and Treto factories and in its commercial and technical assistance offices in Valladolid and Vitoria.

To facilitate this expansion, FEMSA increased its share capital by 50 percent. In addition, a long-term line of credit was arranged with Bankers International Financing Company, Inc., an Edge Act subsidiary of Bankers Trust Company of New York which had participated in the first IFC loan in 1962.

The IFC subscribed to an equivalent of $225,444 of the new issue, an amount commensurate with the new issue rights formula of one new share of 1,000 pesetas par value for each 2,000 pesetas par value of stock owned by the subscriber.

Eight financial institutions participated in the first two IFC commitments. These banks were located in Europe, the Middle East, and the United States and participated in nearly $1.5 million of the original IFC loan of $2.5 million. In addition, the IFC sold $275,000 of the shares obtained in the two financings.

A third expansion was approved by the company in 1966 which totaled $10.8 million. A new share offering of $2.17 million was carried out. This third expansion was forced by the growth in the automobile and automotive replacement parts industries in Spain. At that time, FEMSA had become the third most important producer of automotive electrical equipment in Europe and had 4,000 employees. The IFC participated in this third expansion.

FEMSA grew rapidly in the early 1960s. Its production increased by more than 900 percent. Assets of the company tripled and its net profits increased by more than 400 percent. These results were achieved by a company which was unable in 1962 to acquire adequate expansion financing from any other source. The IFC was the catalyst which encouraged foreign private investment, broadening of ownership, and expansion of the company's plant and equipment. FEMSA has since become one of Europe's largest manufacturers in one of the most important industries in Europe. It is doubtful that this could have happened without the involvement of the IFC, which no longer holds any investment in FEMSA in its portfolio.

IFC Activities in Eastern Europe and Yugoslavia

The political events of the last few years in Eastern Europe have created a need for new programs initiated by agencies such as the IFC. These countries have had socialist-oriented governments and state-controlled and -owned enterprise. The new trend is toward the formation of democratic governments and introduction of private ownership of industry operated under some form of capitalism.

The IFC has had a history of operations in Yugoslavia in the past. However, its Eastern European exposure has been implemented primarily in the late 1980s in Hungary and Poland. Discussions have been held between IFC officials and the governments of Bulgaria, Czechoslovakia, and Romania to prepare these nations for membership in the IFC sometime in the near future.

The IFC made investments in Yugoslavia in the early 1970s and still holds several investments in Yugoslavian projects in its portfolio. This country has always had an enterprise structure different from the Eastern European countries (IFC, *IFC in Eastern Europe and Yugoslavia*, 1990, p. 4). For example, Yugoslavia has not had a centrally directed ownership, management, or investment planning system. Such plans have been formulated by companies themselves and funded through a financial system which has some elements of competition. Foreign joint ventures have been encouraged. On the other hand, in the Eastern European countries, the move from public to private enterprise has had to begin from ground zero. Firms have to be financially restructured and privatized. The IFC possesses some strong expertise in these areas.

Eastern Europe

The IFC approach developed for Eastern Europe has led to major investments in Hungary and Poland. In addition, the IFC has advised government officials in Bulgaria, Czechoslovakia, and Romania toward becoming members of the IFC. The agency's work in the region has focused on the promotion of the private sector by means of loans for projects, joint venture investments which provide access to foreign markets, development of local capital markets, savings institutions, and banks, incentives for private investment, and privatizations ("The IFC Approach," 1990).

Hungary was the first COMECON country to join the IFC in 1985. The country had welcomed joint ventures and pursued the assistance of the IFC in this business area as well as development of the nation's financial system. In its operations in Hungary, the IFC assisted seven ventures which are now in operation or under construction. These include Unicbank—$20 million project cost with the foreign equity partners DG Bank of Germany and GZB Bank of Austria, Agroferm Lysine—to be discussed in more detail below, Dunamont Polystyrene—$78.8 million project cost with the foreign partner Montedison of Italy, Salgotarjan Glass Wool—$20.4 million project cost with Nitto Boseki and Toyo Menka of Japan as foreign partners, Tetrapak Hungary—$48.4 million project cost with Tetrapak International of Sweden as foreign partner, First Hungary Fund—to be discussed in more detail below, and Dexter Plastic Molds—$11.8 million project cost with Wilden KG of Germany as foreign partner (IFC, *IFC in Eastern Europe and Yugoslavia*, 1990, p. 3). The IFC committed a total of $70 million of investment funds to these projects including $22 million of equity subscriptions.

First Hungary Fund, Ltd.

One significant IFC operation in Hungary deserves to be singled out for discussion. The announcement to launch an investment fund, First Hungary Fund Ltd., to invest exclusively in Hungarian stocks and bonds was announced in 1989 ("Bear Stearns," 1989). The $70 million offering of shares was made by Bear, Stearns & Company and the IFC by private placement in July 1989. The issue was oversubscribed and a total of $80 million was raised from shareholders who were required to invest a minimum of $500,000.

This was the first investment fund which dealt with investments in a Communist nation. Hungary liberalized its investment laws to enable foreigners and Hungarians to own stock. The fund's adviser is First Hungarian Investment Advisory Rt., partly owned by an American investment adviser who manages $2 billion in assets. This fund manager and co-founder of the fund, George Soros, resigned from the fund's board because of potential conflicts from investing in Hungarian stocks for his own investment fund. In addition to the departure of this official, the fund's investment manager, Robert Smith, was ousted by officials of the fund. The $80 million raised from the initial subscription is still uninvested as a result of the lack of enthusiasm among investors in Eastern European investments in general (Siconolfi, 1991). The current riskiness of this region because of experiments with free market systems has resulted in such turmoil among capital market institutions interested in the area.

The IFC invested $7.5 million in the fund for 15 percent of its shares. In addition, the IFC furnished $40,000 to finance a related Hungarian investment advisory company which manages the fund's investment in Hungarian business ventures. A minimum purchase of the fund is $500,000, limiting its shares to sophisticated institutional investors. However, these shares must be held for a 5-year period and the current turmoil in the fund's management makes these holdings quite risky. Hungary's central bank has a 50 percent holding in the advisory company which runs the fund. The IFC, along with Andrew Sarlos, a Toronto-based money manager who has just been named the replacement fund manager, Mr. Soros, and

Bear Stearns each have a 10 percent interest in the fund's adviser (Siconolfi, 1991).

Another problem with investments such as this and others considered by the IFC stems from the cultural and language differences between foreign investors and the project or local partners. In this case, Mr. Smith was ousted because of his inability to speak Hungarian. The original founders had decided on Mr. Smith as fund manager because of his investment experience and overlooked the cultural experience which would be needed in an Eastern European country (Siconolfi, 1991).

Agroferm Lysine

A second representative IFC project approval in Hungary was a joint venture announced in 1988 between Japanese investors, Toyo Menka — a Japanese trading house and Kyowa Hakko — a Japanese fermentation technology firm and two Hungarian concerns including Hage — an agricultural co-operative, along with the IFC ("Japanese Firms Boost Lysine," 1988). The $45 million project expands lysine production capacity to meet the world's growing demand for this amino acid used as an animal feed supplement. When added to animal diets, especially pigs and poultry, lycine increases productivity. The joint venture is the Hungarian Japanese Fermentation Industry. In Hungary, it is known as Agroferm Lysine.

The Japanese partners supplied the technology for construction of a new plant with annual capacity of 5,000 tons. The plant went on stream in 1990. The Hungarian investors took 65 percent of the ownership interest in the venture with the IFC subscribing to 15 percent and Kyowa Hakko taking 13 percent. The IFC made a loan of $8.55 million to the project and took an equity position amounting to $2.7 million (IFC, *Annual Report*, 1987, p. 57).

IFC Investments in Poland

The IFC has been active in Poland only since FY1989. In late 1988, the IFC made a $14.76 million loan denominated in Deutsche Marks to Centrala Spoldzielni Ogrodniczych i Pszczelarskich — Hortex Cooperative Enterprises, a cooperative owned by 300,000 private farmers (IFC, *IFC in Eastern Europe and Yugoslavia*, 1990,

p. 2). This represented the first World Bank Group loan in Poland. The Hortex project, whose total cost amounted to $56.9 million, was to expand its frozen fruit and vegetable processing facilities to produce high quality frozen products for export to Western Europe. The plant's capacity was adequate but processing facilities were obsolete and inadequate. The IFC-assisted project is under construction and will improve efficiency. At the same time, the IFC is advising Hortex on a long-term strategy for future growth.

Two other projects were approved by the IFC in FY1990. The first of these was a total investment of $29.6 million – loan proceeds of $23.68 million and quasi-equity of $5.92 million, denominated in Deutsche Marks, made to the Export Development Bank (EDB) for onlending to small private exporting companies in the form of long-term loans or quasi-equity investments in amounts too small for the IFC to finance directly (IFC, *IFC in Eastern Europe and Yugoslavia*, 1990, p. 2). Such loans will be in amounts ranging from $50,000 to $4 million, thus giving small Polish firms access to IFC funds. Assistance will be focused on enterprises which export, thus earning foreign exchange reserves for Poland. The total project cost is $60 million. EDB will receive consultations from the IFC to improve its internal systems and procedures.

The second FY1990 IFC investment in Poland involves a $36.2 million renovation of Warsaw's Bristol Hotel by means of a joint venture between Trusthouse Forte, U.K.-based international hotel group, and Orbis, state-owned Polish tourist agency (IFC, *IFC in Eastern Europe and Yugoslavia*, 1990, p. 2). The IFC made a loan of $10.22 million to this project (IFC, *Annual Report*, 1990, p. 73). The project is essentially a privatization since Trusthouse Forte will hold a majority of the equity. The IFC structured the financial plan and is advising Polish authorities and the U.K. partner during the negotiations.

IFC Investments in Yugoslavia

Yugoslavia joined the IFC in 1968 and, shortly thereafter, the IFC began investing in projects in the country. In total, the IFC has made investments totaling $700 million in 35 projects including package loans to local banks for onlending to domestic firms. As a result, several hundred firms have been financed in some way by IFC commitments. As of the end of FY1990, the IFC still held investments in 17 Yugoslavian enterprises with total book value of more than $333 million (IFC, *Annual Report*, 1990, p. 90).

One representative IFC investment in Yugoslavia involved a loan of $39.5 million toward a $202 million project to develop the Molve Gasfield in Drava Basin owned by INA-Naftaplin ("IFC Provides $39.5 Million Financing for Yugoslav Gas," 1984). This field is the largest gas reservoir in Yugoslavia. Natural gas production from the field was increased with this project from 137 millon cubic meters/year to 1.105 billion cubic meters/year. Eleven new wells were drilled in the field and six other wells were reconditioned. Gas-gathering and treatment facilities were completed and general service equipment was acquired in the project. At that time, the field, discovered in 1974, had an expected life of 14 years.

The IFC loan was the first energy loan to Yugoslavia and included a syndication with participating banks including Union Bank of Switzerland, Den Norske Creditbank of Norway, and the American Security Bank of Washington, D.C. The U.S. Export-Import bank loaned $33 million to the project and guaranteed $10.2 million of the loans in which Union Bank and American Security Bank participated. The project greatly reduced the nation's dependence on imported energy.

SYNDICATIONS, ADVISORY,
AND MISCELLANEOUS IFC OPERATIONS
IN EUROPE

As in previous chapters concerning the IFC's regional operations, discussion in the following sections will concentrate on the new activities initiated by the IFC during the 1980s. A few selected cases will be analyzed in these operations. Before turning to these activities, some discussion should be made about IFC syndications of loans to European projects.

Syndications

The IFC has had a successful history of syndicating its loans to projects in earlier years of operations in Europe. For example, in both the General Cement Company and FEMSA investments covered earlier in detail, international financial institutions participated in the IFC loans. In fact, other European loans have been syndicated and all but a few investments in what are now considered developed nations have been sold from the IFC portfolio or have matured and been paid off in the case of loans.

Of the loans made to projects in Hungary and Poland, only one syndication has been done in the case of an investment still held in the IFC portfolio. This was a syndication of $11.375 million in loans to a Hungarian project, Dunamont Polisztirolgyarto Rt., a textiles joint venture. On the other hand, the IFC has been quite active in syndicating its loans to projects in Yugoslavia. More than $144 million of loans have had participations by international banks in 10 projects still held in the IFC's portfolio. Three of these totaled more than $30 million: loans to Belisce-Bel Tvornica Papira, Polu-celuloze i Kartonaze-Belisce, a timber, pulp and paper firm; Ljubljanska Banka-Zdruzena Banka, financial services firm; and Vojvodjanska Banka-Udruzena Banka, financial services firm (IFC, *Annual Report*, 1990, p. 90). The large difference in syndication activity between projects in Yugoslavia and in the Eastern European countries can be attributed to two factors: the long history of Yugoslavian business operations has been uniquely different from those of communist countries and the revolution in Eastern European countries is so recent. Thus, the political risk inherent in countries such as Hungary and Poland remains sufficiently high to cause international banks to avoid increasing their loan exposure in these countries.

Corporate Finance Services

The Corporate Finance Services (CFS) Department was established in FY1989 to assist in financial restructuring and privatizations in LDCs. The operations of CFS are too new to be able to evaluate them with regard to Eastern Europe and Yugoslavia. CFS did work with the Polish Government to create legislative and institutional frameworks necessary to establish private ownership and to facilitate privatization by selecting candidates for privatization as well as advice on techniques. The pricing of assets will need assistance from the IFC because Polish authorities, in selling assets to private firms, will desire fair prices. A large proposal being assisted by the IFC in this area is the $150 million project to finance a facility which will produce 140,000 tons of float glass for both the domestic and export markets.

CFS officials have also held discussions with the governments in Hungary and Yugoslavia as well as with firms in those countries concerning restructuring and privatization. Informal advice was given to the Hungarian Government on the drafting of privatization legislation, that was subsequently enacted in early 1990. It established a National Property Agency to be responsible for privatizations.

Energy Program

The Energy Program (EP) was set up by the IFC in 1984 to assist member countries in the exploration and development of additional energy sources. No operations to date by the EP have been aimed at Hungary or Poland. The INA-Naftaplin project in Yugoslavia in 1985 was the only energy-type program in that country since the EP was established but this project was not directly considered an energy project.

Foreign Investment Advisory Service

The Foreign Investment Advisory Service (FIAS) works in conjunction with the Multilateral Investment Guarantee Agency (MIGA), a World Bank affiliate to encourage foreign investment in LDCs by offering investment guarantees to protect against primarily political risk. FIAS advises member governments in ways which will encourage foreign direct investment (FDI).

In Eastern Europe and Yugoslavia, FIAS has been active. FIAS advised the Polish Government on legal and regulatory frameworks needed to encourage FDI and helped to develop a promotional strategy and monitoring and screening procedures for such FDI ("The IFC Approach," 1990). In Hungary, FIAS is assisting the Ministry of Finance and the Central Bank to design incentives to attract FDI and to develop screening procedures for such FDI ("The IFC Approach," 1990). In Yugoslavia, FIAS is advising the government on structural reforms to establish a more fully market-based economy. As a result, Yugoslavia has improved its foreign investment law and is revising its labor laws to give management more flexibility in plant operations (IFC, *IFC in Eastern Europe and Yugoslavia*, 1990, p. 4).

Technical Assistance and Technology Service

Technical assistance is offered by the IFC through its Technical Assistance (TA) Trust Funds program, financed by donations from other international development finance agencies. It identifies, evaluates, selects, and acquires technologies for businesses in member LDCs with its Technology Service (TS).

These operations in Eastern Europe and Yugoslavia have not been very active. During the past few years, the IFC has assisted only Hungary and Poland with TA or TS activities. Poland is in the second stage of a multi-phase study to identify investment opportunities and is receiving promotional/technology transfer/technical assistance in pollution control. Hungary is in the advanced stage of the multi-phase study to identify investment opportunities.

SUMMARY AND CONCLUSIONS

The IFC has had a mixed history of operations in Europe. In its early years it assisted several firms as well as development finance companies in Finland, Greece, Spain, and Yugoslavia. Currently, it is active only in the latter country and in the new emerging markets of Eastern Europe. At the present time, only Hungary and Poland of that region are members of the IFC. However, in the near future, Bulgaria, Czechoslovakia, and Romania may become members of the IFC. Governments of these nations are now being advised by the IFC about their future role as members.

Thus, with the revolution so close at hand, the IFC's role in Hungary and Poland has been very preliminary. Some investments have been made by the IFC and these are smaller in average size than similar commitments to projects in other regions. However, the projects financed have average total project costs which compare favorably with those in other regions. The IFC is active through CFS and FIAS in advising these governments about financial re-structuring and privatization of state-controlled enterprise. In time, international financial institutions will also become active in syndications of investments to projects in these countries.

In Yugoslavia, the IFC has been active for the past 20 years. It still holds portfolio investments totaling more than $333 million in 17 projects located in that country. And international banks have participated in loans to the extent of $144 million in these projects. The Yugoslavian business environment has always been more con-ducive to FDI than have the environments of the Eastern European nations.

The IFC has played a very important role in these countries and will continue to do so in Eastern Europe particularly as these na-tions enter the world of private enterprise more and more. In fact, a senior executive of a large Japanese firm which participated in one Eastern European joint venture stated that the company is planning other investments in Hungary and Poland and would not contem-plate these projects without the backing of the IFC ("The IFC Ap-proach," 1990, p. 7).

Chapter 12

Development Financing Benefits: An Evaluation of the International Finance Corporation

INTRODUCTION

During its 35 years of operations, the International Finance Corporation (IFC) has mobilized more than $50 billion for investment in well over 1,000 business ventures in more than 90 countries, while working with more than 2,000 companies and financial institutions which have participated in these ventures. This brief synopsis of its history demonstrates the significance of a multilateral development finance agency which began life with only $100 million in subscribed capital from its member countries. The organization has evolved from a simple project investment agency to a very diversified group offering a wide range of advisory and management services which rival the best of Wall Street's or London's investment banking firms. However, project investment is still its major activity.

The benefits accruing to LDCs from the IFC's efforts are immeasurable. For example, the total cost of the projects financed by the IFC is more than $50 billion. However, this is a book value figure. The market value of these projects should definitely be well over their book value.

The IFC's general purpose, as restated from its Articles of Agreement, is to foster economic development through investments to the private sector in member countries, as a supplement to the aid given by the World Bank. This objective is administered by the IFC in three ways: (1) commitments, loan and/or equity investments, to private enterprise projects in LDC member countries without government guarantee when insufficient private capital is available on reasonable terms; (2) acting as a catalytic effect by combining investment opportunities in these countries with domestic and foreign private capital, experienced management, and appropriate technology; and (3) the stimulation and creation of conditions conducive to the flow of private domestic and/or foreign capital into productive investments in these areas.

During its 35 years of operations, the IFC, in its private sector investment activities, has passed through a metamorphosis of three stages. In its first 10 to 15 years, the agency had little or no real equity investments, committed funds to small projects, and offered few other investment products. In the middle 10 to 15 years of its operations, the IFC committed to larger projects, did subscribe to equity in some projects but was not very aggressive, and offered few other types of investment products. During the last 10 years of its activities, the IFC has committed to very large projects, has taken aggressive equity positions, and has greatly diversified its products and services. Through these three stages of operations, the IFC, despite the fact that it does not require a government guarantee of its investment commitments, has incurred very few losses on its investments. It had to write off about 0.5 percent of its loans and about 3.7 percent of its equity during its first 25 years of operations ("IFC: Finding 'Bankable' Ventures," 1982). Indications are that the organization has done even better during the 1980s.

An evaluation of the IFC's fulfillment of its major goal and the strategies by which it is implemented can be done by examination of four major activities of the IFC. These are capital market development, encouragement of international banks to participate in LDC projects, encouragement of entrepreneurship in LDCs, and the catalytic effect of the IFC's participation in LDC project investments. These four activities, as they relate to the IFC, furnish the major focus of the remainder of this chapter.

CAPITAL MARKET DEVELOPMENT

The Capital Markets Department (CMD) was established to assist member countries in three ways. First, the IFC, in this area, advises governments on the fiscal, legal, and regulatory framework needed by a viable private sector financial system. Second, the IFC provides funds and technical assistance to local financial institutions, often assisting their establishment. Third, the IFC acts as an intermediary between international investors and the emerging markets by sponsoring, underwriting, and distributing, in international financial markets, country investment funds and new securities issues of LDC companies.

In order to make these goals, strategies, and policies operational, the IFC established the CMD in 1971. The activities of this department were discussed in Chapter 5. Operations of the CMD for FY1990 were at record levels and a list of individual projects for that year were shown in Table 5-2. The IFC's capital market operations actually began a decade before the Department was formed when its Articles of Agreement were amended permitting direct equity investments and new issue underwriting.

The CMD has been a very active operation for the IFC. Its experience includes more than 200 advisory assignments in 60 countries. It has made investments in 110 financial institutions in 40 countries. The CMD has been promoter, underwriter and/or has placed securities of 24 single or multi-country investment funds as well as a large number of international equity and debt issues. It has also developed the Emerging Markets Data Base which analyzes 20 emerging securities markets and more than 700 companies in LDCs on an on-going basis.

Underwriting Operations

One of the earliest underwriting operations undertaken by the IFC was done in 1971 for a Venezuelan firm, Consolidada de Cementos, C.A. (Conceca), a leading cement producer in the country at that time (IFC, *IFC: What It Is, What It Does, How it Does It*, 1973, p. 12). The company made an issue of 10-year mortgage bonds for Venezuelan investors. The IFC made a standby commitment to purchase up to $2 million of bonds from an underwriting syndicate led by C.A. Venezolana de Desarrollo, a development finance company whose establishment had been assisted by the IFC in 1963. The entire issue was sold to Venezuelan investors within 30 days, as a result of the participation by the IFC.

Another prime example of the IFC's early underwriting activities involved Compañia Fundidora de Fierro y Acero de Monterrey,

S.A. (Fundidora), a Mexican steelmaker. The IFC underwrote several issues of the company's stock before the company was essentially taken over by the Mexican Government. This company's IFC relationship was discussed in Chapter 7.

Development Finance Companies

Another capital market development activity in the early years of the IFC's operations involved the assistance of development finance companies (DFCs) in member countries, which were discussed in Chapter 5. These were the first of several types of financial intermediaries developed by the IFC, in addition to mortgage companies, securities firms, merchant banks, leasing firms, and consumer finance companies. Such intermediaries were needed to mobilize savings in LDCs and to invest these funds in productive projects, most of which were too small for direct financing by the IFC (IFC, *IFC After 25 Years*, 1982, p. 14).

These intermediaries were still inadequate in the growing financial systems of LDCs because of the complexity of development finance. New markets and instruments were needed to fill the gaps. Thus, the IFC expanded its Capital Markets Department operations, especially during the 1980s.

Specifically, the CMD presently acts as both adviser and investor in developing financial markets and systems. Its operations are much more comprehensive than the earlier operations with DFCs and underwriting new issues. These services include advising, investment and financial support for financial institutions, and sponsorship, structuring, and investment for local companies seeking access to international capital markets. The CMD often works in conjunction with other multilateral development finance institutions, particularly the World Bank.

Examples of these joint operations shows a diversity that has benefited all regions of the world's LDCs. They include a privatization program in Nigeria, design of venture capital policies in India, financial restructuring and debt conversion programs for firms in Jamaica, as well as advising countries with centrally-planned economies, such as Hungary and China, about the establishment of securities markets or the regulation of such securities markets in other LDCs (Sethness, 1988, p. 33).

Country Investment Funds

One of the fastest growing tools for mobilizing worldwide investment capital has been the investment fund which concentrates its investment portfolio on the securities of one or more countries. These are generally closed-end investment companies whose securities often trade on organized securities exchanges in New York, London, and other major financial centers. By 1990, at least 131 of these funds had been established with an estimated market value of $11.2 billion ("Emerging Markets," 1990).

Global investors have shown much interest in country funds, particularly those made of stocks traded on emerging markets. These markets as a whole consistently outperformed all developed stock market indices during the second half of the 1980s, including the Japanese market ("Emerging Markets," 1990). In 1989, four of the top five performing markets were in LDCs. With investors continually turning to the practice of global asset management and with ample liquidity to absorb increasing foreign investment flows, country funds, especially those in the LDCs, will remain popular.

The IFC, through the work of the CMD, has pioneered in the establishment of some of the best-performing of these country funds. Its first such fund was the Korea Fund, first of several funds dealing with Korean securities, which was developed in 1984. Since then, the IFC has been quite active in this area of finance. In FY1990, it developed 11 country funds which mobilized more than $1 billion in the international capital markets. These included the First Hungary Fund, first such capital market security in a former communist country and discussed in Chapter 11. In previous years, the IFC was lead or co-lead manager of, for example, the Thailand Fund in 1986, the Malaysia Fund in 1987, and the Thai Fund in 1988. Overall, the IFC has assisted in the formation of 45 country funds which have mobilized new capital amounting to more than $2.5 billion.

Finally, the IFC, through its CMD, established the epitome of LDC country funds, the Emerging Markets Growth Fund. This fund was established in 1986 and is a multinational investment fund with a portfolio of companies located in the emerging markets of LDCs.

Emerging Markets Data Base

Another extremely interesting IFC enterprise is the Emerging Markets Data Base (EMDB), now marketed commercially by the IFC ("Emerging Markets," 1990). It is a unique computerized data base which includes the most actively traded stocks in 19 emerging stock markets. The EMDB offers information on stock prices, cash dividends, changes in capitalization, trading data, price/earnings ratios, book values, as well as a time-series, on a monthly basis, of more than 400 leading companies among these securities markets, some series going as far back as 1975. This service offers the only indexes prepared on a comparable basis of these emerging stock markets. The service is published in both annual and quarterly reports as well as in computer tape form. The EMDB is becoming recognized as one of the most valuable data bases available on financial market information concerning companies in the LDCs.

In terms of activity with regard to the IFC's objective of developing financial intermediaries in LDCs, the CMD has made more than 150 investments in merchant and investment banks, export finance enterprises, venture capital operations, housing finance, and leasing and insurance companies. The first leasing company in Portugal was established with the assistance of the IFC. The CMD assisted the formation of four Korean companies to carry out money market and securities financing, equipment leasing, and venture capital financial operations ("Emerging Markets," 1990).

The demonstration effect of an IFC commitment has been discussed in several case studies in previous chapters. In many of these private sector projects, domestic and foreign investors as well as international and local financial institutions would have avoided many of these projects without the marginal investments by the IFC. Furthermore, the demonstration effects of the projects, once on stream, have resulted in further investments in many countries, including India, Indonesia, the Philippines, and Sri Lanka — particularly in equipment leasing. Thus, the entire financial system in many LDCs has been made more efficient by the capital market operations of the IFC.

Technical Assistance to Capital Markets

The CMD also disseminates technical assistance to the financial sector in LDCs. This aid is carried out by a variety of means. For example, since the CMD was formed in 1971, it has studied and advised on: financial systems in 28 countries, the securities markets of 43 countries, the regulatory systems in 28 countries, the accounting systems in nine countries, tax policies in 22 countries, as well as the means to increase access to international capital markets in 14 countries (Economics Department, 1989, p. 15). These activities are divided into two types: (1) broad, general, open-ended studies which review capital markets partially or entirely and which identify problems and make recommendations; and (2) studies which are more focused and specific and in which the local government has some goal to be achieved through specific policy advice from the IFC (Economics Department, 1989, p. 15).

Several specific case studies can be cited. The following are representative examples of technical assistance rendered LDCs by the CMD. The Kenyan financial sector has received IFC assistance in developing money and capital markets. A study was done in 1984 which led to the establishment of a Capital Market Development Authority by the Kenyan Government to implement the CMD's recommendations. In Pakistan, the financial sector was reviewed as part of a World Bank Mission and a specific report was issued concerning the Pakistani capital market. Several recommendations have been adopted by the Pakistani Government. The IFC gave the country a bonus when it also reviewed the Karachi Stock Exchange in order to improve the trading, clearing, and market information systems of the Exchange. Also the Government issued regulations which will facilitate privatization of the country's banking system, now dominated by nationalized banks. A new investment bank for the nation has also been recommended by the IFC's comprehensive capital markets study carried out through its CMD (Economics Department, 1989, p. 15).

International Securities Group

Finally, another recently established activity within the CMD, the International Securities Group (ISG), is worthy of mention for its work in assisting companies in the acquisition of financing by means of international offerings of investment funds and individual corporate securities. The ISG was formed in FY1989 and brings together the four vital elements in the development of the private sector in LDCs with international investment: (1) corporations in LDCs which issue securities to international institutional investors, (2) investment banks and securities houses which provide knowledge of and access to the international capital markets, (3) international institutional investors which seek portfolio investment opportunities in LDCs, and (4) governments of these LDCs which regulate the investment of foreign capital in the domestic private sector (IFC, *International Securities Group*, 1990, p. 3).

The ISG works to reconcile the problems which are prevalent in this matrix of conflicting parties. Its functions include: (1) representing the IFC in international capital markets, (2) focusing on individual corporate securities issues from LDCs, (3) working closely with commercial partners, (4) making early commitments to transactions and the playing of a major role in structuring them, (5) performing underwriting and placement of securities, (6) making investments where appropriate.

The role of the ISG may, no doubt, be eliminated in years to come because, if it is fully successful, the private sector in LDCs will be developed to the point whereby many if not most of these LDCs will become, like the early nations assisted by the IFC, sufficiently well off to lose eligibility for World Bank Group assistance.

CORPORATE FINANCE SERVICES

Corporate restructuring and privatization activities are relatively new services offered by the IFC through its Corporate Finance Services (CFS), created in FY1989. These activities will continue to grow in number and should become a significant operation of the IFC as fulfillment of its objective to develop the private sector in LDCs continues to be its major role. As more and more socialist countries desire to change from public enterprise to private enterprise, the privatization movement will continue to grow. Companies in LDCs whose management desires to remain viable in terms of their core business will continue to attempt financial restructuring in order to reduce their emphasis on debt capital. Both activities should continue to require the expertise of the CFS.

Financial Restructuring

Financial restructuring operations had been carried out within the IFC earlier, especially after the 1982 debt crisis which began when the Mexican Government decided it could not service a jumbo loan. When it became clear to top officials at the IFC that company restructuring may become a necessary ingredient in the development of the private sector in many LDCs, centralization of the activity in the CFS was implemented. Many private firms in LDCs have taken on too much debt, as a result of the global debt crisis which ensued, thus restricting their financial and production activities.

The CFS attempts to identify fundamentally sound companies in member LDC countries and to restructure them financially, assisting them to reduce their debt capital while increasing the equity capital in the company. The IFC has been able to recruit the help of other financial institutions in such endeavors and to mobilize funds for these revisions of company capital structures. Since it began its operations in this area, the IFC has participated in 48 restructurings while providing technical assistance to another 14 firms. Half of these firms have been located in Latin America with the remainder in Asia and Africa.

One representative example of the IFC's work in this area is that of the Visa Group in Mexico, discussed in Chapter 6. The Visa Group restructuring operation was one of the largest in Latin America and was facilitated by the work of CFS. The Visa Group, a Mexican conglomerate comprised of Visa Holding, Fomento Económico Mexicano S.A. de C.V., and Grupo Cermoc S.A. de C.V., committed to a $1.7 billion restructuring designed to reduce the Group's debt.

Privatizations

During the past few years, the desire to privatize state-owned enterprises in LDCs and in Eastern Europe has become a frenzied activity. The supply-side economics of the early Reagan Administration in the United States has become a guiding principle in the development policies of many of these countries. The IFC has become quite active in privatization assistance through its CFS. As discussed in Chapter 6, privatization discussions have been carried on, in some cases successfully, with the Pakistani Government to study the feasibility of privatizing part of the Pakistani International Airlines, with the Philippines Government to privatize the Philippines Airlines, and with Poland and Hungary to privatize many state-owned firms.

The latter two countries, and particularly Hungary, can keep CFS very busy in restructuring and privatization operations during the next several years. In Hungary, the Government plans to transfer $30 billion of firms now in state hands to private control but no master plan exists to implement such an ambitious program ("Raising Capital for Eastern Europe," 1990, p. 90). The Hungarian process will begin small with 30-40,000 small enterprises such as hairdressers and gasoline stations being converted to private firms. Large, poorly run and inefficient firms such as steel and chemical companies may be liquidated or allowed to become bankrupt with government subsidies. Local partners will be found to enter joint ventures with foreign investors ("Raising Capital for Eastern Europe," 1990, pp. 90-91). In each of these areas, the expertise of the CFS in financially restructuring firms and privatizations should benefit the Hungarian economy in the new world of private enterprise.

Specific proposals for privatization procedures have been received by the IFC from several governments. Among them are Antigua, Argentina, Bolivia, Egypt, Greece, Hungary, India, Jamaica, Malaysia, Mexico, Morocco, Nigeria, Paraguay, Thailand, Turkey, Uruguay, Venezuela, and Yugoslavia.

PROJECT DEVELOPMENT FACILITIES

During the 1980s, the IFC established new project development facilities for specific regions of the world. In 1981, the Caribbean Project Development Facility (CPDF) was formed and, in 1986, the Africa Project Development Facility (APDF) followed. These facilities were established under the auspices of other development finance institutions, principally the United Nations Development Programme (UNDP) and are responsible for the preparation of market and prefeasibility studies and other documentation needed in identifying and evaluating project proposals. Both facilities were discussed in Chapter 6. Finally, in FY1990, a South Pacific Project Facility (SPPF) was established modeled after the two earlier formed facilities, to assist development of small and medium-sized firms in South Pacific island nations. Projects will average $1 million in size. This facility did not begin operations until August 1990 so no evaluation is possible.

The African and Caribbean facilities have received overwhelming response to their services from entrepreneurs in those regions. The CPDF has assisted project sponsors in 21 Caribbean nations and territories, acquiring debt and equity funds for some of them. A total of 45 projects have been financed with total investments of $100 million while generating jobs for 3,300 people. The projects are located in 15 countries and involve the agriculture, agro-processing, manufacturing, and tourism sectors. The vast majority of these projects were $2 million or less in size, too small to receive direct financing from the IFC. The APDF has so far received more than 1,000 proposals resulting in 30 projects accepted for funding. Total cost of these projects is $47 million — average project cost of $1.6 million — of which $32 million was secured by the APDF. A total of 2,300 jobs have been created and foreign exchange savings of $22.3 million have been generated.

Insufficient time has passed for an evaluation of these projects but some side benefits have surfaced. Local consultants have improved their ability to advise domestic entrepreneurs. In addition, projects have been found to need redesign of the proposal and the facility assists in this phase. One example of the benefits from proposal redesign was mentioned earlier and concerned the Nigerian flower export project which had been designed to grow anthuriums for the North American market. The APDF advised that the European market for roses was a much better market and a test market for the redesigned project was carried out successfully in FY1989.

GOVERNMENT ADVISING

The IFC has begun to directly advise government of member countries or, in the case of some Eastern European countries, future members of the agency. This activity is carried out under the auspices of the Foreign Investment Advisory Service (FIAS) and was created in FY1989. It is operated jointly with MIGA, the Multilateral Investment Guarantee Agency, a World Bank affiliate.

This particular operation seems to be in juxtaposition with the IFC's unique character, development financing of private sector projects without government guarantee or influence. However, without direct advisory services for member governments, the restrictions imposed by these governments on private enterprise in some countries will remain in place. The FIAS will give technical advice and conduct research designed to encourage private investment and close contact with the host government is necessary in most cases in order to fulfill this objective.

In its first two years of operations, FIAS has been extremely busy in carrying out its mandate. It has advised 15 different governments on promotion and regulation of foreign investment and in six of these countries, a repeat project was undertaken. Two major activities sponsored by the FIAS have involved: (1) a seminar in China in which comparative business practices were discussed as well as an analysis of foreign investors' views of China by several experts and (2) a major conference on foreign private investment in sub-Saharan Africa.

Governments do not have to follow the advice of any outside agency, including the FIAS. However, the involvement of the IFC brings with it not only expertise but also prestige. The record of the first two years of FIAS activities shows that it has been successful. In seven of the 11 countries in which FIAS has completed its advisory process, its recommendations have been accepted by the host government. One of these, if successfully implemented, may result in the establishment of a secondary market in foreign exchange in China.

PROJECT FINANCIAL ASSISTANCE

The major activity of the IFC is, of course, regular participation in project financing (Economics Department, 1989). From the inception of the IFC, its major objective has been to develop the private sector in member country LDCs by approving catalytic investments, either debt or equity or both, made to private enterprise projects. This has been, and will continue to be, the major operation carried out by the IFC. The activities mentioned in the preceding sections have been organized in the manner discussed as a means to rationalize the various parts of the private sector development equation and make its operations more efficient and streamlined.

As stated at the beginning of this chapter, from its inception in 1956, the IFC has invested in projects in LDCs whose total capital cost is estimated to be more than $50 billion. Such projects have involved more than 2,000 enterprises and financial institutions in support of more than 1,000 businesses in more than 90 countries. At the end of FY1990, the IFC held a well-diversified portfolio of investments in some 495 firms or financial institutions located in 80 countries, along with some six regional investments, whose original total IFC investment was $6.428 billion. The IFC currently holds investments in these projects totaling $4.752 billion, after sales and payoffs of investments.

Quantitative Returns

Some attempt has been made by the IFC to analyze the profitability and benefits which have accrued from its investments. In one such study, the organization measured the ex-ante economic rate of return from a sample of its investments. This return measures the real added value expected to come from the particular investment activity. If this measure does not exceed the real cost of capital including a premium for risk, the IFC will not pursue the project. The economic return from the projects in this study were measured before the project investment was approved, i.e., the returns were assumed to accrue from the project as though it had been approved.

Before 1970, the IFC did not have available any systematic procedures for assessing or screening projects; or, at least, it did not apply any of the accepted financial techniques for screening investment projects. It has been since 1970 that the art of capital budgeting techniques — net present value, internal rate of return, and other methods — have been discussed to any extent in the financial management literature. After 1970, the IFC began to apply economic cost/benefit analysis to its projects and has since used the technique in all of its investment approvals.

The IFC's acceptance criterion is that projects must have a satisfactory economic rate of return. However, expected benefits from approved projects must also have satisfactory expected financial returns. Occasionally, the latter are distorted by policy-induced protection or subsidies and, thus, financial returns will differ from economic rate of return on a given project. However, the IFC approves only projects which have satisfactory results on both economic and financial returns.

In a sample of 110 projects, the IFC found that all had similar economic rates of return and financial rates of return. These projects were selected from two sources: data on 57 projects were obtained from sectoral studies undertaken by the IFC's Operations Evaluation Unit (OEU) while data for the other 53 projects were gained from project completion reports (PCRs). The ex-post estimates of both economic and financial returns were available for all 110 of the projects. See Table 12-1 for a sector-by-sector breakdown of the distribution of real ex-ante returns by sector. In addition, the economic rates of return were significantly above the financial rates of return in nearly all cases. In nearly two-thirds of the firms in this sample, the distribution of benefits tended to favor the host economy. The ex-post returns on the 110 projects by sector is shown in Table 12-2.

By applying such investment evaluation techniques, the IFC insures that the ex-ante benefits of projects in which it invests will be economically and financially beneficial. In addition, such projects will insure that scarce resources are allocated in an efficient manner

TABLE 12-1. Distribution of Real Ex-Ante Returns by Sector

	Number of Projects	Ex-Ante Ex-Ante ERR(%) FRR(%)
Agricultural Production	15	2120
Agricultural Processing	19	2420
Cement	20	2719
Chemicals	5	2225
Mining	13	2825
Manufacturing	11	2121
Pulp, Paper	4	1723
Textiles	15	1919
Tourism	6	1914
Other	2	1817
Group Average (unweighted)	**110**	**2320**

Note: Data refer to 100 projects from combined OEU and PCR samples.

Note: From The Development Contribution of IFC Operations.

Discussion Paper No. 5, p. 22, by Economic Department, 1989, Washington, D.C.: International Finance Corporation. Copyright 1989 by the International Finance Corporation. Reprinted by permission.

TABLE 12-2. Ex-Post Returns on IFC Projects by Sector (in percent)

Sector	PCR Sample			OEU Sample		
	Number of projects	Ex-Post ERR	Ex-Post FRR	Number of projects	Ex-post FRR	Ex-post FRR
Agricultural production	2	2	-3	13	2	3
Agricultural processing	6	11	14	14	7	4
Cement	11	11	7	9	20	11
Chemicals	4	15	15	--	--	--
Mining	4	8	11	9	16	13
Manufacturing	11	8	10	--	--	--
Pulp, paper	4	14	15	--	--	--
Textiles	3	17	20	12	10	8
Tourism	6	11	9	--	--	--
Other	2	17	16	--	--	--
Group Average	**53**	**11**	**11**	**57**	**10**	**7**

Note: Project Completion Reports and Operations Evaluation Unit samples are not overlapping.

Note: From "IFC and Development," by Guy Pfeffermann and Gary Bond, 1989, December, Finance & Development, 26, p. 42. Copyright 1989 by the International Monetary Fund. Reprinted by permission.

and that government-imposed distortions do not dominate the returns from these projects.

Another measure of the success of the IFC's project investments can be obtained from an analysis of the return on assets for its active portfolio. The average nominal return on assets before taxes for its portfolio has been estimated to be 9.5 percent, if only those investments which have had no IFC commitment of funds for at least six years are considered. Its portfolio of 490 holdings has 136 companies which meet this criterion (Pfeffermann and Bond, 1989, p. 42). Such return compares quite favorably with the average return on assets before taxes of 8.6 percent reported for developing country affiliates of U.S. firms in 1986. Of course, the IFC criterion of investing only in companies which offer a satisfactory ex-ante economic rate of return insures that government-imposed investment distortions such as subsidies and protection will be more than offset.

Miscellaneous Returns

Throughout the discussion of specific case studies of projects assisted by the IFC, several instances of non-quantifiable benefits have been discussed. The process of economic transformation from the development finance assistance rendered by any of the multilateral financial institutions is of a complex nature and has many ingredients. Change emanating from expert financial assistance elicits improved technologies, better management techniques, greater employee skills, and new and exotic financing techniques. The project approval itself generates iterative experience with greater and greater efficiencies in project design, choice of technologies, market and environmental analysis, cost-cutting, and the myriad of government-imposed obstacles presented by the bureaucracy generally found in LDCs.

The IFC brings many skills into the development process, given its 35 years of experience in dealing with private sector development within the bureaucratic environment of its client member countries. In the project approval decision, the agency can draw on expertise from other agencies including the World Bank and the United Nations Development Programme as well as from the regional multilateral development banks. This expertise includes financial and economic analysts, engineers, legal experts, officials with marketing, manufacturing, and human resources management experience, and political analysts who can measure country risk. Thus, the expertise brought by the IFC to bear on project proposals eliminates inefficient and uneconomic projects and improves those found acceptable through redesign and restructuring.

Once a project is approved for assistance from the IFC, the sources of funding have already been found. The IFC is merely the "lender of last resort" filling in the final 25 percent or less of financing needed to top off the project. However, the presence of the IFC in the project planning stage encourages many international financial institutions to participate in the project, either as a principal partner or in a syndication of the IFC portion of any loan to the project. The prestige accruing to a member of the World Bank Group created this encouragement in the early years of the IFC's operations. However, during the last decade especially, it is the prestige of the IFC itself, garnered from years of expert and successful development finance operations, that now reduces the perceived risk of international financial institutions in deciding to enter projects approved by the IFC. Such perceived prestige has been inferred from the discussion of many of the project case studies included in preceding chapters. In fact, many international banks and foreign firms will not enter projects in LDCs without the presence of the IFC.

The synergy generated from the pool of resources in many areas of development project finance at the IFC creates immeasurable non-quantifiable benefits to the member country clients of the agency. FIAS is able to advise member country governments about means to encourage foreign direct investment. This department can pool its resources, with the help of MIGA, and hold seminars and major conferences on the problems of regional areas needing development finance and foreign direct investment, e.g., sub-Saharan Africa. The global movement toward financial restructuring of private firms in LDCs which have become overburdened from excessive debt levels and the privatization rampant in some countries, especially Eastern Europe, is facilitated in many ways by Corporate Finance Services, a new fee-based advisory service offered by the IFC. Billions of dollars of global funds can be mobilized through country investment funds formed by the Capital Markets Department at the IFC. The International Securities Group can operate on a competitive basis with Wall Street investment firms in finding international capital markets for securities issued by firms in LDCs which have been assisted by the IFC.

Project development facilities in the South Pacific, Caribbean, and African regions have been established to formulate projects in these areas which lead to private sector development and to identify such projects which are too small for direct financing from the IFC but which can obtain funds from other international development financial institutions or local development agencies interested in funding relatively small projects. The African Management Services Company is able to find ways to train and develop managers for IFC-financed projects.

Projects in the private sector which have not been found can be identified by the technical assistance section of the IFC, thus resulting in entrepreneurial efforts which might have gone unnoticed if not for the presence of IFC expertise. Projects dealing with the exploration and development of energy sources have been centralized in an Energy Department which should alleviate one of the most severe problems found in the developing world.

The results of these many IFC-related operations is immeasurable. Only the trends over time can be analyzed to obtain an inference of the value of the IFC's presence in economic development. In each decade, the organization has grown larger, financed more projects with greater average total costs, diversified into more and more industrial sectors, and established more services.

SOURCES OF FUNDS

Another sign of the IFC's success is found in its ability to obtain funds in more comprehensive ways than either from member country subscriptions or borrowings from the World Bank as well as from the sales of its investments. It has received AAA rating from leading bond rating houses for its capital market issues and, during the past few years, has begun to aggressively source its longer-term funds from the leading financial markets around the world. Funding management at the IFC has evolved into a well-diversified operation as can be seen by its activities in FY1990. And it has found more willing buyers of its investments in the international financial community.

Borrowing in International Capital Markets

The IFC was able to borrow 81 percent of its funding needs from the international markets in a variety of ways. Its first public bond offering, a $200 million issue of 7-year bonds, was underwritten by Credit Suisse First Boston, the Industrial Bank of Japan, Deutsche Bank Capital Markets, J.P. Morgan, and Kidder, Peabody. The issue carried a triple-A rating from both Moody's Investors Services and Standard & Poors ("World Bank Affiliate Sets Public Bond Sale Totaling $200 Million," 1989).

IFC financing also involved other public issues on the international capital markets. These included a $300 million Eurobond issue underwritten by many of the leading international bond underwriting banks, an issue denominated in Spanish pesetas, and two reverse dual currency Samurai issues in Japan. These latter included a so-called daimyo bond issue, 20 billion yen ($144 million) of 5-3/8 percent, 10-year bonds in the Japanese market, which were also triple-A rated and priced to sell at a premium ("World Bank Affiliate Issues Bonds in Japan," 1989). Its asset/liability management prowess in years to come should become quite sophisticated and include many of the means of interest risk management including gap management and use of futures, options, and other derivative financial instruments.

Sales of Investments

Although the IFC still holds nearly 500 investments in its portfolio, these holdings represent less than half of the individual commitments made by the agency. Some of the more than 500 investments no longer shown on the IFC's books have matured and been paid off by the borrowing firm. Many have been sold to private investors, primarily international financial institutions. The funds from these investment sales are recycled back into new investment commitments. In FY1990, the IFC closed out 46 investment accounts and reinvested these funds in 67 new projects ("IFC Goes into New Markets for Nascent Enterprises," 1990, p. 60).

SUMMARY AND CONCLUSIONS

The IFC started as a very small development finance agency, operating globally, with initial capital of only $100 million. Its earliest investments were in the less-than-$5 million category and total cost of the projects approved seldom amounted to more than $10-15 million. It was restricted from directly investing in the equity of its client firms and could not underwrite equity issues made by such firms. By 1970, it had achieved permission to take equity positions in project firms and to underwrite securities as well as to borrow directly from the World Bank. In that year, it financed 40 projects. By FY1989, it had made in one fiscal year as many as 90 investments, committed as much as $1.3 billion of its funds, and mobilized an additional $8.4 billion from other international investors in syndications, country fund formations, and sales of its securities. It has, thus, evolved from the simple multilateral development financial institution into one which furnishes a broad range of investment, advisory, and managerial services for private enterprise in LDCs, while holding a large, diversified portfolio of nearly 500 investments, and funding its operations with international capital market debt issues which are top-rated globally.

The IFC could have been stillborn as a result of the early conservatism of the Eisenhower Administration in the United States. Perhaps without the international community in Washington with its informal communications networks and cocktail party circuit, the IFC might have remained just another interesting international development idea. It did, however, evolve despite the early obstacles in the form of a puny institution and is now one of the world's most successful development finance agencies.

Chapter 13

Problems of the International Finance Corporation

INTRODUCTION

The International Finance Corporation (IFC) is a unique multilateral development finance institution with a history of 35 years of operations. Any international organization which has survived more than three decades of pursuing global objectives with regard to development finance will have acquired much baggage, some good and some bad. Any such institution which, furthermore, makes investments in LDC private enterprise projects without government guarantee will have garnered many problems, some perceived, some real. Most of these problems are inherent in the nature of development finance and the clients with which one deals, the LDCs.

The discussion in this chapter will turn to the major problems facing the IFC in the implementation and fulfillment of its major objective: private sector development in LDCs. These problems include those stemming from LDC government practices and policies such as the IFC's conflicts with the anti-government guarantee objective, government bureaucracy, and government restrictions on foreign private investment. Problems dealing with private enterprise in LDCs will be discussed and analyzed. These include conflicts with the World Bank on jurisdiction, the lack of managerial and entrepreneurial talent in LDCs, and cultural problems. Another problem to be examined is the difficulty in mobilizing funds to LDC projects in light of sovereign lending problems. This problem affects the IFC's syndication operations and creates obstacles to its satisfactory entry in some regions of the world. World Bank bureaucracy which affects the lesser affiliates has been a problem for the IFC, especially in its earlier years, and will be examined.

Finally, three operational problems will be covered. These involve the apparent conflict in the IFC's Directors' backgrounds and relation to their roles, inadequate staffing for the diverse and growing operations carried out by the IFC, and the relatively obscure nature of the institution. Many international banks, multinational companies, and development analysts have a relative lack of familiarity with the IFC and its unique operations and focus. The discussion of these problems will include countermeasures, many already implemented, which have resulted or should result in their solution.

THE ANTI-GOVERNMENT GUARANTEE CONFLICT

The IFC makes investment commitments only if no government guarantee is present in the project. On the other hand, the World Bank and the International Development Association, the other two World Bank Group development finance agencies, will enter no project without government guarantee. The IFC, in adopting this policy at the time of its inception, did not want government interference with its principal objective, development of the private sector in LDCs.

Importance of the Public Sector

The major conflict which is present in much of the IFC's operations and investment commitments concerns the importance of the host government in most if not all LDCs and certainly in the Eastern European nations which, through recent revolutionary process, have decided to move away from a history of communist- and state-controlled economic sectors, especially in those IFC members, Hungary, Poland, and Yugoslavia. To be precise, the IFC cannot participate in any project without the implied consent of the government. In order to fulfill its major goal of private sector development, its investments in private sector projects would not be feasible if the local government failed to permit the investment. Thus, some discussion with the local government or some agency in that government is a necessary ingredient in the project proposal and its analysis.

Another facet of life in many LDCs is that the public sector is the only or, at least, the most important professional area of employment. Many government officials, thus, practice a very aristocratic life-style. In fact, some of these countries have what some analysts call a banana republic mentality. When foreign investors, or for that matter the IFC, encounter this behavior, some compromise must be practiced if development finance objectives are to be accomplished.

Some have argued that the IFC does, in fact, make many of its loans to government-controlled enterprises (Bovard, 1988). The complaints have been directed primarily at the IFC-financed projects in Eastern Europe and China, where state-control has been the accepted policy. For example, the IFC made a $17 million investment in a Chinese automobile plant in 1985 in which Peugeot made the only private investment, taking less than 10 percent of the company's ownership. Yugoslavia has been singled out as a country in which the IFC has been quite active during a period from 1962 to 1986 when the country's private sector contribution to gross national product fell from 27 percent to only 5 percent (Bovard, 1988). In another Eastern Europe example cited by IFC critics, a $3.2 million IFC investment was made to a new government-controlled bank in Hungary for the purpose of making loans to state-owned enterprises and cooperatives.

Poland is another IFC member country in which the IFC was one of the earliest investors in, again, state-controlled enterprises. In fact, the critics point to the guarantee by the Bank Handlowy, a financial institution fully owned by the Polish Ministry of Finance, of an IFC loan made to a new Hungarian bank, as well as the further criticism that this particular loan was based on the borrower's net worth, calculated at the official exchange rate of about one-eighth that of the black market exchange rate in Poland at that time.

These examples can be explained in a number of ways. First, the government guarantee problem may be skirted by "lip service" but, as was mentioned earlier, an implicit approval for IFC's presence is mandatory for its investments to be feasible. The guarantee referred to here is not the same as the World Bank guarantee. It is an approval to enter the scene. The IFC does not require any guarantee of the payment once the funds have been committed. This procedure is based on common sense. Second, in the case of the Bank Handlowy guarantee of the IFC loan to the new Hungarian bank, the latter is intended to attract foreign private investment, well within the objectives of the IFC (Owen, 1988).

In the case of the Eastern European investment commitments, enterprise in these countries has been state-controlled. No viable privately-held firms have been operating, at least not of the size in which the IFC will participate. The privatization movement, however, is underway in these countries and the IFC is assisting this movement, particularly by means of its Corporate Finance Services Department. In terms of valuation of projects in these countries, although black market foreign exchange rates may be operational, book values must generally be at official rates. The difference is, from a practical standpoint, generally incorporated into the total project cost. At any rate, as discussed in Chapter 12, the IFC now applies both ex-ante economic rate of return analysis as well as ex-post financial rate of return analysis to its projects and makes commitments only if projects' returns are satisfactory after both analyses. Black market costs would be factored into these analyses.

Another answer to the criticism that many of the IFC's investments are made to sectors in which government control is dominant and often overlooked is the fact that the IFC will demand local government shareholders to reduce their share of ownership in the firm by selling to local private interests. In fact, the IFC also desires to spin off its investment interest in well-performing businesses to both local and foreign investors. From 1956 to 1987, the IFC did make 283 sales of its investments whose total value was $117 million (Owen, 1988). In addition, more than 235 international financial institutions, including at least 50 U.S. banks, have participated in syndications of its loan investments.

Yet another criticism of some of the projects in which the IFC participates is the seemingly low economic benefits from some areas. For example, the IFC investments of $6 million in the Ramada Renaissance Hotel in Grenada, $7 million in a Sheraton Hotel in Fiji, and $3.6 million to expand an Intercontinental Hotel in Kenya were questioned as international versions of Urban Development Action Grants (UDAGs), once popular in the United States before the U.S. Reagan Administration curtailed their use with budget reductions (Bovard, 1988). Another IFC commitment to the tourist sector involved a $28 million P.T. Bali Holiday village resort in Indonesia characterized as a project which would create 300 additional direct jobs. The critics estimated that, with Indonesian per capita income of $550, the returns did not match the project cost of $90,000 per job created.

The criticism of these tourism projects assisted by the IFC fails to take into consideration the synergy created by these projects. First, the projects are aimed at increasing the foreign tourist business in the assisted countries. This is a foreign exchange generating industry. The increase in foreign tourism in these countries also benefits other sectors of these nations, including local taxi and car rental businesses, local restaurants, shops which cater to tourists, and a myriad of other enterprises. The increase from the increased employment directly related to the IFC-assisted projects is just the tip of the iceberg in terms of the benefits contributed to the host country of an IFC-supported project, particularly in the tourism sector.

Still another criticism leveled at the IFC and its investments is concerned with countries which do not have adequate financial systems. In these countries, for example Poland, because of the lack of security stemming from an adequate system of banks and other financial institutions, private savings is hoarded by private citizens and kept at home. Thus, these savings are not mobilized into productive investments because of the lack of security. The recent Government confiscation of large denominations of domestic currency in Russia is an excellent example where Russians lacked confidence in their financial institutions and, thus, kept currency at home "under the mattress" and usually in large denominations. Many had life savings wiped out by this policy action.

However, through the IFC's efforts at institution-building, necessary financial intermediaries are being established. As discussed earlier, the IFC assisted in the formation of the First Hungary Fund, a country investment fund, to mobilize foreign investments into holdings of Hungarian enterprises. After all, the history of the modern private sector in Eastern Europe is less than 2 years of age. These nations are starting from a position not unlike South Korea's in 1962.

A majority of the IFC's investments may be prone to these criticisms. However, the fulfillment of the major IFC objective of development of the private sector mandates some minimum dialogue with local government officials. Again government bureaucracy and control is a way of life in most client countries that need IFC assistance.

Two departments established in recent years by the IFC are designed to facilitate the problems inherent from government control of foreign investment or assistance from multilateral development finance institutions. These are Foreign Investment Advisory Service (FIAS) and Corporate Finance Service (CFS). FIAS directly advises governments about ways and means to encourage foreign direct investment while CFS advises companies and governments about methods to financially restructure companies and to privatize state-controlled firms.

GOVERNMENT RESTRICTIONS AND POLICIES

An area closely related to the problems discussed in the preceding section is concerned with government restrictions and policies practiced in LDCs which lead to further problems. In the case of these problems, they are not so much restrictions on the operations of the IFC as they are challenges to be overcome by the fulfillment of the agency's objectives.

Three major problems are deep-rooted in nearly all LDCs and, thus, are major concerns for potential foreign investors. These are: (1) the inadequacy of foreign exchange reserves and the concomitant foreign exchange controls imposed by the host government, (2) the fear of expropriation or nationalization of direct investments, and (3) the inadequacy of skilled management or employees as well as entrepreneurial skills.

Foreign Exchange Controls

Most LDCs have inadequate foreign exchange reserves. Because of the stage of their development and, in general, adverse terms of trade with, especially, the industrialized nations, these countries have trade deficits which result in severe diminution of their reserves and, thus, an inability to service their foreign debt. Thus, the monetary authorities in these countries impose foreign exchange controls designed to restrict the use of scarce foreign exchange. Firms may be licensed to use foreign exchange for imports. Multiple exchange rates may be imposed, thus resulting in more restrictive exchange rates implemented for different classes of imports. The more luxurious the goods, the more foreign exchange is needed to pay for the imports. As a rule, these foreign exchange controls lead to black markets for foreign exchange and, therefore, possible corruption of government officials and misallocation of scarce economic resources.

In many cases, IFC assistance to private sector projects become entwined in these foreign exchange controls. Foreign investors perceive the country, or political, risk to be sufficiently high to merit foreign direct investment. A prime example of a region in which such perceptions are prevalent is sub-Saharan Africa. This was pointed out in Chapter 10 as a major reason why the level of foreign investment is only one-third of the average for all LDCs relative to gross domestic product.

However, the presence of the IFC in private sector projects in these countries is more and more perceived to be sufficiently prestigious to reduce the risk threshold of many foreign investors so that they will be encouraged to participate in investments approved by the IFC. In time, many of these projects lead to either the generation of foreign exchange or a significant savings of reserves, thus leading to a reduction of such foreign exchange controls.

Fears of Nationalization of Investments

Another problem feared by many investors, especially foreign investors, is the nationalization or expropriation of investments made in LDCs. Many examples are available which furnish the evidence why such fears are warranted. The Castro Revolution in Cuba in the late 1950s led to the nationalization of many foreign investments. The Chilean Government expropriated the foreign copper producers in the 1970s. One of the companies assisted by underwriting operations of the IFC on a number of occasions, Fundidora de Monterrey, a Mexican steel producer, was essentially taken over by the Mexican Government. This former IFC client was discussed in more detail in Chapter 7.

It is, however, the role of the IFC to develop the private sector of its LDC members. To do this, the IFC accepts risks which take into consideration the level of political risk in the host country. One of its present successful tools which alleviate the fear of this problem is the FIAS and its direct advisory service to LDC governments aimed at the encouragement of foreign direct investment. The project development facilities created for the South Pacific, Caribbean, and African regions also perform the function of identifying feasible projects which can be developed on the local level, thus reducing the penchant for the host government to consider nationalization of such development projects.

In addition, a new global means for insuring against expropriation and other confiscatory decisions by local governments has become available for use by foreign investors. This is MIGA, the Multilateral Investment Guarantee Agency, an affiliate of the World Bank, which will offer guarantees against nationalization by less-developed country governments of foreign investment when both parties are members of the World Bank (World Bank, *Convention . . . ,* 1985). MIGA is not an IFC affiliate but works quite closely with FIAS.

Facilitation of the IFC-No Government Influence Policy

It is apparent from the discussion of a number of case studies that conflict has always been inherent in the principle practiced by the IFC in its private sector assistance that investments will be made only without government guarantee. As mentioned earlier, approval by the host government is crucial before the IFC will approve a project for an investment. However, this is not a guarantee of successful operations, as demanded by the World Bank in its loan approvals. In fact, in most if not all cases of the IFC's project approvals during its history, some degree of government influence, no matter how small, can be found.

The IFC has formulated a method of easing this problem so that future project approvals may be undertaken leaving no stone unturned, so to speak, in gaining government approval of its operations in the host country. In some cases, this government approval may mean merely that the host government will in no way interfere with the IFC-assisted project. In fact, it could lead to "greasing the skids." This method is carried out by the work of the FIAS, an IFC department which carries on direct discussions with the host government on methods to encourage foreign direct investment. For example, the FIAS has been quite active in selected African nations. In Senegal, it assisted the government to identify policy changes aimed at the encouragement of foreign direct investment in agricultural ventures in the Senegal River Basin. In Ghana, the FIAS assisted in the implementation of a new investment code. In Kenya, it reviewed the work program and training needs, investment reforms, tax regime, and government incentives, and assisted in the formulation of an investment code for the Investment Promotion Centre of the Kenyan Government.

LDC MANAGERIAL/EMPLOYEE PROBLEMS

Another problem found in most LDCs which discourages foreign investment is the paucity of skilled management and employees capable of successfully implementing development projects in the private sector. The IFC works in a variety of ways to alleviate and solve this particular problem. For example, its African Management Services Company (AMSCo) was established in collaboration with the United Nations Development Programme and the African Development Bank to find solutions to the shortage of well-trained and experienced managers in Africa. Such shortage of skilled personnel has been identified as a reason for the weakness of many African private companies and slow progress of privatization in many African nations. The Technical Assistance and Technology Service programs of the IFC are also designed with the objective of identifying feasible projects and technologies and acquiring such as needed to begin a new venture or to modernize, expand, or diversify operations.

PROBLEMS STEMMING FROM LDC
SOVEREIGN LOANS

Sovereign Lending

The sovereign lending crisis in the LDCs, especially since 1982, has increased the difficulty in mobilizing funds for private sector projects in many of these countries. This problem is the result of the rescheduling of country loans or the moratorium placed by some nations on their debt service. It may also be attributed to cultural differences in some regions, such as the Arab world in the Middle East where Islamic principles based on the Koran may create problems with traditional investments.

Where the IFC may be affected directly is in its charter mandate to encourage the participation of the international private financial community in its investments. It fulfills this objective by syndicating portions of its loans to international financial institutions. In some areas, the Middle East and Eastern Europe for example, it has encountered resistance from the international financial community to enter such syndications. However, through its examples and those of syndications in other regions of the world, IFC investments in these regions will, in time, become attractive as syndication candidates. It has a history of syndication operations in which well over 200 international financial institutions have participated in its investments. Another fact worth mentioning here is that no IFC loan syndicated to international banks has had to be rescheduled.

Cultural Problems

In some cases, specific cultural problems may have an impact on the IFC's ability to mobilize foreign capital into private sector projects in a given regional area. This may be especially true in the Middle East where the religion of Islam is practiced very prevalently. Islam requires different practices involving financial transactions. For example, no interest can be paid on loans, because all interest is considered by the Islamic code to be usury and usury is prohibited, at least according to some Moslem financiers. The actual teaching from the Koran is that Moslem canon law bans all transactions with a guaranteed return except when the loan is made for charitable purposes (Cooper, 1982, p. 123). Thus, traditional loans, one of the major investments made by the IFC, may have to be modified in private sector projects assisted by the IFC in Moslem countries. International banks may be discouraged from entering such arrangements. However, the solutions are usually quite simple. Profit participation in the investment may be the acceptable means of countering the cultural or religious practice in such cases.

These religious teachings from the Koran actually define what an Islamic financial institution is (Cooper, 1981; Kassem, 1981; Khouri, 1987). The growth of such institutions in the Arab world demand that foreign investors be aware of the Moslem teachings. As the Arab world becomes more and more a geo-political and strategic region, especially with its oil, the IFC will become more active in the countries of the Middle East. Its lending policies may need to be modified to deal with Islamic teachings.

Religion is just one area of culture which may have a tendency to interfere with private sector development as practiced by the IFC. Racial differences may also create problems. For example, in some Asian nations, local animosities against Chinese immigrants may create prohibitions against assistance from the IFC if the proposed project is operated by Chinese. Malaysia and Indonesia are two such countries. Hindu and Moslem animosities in India and Pakistan may also create problems which have to be handled in a very sensitive manner as may tribal differences in some sub-Saharan African nations.

Finally, language differences have been a stumbling block to some foreign investment projects. The role of the IFC in the establishment of the First Hungary Fund, a country-based closed-end investment company and the first fund designed to invest in Eastern Bloc stocks, has been discussed in a number of places in this study. This fund was highly touted but has had top management problems in its advisory board (Siconolfi, 1991). Its investment manager, a person with deep investment experience, was fired by fund officials because his inability to speak Hungarian created problems in the management of the fund.

On the other hand, such problems have been overcome in some projects. A prime example of such success is that of the Arewa Textiles Company project in Nigeria whose establishment was assisted by the IFC in 1964. This project had technical partners from Japanese textile companies and local partners who were from the Yoruba tribe in Nigeria. The Japanese spoke no Yoruba and the Yoruba spoke no Japanese at the outset. However, the project was on stream in 1 year and paid its first dividend shortly thereafter in spite of these cultural differences.

WORLD BANK BUREAUCRACY

Early Years of IFC Operations

As an affiliate of the World Bank, and a junior affiliate at that, the bureaucratic effects of this relationship with an extremely large organization has had adverse effects on the IFC at times. These conflicts were manifest in the early years of the IFC's operations in its inability to borrow capital funds, as it does very well today, in the international capital markets. Although its Articles of Agreement permitted the IFC to obtain funds in such a manner, the World Bank management essentially prohibited the IFC from doing so because they believed such funding operations would come in direct competition with the prestigious international bond issues of the World Bank. Finally, a way was found to circumvent this prohibition. The IFC Charter was amended enabling it to borrow directly from the World Bank in amounts which were multiples of its subscribed capital. Of course, in recent years, further changes have permitted the IFC to make international capital market issues directly. In addition, the IFC has been granted the highest debt rating by the two leading debt rating agencies in the United States in the last few years.

World Bank Attitudes Toward the IFC

The World Bank has demonstrated on occasion an adverse attitude toward its junior affiliate. This was true in the early stages of the IFC's operations and its seems to be recurring in the present. During the first 15 years of the IFC's operations, it was said that Bank missions rarely turned up investment opportunities of interest to the IFC and, on the other hand, IFC personnel were rarely included on World Bank missions. The Bank was not very interested in the private sector at the time and some Bank staff seemed to consider the IFC as a relatively insignificant appendage (Mason and Asher, 1973, p. 745).

During those early years, the organizational structure within the World Bank and at the IFC also created bureaucratic problems in the fulfillment of the IFC's objectives. For example, the IFC was inadequately represented overseas. Investment policies of the IFC were imperfectly adapted to the changing views found at that time in LDCs as to what were acceptable forms of foreign investment. IFC executives kept their distance from World Bank and International Development Association bureaucrats (Mason and Asher, 1973, p. 745). It was felt then that the IFC needed to exercise leadership in forcing LDCs to be more receptive toward arrangements adapted to changes in the traditional types of foreign investment (Mason and Asher, 1973, p. 746).

The apparent conflicts between the Bank and the IFC seemed to have surfaced again at the beginning of the 1990s. The success of the IFC in private sector development, especially under the leadership of Sir William Ryrie, has been recognized by some World Bank officials as the profitable path to take in development finance. The public sector programs of the Bank are declining in importance and some Bank officials have expressed a desire to move into private sector development (Westlake, 1990). This may be done by the Bank at the expense of the IFC with its higher level of expertise in private sector activities.

Bureaucracy at the IFC

The IFC has inherited some of these bureaucratic tendencies from the World Bank. The organization, despite a relatively small professional core staff, has established several diverse new functions which have been added to its traditional operations. Thus, it has been criticized for creeping bureaucratization of some of its major activities, including project analyses. The Reagan Administration in the United States, a fan of the IFC and its operations, also criticized the IFC after commercial bankers complained that its analyses were too slow, that it is too bureaucratic, and that its private sector assistance constitutes unfair competition since it can borrow from the World Bank, an institution subsidized by its member governments (Kramer, 1981).

The need to gain local government approval also can become part of the bureaucratic syndrome. For example, the IFC has a need to negotiate political as well as the usual economic barriers when it approves a loan to a private sector project. For example, Asian commercial banks believe that they can finance private sector projects in Asia with lower cost funds than can be borrowed from the IFC at, for example, 10.5 percent. In addition, the IFC has minimum project size requirements and, therefore, local commercial banks can make investments which are smaller in size but which are more efficient for the enterprise concerned. The IFC requires much more thorough documentation from the firms in which it invests, as was discussed in Chapter 4. The agency's credit checks are, therefore, more bureaucratic. And in countries such as Malaysia and Indonesia, few IFC loans seem to be made to Chinese-owned firms because of the need for the IFC to compromise some human rights principles in order to gain the government's approval for assistance from the IFC (Friedland, 1989).

Another project which encountered the IFC's bureaucracy was referred to in Chapter 6 in the discussion of country funds. During 1985, the IFC launched plans for its very successful Emerging Markets Growth Fund. The IFC had encouraged John Templeton, the mutual funds wizard, to work with them on this project. However, after several months of this collaboration, Templeton left the association with the IFC. It was reported that among the reasons for his departure were the restrictions imposed by the IFC bureaucrats. Investments in Taiwan were prohibited because of problems which might arise with the People's Republic of China. Investments made in South America would have to be kept there for a certain amount of time so the local governments would not be offended. Templeton apparently believed the fund would be cumbersome, especially with interference from its 10-man board of directors who were perceived by him to be hands-on advisers (Finn, 1986).

Pass-Through Effects

The pass-through effects of adverse publicity accruing to the World Bank, the effect of criticism of the World Bank which passes through to Bank affiliates, may have affected the IFC in negative ways. In dealing with some local governments, the Bank and the

IFC must deal with a certain amount of bureaucracy and corruption. This was true of World Bank loans to the Philippines when the Marcos family was in power. The IFC presumably developed ties with a number of companies which were partly owned by Marcos acquaintances. These included: (1) the Mariwasa Manufacturing Company, a joint venture of Japanese capital and the local Silverio Group, (2) the Philippine Polyamide Industrial Corporation, a joint venture with Japanese capital, and (3) the Marco-linked Tan-Lee family group. In addition, the IFC made a $5 million investment in a Marubeni-financed copper smelter project. Marubeni had ties with a sugar magnate who also had close relations with the Marco family (Bello et al., 1982, p. 187). As it has been stated previously, the IFC must obtain some type of approval for the projects in which it invests. IFC-assisted projects must not be opposed to the political philosophy practiced in the country. Otherwise, the profitability of these projects may never be realized.

From 1985 to the present, the attitude of the World Bank toward the IFC, except for the seeming jealousy at the present time, has taken an about-face. In that year, the President of the World Bank Group, A.W. Clausen, called for a more balanced approach to development financing, one which would increase the emphasis on the private sector at the expense of public sector development. The IFC was recognized as the major agency in private sector development which could achieve this changed balance (Smith, 1985, p. 48). In fact, when the 5-year plan adopted by the IFC at that time called for a doubling of its capital and an investment program totaling $30 billion, John Williamson of the Institute for International Economics, Washington-based think tank, predicted that the IFC would be the one part of the World Bank Group which would be expanded, especially because it of its popularity in the Reagan Administration (Smith, 1985, p. 48). Then-U.S. Treasury Secretary James Baker had referred to the IFC as "the flagship of the private sector in the Third World" (Bovard, 1988).

OPERATIONAL PROBLEMS

The IFC has incurred a number of operational problems, aside from its funding operations, which have limited the fulfillment of its objectives at times. These include the general background of its

Directors, the size of its staff, and the fact that the organization seems to operate in relative obscurity. These problems are analyzed in the concluding sections.

IFC Directors

The IFC Board of Directors consists of 22 voting members. These are temporary employees of the IFC and meet weekly to, among other matters, vote on projects to be financed by the IFC. Funds will not be committed unless the Board of Directors has discussed and voted on each project. Actually some smaller projects can be accelerated and approved without Board discussion and approval but the Board still has implicit approval authority.

The Board of Directors, thus, is a relatively powerful part of the IFC and represents all of the leading country members of the agency. However, a basic conflict may be inherent in the make-up of the Board. For the most part, Board members have public sector experience. Few have broad private sector experience. This may be inconsistent with the IFC philosophy of focusing on private sector development financing without government guarantee for its investment commitments.

In most LDCs, the public sector is the most important area in which to gain any experience. Much of the enterprise in these countries is state-owned so any such experience could be useful. At any rate, IFC Board members usually have long tenure and generally become acclimated to a private sector culture. In short, such private sector inexperience has not been a hindrance to the fulfillment of the major goals of the IFC.

The IFC Professional Staff

The IFC regular professional staff numbers about 650 at the present time. It includes nationals from some 70 nations, including 50 LDCs. The IFC employs another 150-200 persons which include long-term consultants and temporary staff, staff in the IFC's overseas missions, and other specialized staff.

Given the many departments and functions analyzed and discussed in preceding chapters, the size of the IFC staff may be a problem. In the future, particularly, when the organization begins to digest the various operations such as restructuring, privatization, project analysis and identification, post audits, major funding operations in international capital markets, asset/liability management of interest rate risk using exotic financial instruments, underwriting, syndications, and advisory services the problem may become more apparent. The IFC staff has been classified as highly productive. In fact, some IFC officials have had the opportunity to join Wall Street investment banks doing similar work for much higher salaries but have chosen to remain with the IFC partly because of the prestige of the organization and partly because of the value they place in the results from the roles they play.

A few years ago when Barber Conable was appointed President of the World Bank Group, one of the first policy changes made by Conable was to announce a drastic restructuring of the World Bank. This included a reduction in staffing. The morale of World Bank employees dropped. However, this move did not affect the IFC because, as some IFC officials stated, the organization had no fat to reduce.

Although the IFC staff is as productive as it is, officials there have stated that it apparently takes as much time to check out a $10 million project as it does to analyze a $100 million project. However, the IFC is able to alleviate some of this staffing problem by using temporary consultants. Experts from other development finance agencies also work with the IFC in many of their projects, and the ability to draw on an external pool of expertise and the synergy generated enables the IFC to accomplish much more than its small staff might indicate.

Another method used by the IFC is to rotate staff members from project to project and from function to function so that many of the IFC professional staff are quite diversified in the skills they possess. Sir William S. Ryrie, Executive Vice President of the IFC — essentially chief executive officer, improved the staff organization for the investment portfolio by abolishing the practice of giving supervision of IFC investments to five different regional vice-presidents and, instead, centralizing responsibility in one person (Donlan, 1985, p. 18).

Relative Obscurity of the IFC

The IFC, despite the fact that it has mobilized more than $50 billion for private sector projects, has remained in relative obscurity. The World Bank receives much more publicity as a result of the larger commitments it makes to social infrastructure projects in LDCs and because it makes large debt issues annually in the international capital markets. Even the International Development Association (IDA) gains more publicity, although much of this is negative because of the easy terms of its loans and the many replenishments needed from member countries for its development financial resources. National institutions, such as public sector institutions — bilateral aid or export financing agencies, and private sector institutions — such as large multinational banks, get publicity for the political effects caused by their operations.

A former Executive Vice-President of the IFC, William S. Gaud, once expressed his surprise about this obscurity. His observations about the IFC drawn from his travels found that few people anywhere were familiar with the IFC or with its philosophy or methods to encourage private enterprise in LDCs (Gaud, 1971, p. 567).

On the other hand, the IFC quietly goes about operating under its charter mandates of assistance to private sector projects in member LDCs without government guarantee and encouragement of the participation of the international financial community in its operations. The results of its project financing are disseminated in a broad range of obscure publications, its annual reports and press releases, and occasional research monographs such as this one. The bottom line is that it has been highly successful. (The data in Table 13-1 show how it made its money in FYs1989 and 1990.)

SUMMARY AND CONCLUSIONS

This chapter has included a discussion of some of the major problems encountered by the IFC during its 35 years of operations. It appears in nearly every case that the fulfillment of the IFC's major objective, private sector development in member LDCs, has been sufficiently successful to have offset most if not all of these problems. Some of the criticisms of the IFC stem from lack of under-

James C. Baker
265

TABLE 13-1. How IFC Makes Money (millions of US$)

	FY1990	FY1989
Interest earned and financial fees	297.1	244.4
Dividends and profit	30.7	30.8
Gains on equity sales	90.7	118.6
Service fees	16.8	25.3
From short-term investment of cash and securities	142.2	101.5
Other (losses) and income	7.4	(2.1)
Total	584.9	518.5

Note. From "IFC Goes Into New Markets for Nascent Enterprises," 1990,

15 September, Asian Finance, 16, p. 61. Copyright 1990 by Asian Finance

Publications Ltd. Reprinted by permission.

standing of its operations. Some of the problems for which the IFC has been criticized have been eliminated by the reorganization of the agency in the 1980s during which time several new functions were developed by the IFC to facilitate the achievement of its goals while others were centralized and refocused for more efficient results, especially in light of the fact that the IFC has a perceived shortage of skilled personnel to implement these operations. Smoother and more streamlined operations have enabled the IFC to take advantage of the skills inherent in its small staff. In realistic terms, the IFC is positioning its operations for the 1990s when the challenges in Eastern Europe and Africa will require a futuristic development finance institution.

Chapter 14

The IFC: Its Future

INTRODUCTION

The future of the International Finance Corporation (IFC) appears very bright in its role as a major global development finance agency after 35 years of operations. Such a prognosis probably could not have been made in 1956 when it began operations with 31 member countries and 78 percent of its subscribed capital of a paltry $100 million subscribed and paid-in at that time. At the end of FY1991, it had $1.3 billion of subscribed capital, with another $1 billion approved for FY1992 and contributed by 135 member countries. Its role in mobilizing financing for private sector projects in LDC members without taking government guarantees has been sufficiently successful to create jealousy within other development finance institutions, namely the World Bank. In the remainder of this monograph, the future of the IFC will be analyzed with a commentary on the effects it has had on LDCs.

PRESENT ECONOMIC STATE OF LDCs

High Debt Level

Currently, the world's LDCs have combined debt owed to foreign governments and private financial institutions totaling more than $1.2 trillion. The largest debtor nations among the LDCs are Brazil, Argentina, Mexico, Nigeria, and Venezuela. Most of the top 10 leading debtor developing countries are energy-importing countries. Some, such as Brazil and Korea are classified as NICs — newly industrialized countries, or high-income developing nations, according to World Bank statistics.

During the last 2 to 3 years, the growth rate in debt incurred by these LDCs has declined and it would appear that some of the problem has been alleviated. Much of this debt could be eliminated if three scenarios were to happen simultaneously and continue for a sustained period of time. First, if global interest rates were to decline and stay relatively low for a period of time, the debt service by the LDCs would be much easier. Most of this debt is financed at LIBOR — London Interbank Offer Rate — in the Eurocurrency market or at U.S. prime rate, the interest rate which top commercial banks charge their best corporate customers. Second, if energy prices were to decline and stay low for a sustained period of time, the energy costs of LDCs, especially the oil-importing nations, could be reduced. For most LDCs, energy costs represent a significant portion of industrial and consumer spending. Third, if the industrialized countries would export more from the LDCs, much of the debt could be eliminated. In recent years, the high income countries have cut back on imports in an attempt to eliminate trade deficits and these cutbacks have had adverse effects on LDCs in general. In addition, many of the industrialized nations have had low economic growth and, thus, have reduced imports. In the near future, none of these three scenarios appears to be in the forecast, at least as simultaneous events and, thus, will not hold promise for the LDCs, as will be discussed later.

Low Savings Rates in the LDCs

In most LDCs, savings are insufficient for the investment demand. As a result, foreign investment is needed to enhance productive investment. Two problems arise from the demand for foreign investment. Many LDCs have a political environment which discourages foreign direct investment. This is especially true of the sub-Saharan African nations where foreign private investment is about 1/3 the average of the rest of the world's LDCs. Or foreign investment means borrowing, the problem of the 1980s for LDCs when both foreign exchange rates and interest rates moved against these sovereign borrowers. Another problem stemming from the need for foreign borrowing is that these countries have often invested the funds in the wrong things, spent them on public sector consumption, or used them to service other debts.

A large reason for the low savings rates found in LDCs can be attributed to the financial systems in these countries. Most are tightly controlled by government and financial regulation, thus, causing misallocation of the savings these countries already have. The World Bank has urged reforms which are both microeconomic and macroeconomic in nature ("The Price of Cheap Money," 1989). In the microeconomic sector, the Bank urges governments of LDCs to reduce the rigid ceilings on interest rates. Directed credit — credit aimed at specific sectors by government decree — has also been criticized.

The practice has worked in some LDCs, for example, Korea, but for the most part has been an inefficient use of scarce capital funds. The legal framework for financial market regulation is needed in many of these countries. The entire financial system including intermediaries needs to be overhauled in many LDCs. Again Korea is a good example where many of the top banks were government-owned and inefficient. Foreign banks and other financial institutions entered the Korean economy and their competition created an environment in which most of the largest local banks were privatized and the financial system was made much more efficient (Euh and Baker, 1990).

In the macroeconomic sector, the Bank recommends that the chronic economic instability found in these countries must be alleviated in order for an improved microeconomic sector to perform. Artificially low real interest rates should be permitted to rise. Inflation must be eliminated. Governments must practice sound public finance. Such will lead to more efficient and market-conscious financial systems in LDCs through which increased domestic savings will flow.

Terms of Trade

One of the key problems which affects LDCs in their development manifests itself in the adverse terms of trade between them and the industrialized countries. The economies of low-income countries are usually comprised primarily of one or two major commodities, generally agricultural products, which represent the main exports of LDCs. These exports are usually priced in global commodities markets and such prices are set according to supply and demand conditions. The principal imports of these LDCs are finished machinery and equipment whose prices are negotiated and also relatively higher than the commodity exports prices. In other words, the LDCs must pay more in foreign exchange for finished goods imports than they receive for the commodities which they export. The terms of trade run against such countries, causing their foreign exchange reserves to be depleted and their currencies to be depreciated. Inflation is exacerbated. This condition is alleviated generally only when high income countries have growing economies and import more of the produce of the LDCs, thus alleviating the latter's foreign exchange problems.

The terms of trade problem is a major reason in some areas why foreign investment has been discouraged. Sub-Saharan Africa is one such region. To some extent, particular Latin American nations have experienced this problem. Argentina, Bolivia, Colombia, and some of the Caribbean nations are representative of countries where the terms of trade have adversely affected their economies. In other regions, LDCs have been able to overcome adverse terms of trade. Korea and the ASEAN economies are representative of nations which have had, in recent years, surplus trade balances with industrialized nations, particularly with the United States, thus resulting in large foreign exchange reserves and reductions in their foreign debt totals. These countries diversified their economies and began to emphasize export-oriented manufacturing sectors. The result has been successful growth rates and competition with industrialized nations.

Global Interest Rates

Global interest rates affected the LDCs throughout most of the 1980s. The very high interest rates of 1979-1982 created the sovereign debt crisis which essentially began in 1982 when Mexico announced a moratorium on that country's debt service. A large number of reschedulings of country debt had to be implemented in 1982 and during subsequent years. Later in 1984, Argentina had a massive rescheduling and Brazil followed a few years later with a temporary debt service moratorium.

During the latter part of the 1980s, several proposals were issued which were aimed at alleviating the country debt problem. Some called for a swap of country debt for equity in the private sector of some LDCs. One proposal recommended forgiveness of some country debt owed to foreign private commercial banks coupled with an increase in additional loans to these same countries by some of the same banks forgiving the original debt. In some sense, the private marketplace has, perhaps, taken care of some of the problem by marking down the value of country debt to, in some cases, as low as 20-25 percent of par, or lower. At the same time, the International Monetary Fund has demanded that the governments of some of these high debt countries agree to aggressive austerity plans which are designed to reduce inflation and increase savings. These actions have no doubt been responsible for the decline in the growth of country debt among LDCs in general.

Most loans made to sovereign borrowers are made using either LIBOR, the Eurocurrency rate, or the U.S. prime rate. Both interest rates have declined in recent years but have remained rather sticky in their decline. In fact, economic analysts have shown some concern that these rates may increase globally given the large demand for investment capital and the U.S. Federal Government deficit and its large need for foreign capital. If such becomes the case, especially during a global recession in the early 1990s among industrialized nations, the LDCs may suffer a double-dose of economic adversity.

Energy Costs

Rising energy costs have been a bain for the LDCs throughout the 1970s and 1980s. The demand for energy from the industrialized countries pushed up the price of a barrel of oil several times. Before the Persian Gulf crisis began in mid-1990, the price of oil had seemed for some time to have stabilized. However, the Iraqi invasion of Kuwait and the uncertainty of what may happen more than doubled the price of oil during the latter part of 1990. Prices since the beginning of 1991 have subsided substantially, especially after the beginning of military action by the Multinational Coalition against Iraq. Early success by the Coalition coupled with a world glut of oil has resulted in lower futures prices for oil. However, a prolonged military action and destruction of the Iraqi and Kuwaiti oil fields could have disastrous effects on the world price of energy.

Many analysts believe that a serious armed conflict in the region may have a twofold effect on the global economy and its concomitant effect on LDCs. They believe that the global economy will incur serious inflation which will be caused by rising oil prices and high interest rates, both conditions devastating to LDCs. For example, a 40 percent increase in the present price of a barrel of oil would cost the net debtor countries an additional $13 billion in 1991. Exporters of primary products would lose 4 percent of their exports in 1991, up from a 1.8 percent loss in 1990. By region, Asian nations would lose 3.6 percent of exports in 1991, up from a 1.5 percent loss in 1990, Europe would lose 3.8 percent of its exports in 1991, Africa would lose 4.8 percent of its exports in 1991, and the loss by Western Hemisphere countries would be about 4.7 percent ("A Look into 1991," 1990, p. 21).

THE POLITICAL MOVEMENTS IN LDCs

Increasing Democracy

During the last decade, many of the LDCs as well as Eastern European nations became more democratic. In some, this movement was evolutionary and some, it was revolutionary. Some nations finally gave up dictatorial chains or communist control by peaceful debate, while in other countries the change was violent.

Such change has been witnessed in two areas of the world, Asia and Eastern Europe. The political changes in, for example, Korea and Taiwan in Asia and Poland and Hungary in Eastern Europe are prime examples of such political movement to more democracy. Korea and Taiwan have striking similarities in their economic and political systems. Both nations are small geographically and have dense and homogeneous populations. The economies of both nations have been driven by exports. Both have experienced Japanese military occupation. Both nations have gone through difficult political conflicts since World War II: South Korea has been threatened by North Korea and, in fact, the Korean War was fought because of North Korean and communist Chinese invasions of South Korea. Taiwan has had a political conflict with Mainland China, the People's Republic of China. Both nations have had dictatorial or military governments with heavy centralization of their national governments. Also, both countries have had a long history of successful economic planning directed by their respective governments. As a result, both Korea and Taiwan have gained growing shares of world trade, large foreign exchange reserves, and large trade surpluses with the United States (Euh and Baker, 1990, pp. 78-79). In short, both countries have relied more and more on their private sectors, have deregulated more of their financial systems, have set into process liberalization of business regulations, and increased the efficiency of their manufacturing and financial sectors.

With few exceptions, the Eastern European countries have moved toward democratic institutions and away from communist, state-controlled economies. The prime examples of this movement have been Hungary and Poland, both members of the IFC. Future members of the IFC, Bulgaria, Czechoslovakia, and Romania, have also moved in the direction of greater emphasis on private sector economies. The Democratic Republic of Germany — East Germany — has united with the Federal Republic of Germany to form a new nation, Germany, and is adopting western business practices under a unified government.

These changes in Eastern Europe will require much in the way of financial and advisory assistance. The newly created European Bank for Reconstruction and Development is designed to assist the region in the same manner as the World Bank has done globally. The IFC will be quite active in assisting private sector projects as well as advising on restructuring and privatizations.

Country and Company Debt Reduction

The global debt problem for LDCs, now strapped with some $1.2 trillion of foreign debt, permeates their economic systems and involves the private sectors where many companies are overburdened with debt. The plans discussed earlier in this chapter, supported by the IMF, the governments of the industrialized nations, development finance institutions, and private lending banks, have been designed to reduce the amount of debt owed by these nations. Some progress has been made toward the achievement of this goal in the last few years. However, the progress could be reversed if global interest rates and energy prices rise in the near future.

In terms of restructuring the balance sheets of some of the private firms in LDCs which have high debt burdens, the Corporate Finance Services Department (CFS) of the IFC will be a key factor in furnishing advice aimed at reducing debt and increasing equity in these firms. Mexico has had a long history of a country with sovereign debt problems. In fact, the moratorium by Mexico on its debt service in 1982 is labeled as the beginning of the global country debt problem. In the IFC's FY1989, CFS engineered a $1.7 billion corporate restructuring of the Visa Group in Mexico. This conglomerate, one of Mexico's largest, includes Visa Holding, its largest operating subsidiary, Fomento Económico Mexicano S.A. de C.V. (FEMSA), and its affiliate, Grupo Cermoc S.A. de C.V. The restructuring, one of the largest in Latin America, included an $80 million loan from the IFC to FEMSA and a number of debt-reduction options including debt buy-outs, debt-debt swaps, debt-equity swaps, and asset divestitures. The program reduced the Group's debt from $1.7 billion to only about $400 million, thus also resulting in a reduction of Mexico's foreign debt by $1.1 billion (IFC, *Annual Report*, 1990, p. 35).

The Visa Group restructuring is a prime example of the type of projects carried out by the CFS. Another recent restructuring by the CFS is that begun in FY1990 involving Philippine Associated Smelting and Refining Corporation (PASAR), a state-owned company which will have a viable financial structure when the project is completed. The CFS is also planning several restructurings of Eastern European firms so that they may be privatized and become eligible candidates for foreign joint ventures, the accepted mode of company structure in Eastern Europe at the present time.

Deregulation and Liberalization

Many LDCs have initiated policies designed to liberalize government regulations aimed at business and to deregulate their financial institutions and markets. Korea and Taiwan have been mentioned as prime examples where government policies toward the business sector have been changed for the better. The IFC is able to play a key role in several areas. Its Capital Markets Department and International Securities Group can assist these countries in the improvement of their money and capital market mechanisms, as it has done with, for example, development finance companies in many LDCs and securities markets in countries such as Korea. Its CFS can assist in the restructuring of companies overburdened with debt and with the privatization of state-owned enterprise. The Foreign Investment Advisory Service (FIAS) is able to advise governments directly about policies and legislative changes which, if implemented, will encourage private foreign investment in such countries. Its project development facilities developed for the South Pacific Islands, Caribbean, and African regions are able to identify small enterprise projects and means to finance them so that IFC funds may indirectly flow into these firms.

Privatizations

In most LDCs, a strong trend toward privatization of state-controlled enterprises is being followed in all private sectors except for raw materials industries. This trend ranges from the industrial to financial to public service sectors. Privatizations furnish excellent opportunities for multinational companies to enter formerly restricted industries and to work with state-controlled raw materials firms by means of licensing, management contracts, and other strategic alliances with these firms. This movement to privatize firms is a signal from the LDCs of a willingness to allow a greater role for the private sector in the development of their economies.

This movement is occurring in all major geographic regions and, although most active in the democratization of Eastern Europe, it is underway in the Middle East, sub-Saharan Africa, Asia, and Latin America as well. The Argentinean telephone company was sold to foreign investors. The IFC, through its CFS, has been advising several companies in the Philippines, Pakistan, Nepal and Turkey, as well as several other countries. Several countries have asked the CFS to submit specific proposals for privatization of firms. This will, no doubt, be one of the most active areas of fee-based services performed by the IFC in the 1990s.

THE ROLE OF THE GLOBAL
DEVELOPMENT COMMUNITY

The organized global development community, the World Bank and the International Development Association (IDA), the International Monetary Fund (IMF), the regional development banks, as well as bilateral national aid agencies, have a major role to play in the future of the LDCs. One of the major reasons for low incomes in these countries is the pervasive poverty affecting the entire chain of development process in such countries. The institution building necessary to mobilize the funds needed for social infrastructure, not to mention the private sector, is underdeveloped — affected by the inherent poverty found in the low-income LDCs.

The major multilateral development institution is the World Bank. The Bank has evolved through several priorities since its inception (Chowdhury, 1990). At first, the emphasis was on reconstruction, following World War II. The Bank then shifted to development financing and "projects lending," making loans to large scale industry through government guaranteed intermediaries. Its most recent emphasis has been on structural adjustment programs utilizing the "trickle-down" theory of development. This latter program has not been very successful. The current shift is to a policy of poverty reduction. The Bank, in shifting to this new emphasis, recognized that half the world's poor live in South Asia and that the poor in Latin America and sub-Saharan Africa have become even worse off.

If the World Bank is to be successful in shifting to poverty reduction in the LDCs as a top priority, it will have to become less conservative in its lending policies. If the 1988-1990 period of Bank operations is compared with the 1986-1987 period, some significant changes can be detected. First, commitments have grown from only

about $13.5 billion per year for the earlier period to an annual aver-
age of about $15 billion for the latter period. However, disburse-
ments have increased significantly from the earlier period to the
latter period on an average annual basis. On the other hand, when
the ratio of loans outstanding as a percentage of the Bank's lending
limit is considered, the ratio has fallen from an average of 80 percent annually in 1986-1987 to as low as 62 percent in the latter
period. The Bank has become less liquid in 1990 than it was in
1986, with its liquidity ratio falling from 56 percent to 47 percent.
However, its reserves-to-loans ratio has increased from 8.5 in 1986
to 10.8 in 1990. Thus, the bank has slowed its commitments, has
reduced its loans outstanding as a portion of its lending limit and
become less liquid, but has become more conservative with regard
to its reserves.

During the same period, the IDA has increased its commitments,
disbursements, and net disbursements significantly. Thus, it would
appear that more loans are being made to the poorest LDCs through
the Bank's soft loan agency, the IDA. The Bank, itself, does not
appear to be supporting its priority of poverty reduction by its
action. On the other hand, the Bank has made overtures toward
moving into private sector assistance, the area financed by the IFC.
This potential problem was discussed in the last chapter.

The major institutions of the development community may begin
to shift emphasis in many operations toward the private sector. The
Bank is interested in this area, following the successes of the IFC.
The regional development banks all make private sector investments. The Reagan Administration of the 1980s placed emphasis on
development of the private sector, showing its admiration for the
IFC on several occasions. This Administration definitely influenced
policymakers around the world in its encouragement of forces that
support a market economy. This is confirmed in an *Asian Finance*
survey of selected bankers, businessmen, economists, academics,
and editors from six Asian nations. They endorsed the World
Bank's structural adjustment loans by a majority of 65 percent,
which encouraged shifts in LDCs toward particular areas of the
economies of these nations, although the Bank seems to have
shifted to a poverty reduction emphasis ("Robust Income Helps Big
Jump in Net Disbursements," 1990). Thus, bilateral aid from the

industrialized nations may move to place more and more emphasis on financial assistance to private sector projects as a result of the influence of the conservative Reagan Administration and of surveys such as the one just discussed.

If this scenario becomes dominant in the 1990s, the assistance aimed at poverty reduction through government-controlled agencies will probably need to be disbursed by the IDA. First, its soft loan terms appeal to the low-income LDCs. Second, its mandate will prohibit it from making any loans which are directed toward the private sector or any semblage of it. The role of the global development community will then be to encourage increased replenishments of the IDA's funds while guaranteeing no national political debate, as has occurred during each of its previous nine replenishments.

THE ROLE OF THE PRIVATE SECTOR IN LDCs

The Industrial Sector

Development of the industrial sector provides several benefits to LDCs. The benefits have, in one form or another, manifested themselves in all projects financed or assisted by the IFC. First, industrial projects financed by the IFC have, in many cases, resulted in exports by the company assisted. Such exports not only increase gross national product, but they also generate foreign exchange, reduce any trade deficits, and furnish reserves for debt repayment. Second, many of these projects result in foreign exchange savings because the product produced — steel, cement, fertilizer, etc. — no longer needs to be imported or, at least, such imports can be reduced. Again, scarce foreign exchange reserves can be reallocated to other needed projects or for reduction of sovereign debt. Finally, the projects generate new jobs. As mentioned earlier, the sub-Saharan African nations will need to produce 200 million new jobs during the next 20 years in order to satisfy their high population growth rates.

The Service Sector

The service sector has been assisted by the IFC in many ways since it first funded the establishment of a hotel project for tourism in Kenya. In the case of service sector projects, jobs are also created. In many of the LDCs, the service sector has been established or operated by foreign investors. By developing local services, jobs are created. Foreign exchange can be saved because such services do not have to be licensed from abroad or dividends do not have to be remitted from the country to foreign investors. Foreign exchange can even be generated by some service sector projects by the exports they produce. Nationals of many countries play a role in construction projects in many areas. For example, Koreans are involved in several construction projects in foreign countries as are Pakistanis in some of the Arab countries.

The Financial Sector

The IFC has assisted the financial sector in LDCs in many ways. Its earliest projects involved the establishment or expansion of development finance companies (DFCs), predominantly privately-owned finance companies which essentially do what the IFC does on a local level except the size of their financial assistance is much less than what the IFC will consider. Thus, the IFC is able to indirectly finance small enterprises by having assisted DFCs.

The growth of local commercial banking systems has also been supported by the IFC. In some cases, governments have played or still play a dominant role in local financial institutions. This was true of Korea until the influence from branches of foreign banks and their competition forced the Korean Government to privatize the largest Korean commercial banks.

The IFC, through its Capital Markets Department has played a major role in the development of the capital markets in many LDCs. It assisted the Korea Stock Exchange to become more efficient and the result has been the 10th largest stock exchange in terms of volume traded. Its work with the emerging markets of LDCs, especially with the establishment of the Emerging Markets Investment Fund, its promotion of the formation of 45 single or multi-country investment funds which have mobilized $2.5 billion of funds, and the formulation of its Emerging Markets Data Base, have all been nothing short of phenomenal when the direct and indirect benefits to LDCs in general are considered.

As the financial sector in LDCs becomes more developed and efficient, several benefits will accrue to these economies. Savings will be more easily encouraged because local citizenry will feel more secure depositing their funds in the more efficient institutions. Thus, investment funds will be more easily mobilized. Less reliance on foreign investment funds will be needed. Less foreign exchange will be needed to service country debt. The function of intermediation will be more efficiently carried out by domestic financial institutions, thus creating more jobs.

THE IFC UP-TO-DATE

Role and Functions of the IFC

The IFC is a global development finance affiliate of the World Bank Group which is unique in that it finances private enterprise projects in member LDCs without government guarantee. To reiterate, its general purpose is to further economic development by encouraging the growth of productive private enterprise in member countries, particularly in the less-developed areas, thus supplementing the activities of the World Bank.

It accomplishes this purpose with a number of activities including: direct investments in private sector projects, the underwriting of equity in such projects, the mobilization of funds from international financial institutions in the syndications of its loans, intermediation of investment opportunities with domestic and foreign private capital as well as experienced management, and the stimulation of private domestic and foreign capital flows into productive investment in member countries. Such stimulation may be accomplished by assistance in the improvement of domestic stock markets or the formulation of country investment funds designed to mobilize capital from global investors. In recent years, the IFC has added fee-based services including assistance in restructuring of companies overburdened with debt, privatizations, and advice given directly to governments which may result in the encouragement of foreign investment.

Summary of Project Investments

In its 35 years of operations, the IFC has fostered results that for the most part are quite immeasurable. For example, the market value of the projects which it has assisted and which are still viable, going concerns is not available. However, the IFC has invested $14.4 billion in 1,334 projects, as of the end of FY1990, whose total capital costs amounted to more than $61 billion. Such projects have involved more than 2,000 companies and financial institutions in support of more than 1,000 business operations in more than 90 countries. At the end of FY1990, the IFC held 495 investments in its portfolio whose total book value was more than $4.7 billion.

Syndications and Sales of Investments

The IFC has syndicated many of its loans with more than 200 international financial institutions, most of which have been head-quartered in Europe. These international banks participated in IFC loans totaling nearly $3 billion during the agency's 35 years of operations. In addition to syndications of its loans and its investment portfolio now held, from 1956 to 1987, the agency made 283 sales of its investments whose total value was $117 million (Owen, 1988).

Syndications of its loans and sales of its investments represent two important means for the IFC to recycle its investment funds by turning them over into new investments. As the private sector of the IFC's member countries becomes more efficient, thus enhancing their financial markets, and as global investment becomes more and more diversified in both industrialized and emerging market commitments, the IFC should be able to encourage more international financial institutions into syndications of its loans and should incur more success in spinning off its most profitable investments.

New IFC Operations

The new operations of the IFC have been discussed in detail in Chapter 6 and case studies have been included in each of the chapters covering regional operations of the IFC. They have been evaluated in Chapter 12. These activities will become more important in the 1990s as the private sector in LDCs becomes relatively more important because of the decline of state-controlled enterprise in many developing countries. The activities and comments about their future are discussed in the following sections.

Corporate Finance Services (CFS)

Two significant trends in the LDCs and Eastern Europe emerged in the late 1980s. A genuine desire on the part of countries to reduce their foreign debt burdens has been accepted as the modus operandi of the 1990s by business enterprise in these countries. In addition, government officials of many of these countries have come to the conclusion that private enterprise based on market-oriented principles is more efficient than public enterprise or state-controlled firms.

The IFC established the CFS to assist companies in LDCs and to advise their governments in the solutions to these two activities, restructuring of companies and privatizations. Given its success in a few short years of operations and given the demand for its services from Eastern Europe, for example, in the area of privatizations and Latin America with the need to restructure the debt/equity position of many companies, the CFS should continue to remain active for years to come. The only question which clouds the issue is whether its small staff will be adequate for the task.

Capital Markets Department (CMD)

The Capital Markets Department (CMD) demonstrated its prowess in the first 25 years of the IFC's operations in the assistance rendered foreign stock markets. In recent years, its work with the formation of country investment funds designed to mobilize capital funds from global investors and the establishment of the Emerging Markets Data Base (EMDB), among other operations, has established the future role of this department. In addition, the existence of more than 130 country funds along with the demand for global investments should keep this market instrument popular for the next decade. New funds will be formed and the CMD will have the expertise to be able to compete, at least on a small level, with investment banks on Wall Street, in London, and in Tokyo in the establishment of such funds. The EMDB gives market analysts another tool for measuring emerging markets. Academicians will be able to use the data tapes to analyze and measure the efficiency of these markets. The long-term result should be an increase in participation of global investors in the securities of the emerging markets as new markets take the place of more mature trading places (Westlake, 1990).

The International Securities Group (ISG)

One significant phenomenon in global finance during the past decade has been the explosion of new financial instruments with which investors can invest, trade, and hedge risks. This trend should continue for the next decade. The ISG was formed in 1989 to advise companies in LDCs about new and diverse financial instruments available in global capital markets as well as ways to market issues made by them. This IFC operation has a long and bright future as the world of finance becomes more complex and as private firms become more aware of the financial tools available to them.

Project Development Facilities

A major problem found in many LDCs is the inability of local entrepreneurs to identify viable and profitable projects. The project development facilities established by the IFC for the South Pacific Islands, the Caribbean Region, and Africa were specifically designed to assist local businesses to do just that: identify projects and assist in the search for investment funds. In some cases, these facilities have already been successful in advising clients about new projects including the modification of business plans to make them more profitable. These facilities can also find local and foreign funds to finance projects too small to be eligible for an IFC approval. Given the fact that the three areas in which project development facilities have been established by the IFC are the lowest income regions of the world and that foreign investment is relatively low in all three areas, these IFC functions should remain quite active and successful in the decade ahead.

African Management Services Company (AMSCo)

Sub-Saharan African countries have several problems as outlined in Chapter 10. Foreign investment in the area is about one-third the amount for other developing regions of the world. These countries have high population growth rates. Their national governments are young and, in many cases, inefficient. The public sector is better supported by many African governments than the private sector. Most African countries have a shortage of skilled managerial and entrepreneurial personnel.

AMSCo was formed by the IFC to alleviate many of these problems, especially the lack of skilled managers. This unique venture in collaboration with the United Nations Development Programme brings together public sector funding and private sector investment and management expertise. With the help of many other multilateral and national agencies, AMSCo will promote profitable and competitive companies in Africa that are locally managed by providing them with foreign executives who will be succeeded by African managers and by offering management training programs for African nationals.

Because of the high population growth rate in sub-Saharan Africa, 200 million new jobs will be needed by the year 2010. Consequently, as many as 10 million or more new managers will be needed. AMSCo should remain extremely active for the next 20 years in the creation of these new managers. Since it is a self-supporting operation in collaboration with many public and private institutions, it should have sufficient funds and staff to meet this challenge.

Other Programs

Three other IFC programs should also have active and successful futures. These are the Energy Program (EP), Technical Assistance (TA), and Technology Service (TS). All three programs will be important tools for the IFC in the next decade.

The EP was formed for the purpose of exploration and development of new energy sources in member countries. The cost of energy is a major problem for most LDCs. With the uncertainty from the Persian Gulf crisis of 1990-91, any operation which encourages more exploration and development of energy in LDCs will be mandatory in global development.

The TA program uses funds contributed by the European Community and other industrialized nations to provide companies in LDCs with technical assistance to insure that their operations are financially, managerially, and technologically sound. Such potential projects can be found in most LDCs. One example of an IFC-planned technical assistance project is located in Argentina involving the commercial application of satellite telecommunication technology. Some are smaller in scale, e.g., the IFC development of a small biotechnology project in the Cameroons to transfer U.S. know-how in the provision of medical test kits for household use (IFC, *Annual Report*, 1990, p. 45).

The IFC's TS assists business firms in member LDCs with the identification, evaluation, selection, and acquisition of technologies. It has been successful in several countries in preparation studies, updating of process technologies, and helping them find new products, processes, and business activities. Food preservation technologies and processes are needed in nearly every LDC. These need to be state-of-the art in order to process the food needed for their burgeoning populations and to enable them to access world markets for their produce. This is a principal area in which TS will play a major role. The TA operation is a necessary ingredient in project identification, feasibility studies, and project rehabilitation in many of these countries, again a service highly necessary in all low-income LDCs.

THE FUTURE OF THE IFC

Larger Projects

The average size of the project financed by the IFC has grown significantly in each decade of its operations. In recent years, the IFC has financed projects with average total costs of $52.7 million in FY1988, $105.4 million in FY1989, and $75 million in FY1990. During the past three years, several projects have had total project costs of more than $500 million. Three of these, Escondida and CTC in Chile and Aracruz Celulose in Brazil, had total project costs of more than $1 billion each. In fact, in its most active year to date, FY1989, five of its approvals had total costs of more than $500 million.

Projects approved by the IFC will be even larger in the future. A number of reasons can be attributed for this trend. First, the IFC plans to increase its subscribed capital to $2.3 billion. Second, the agency now uses its top rating to borrow on the international capital markets. A profile of these borrowings for FYs1988 and 1989 is shown in Table 14-1. The IFC may become even more aggressive in such public issues and will be able to fund much larger investments. The number of international financial institutions which will participate in syndications of the IFC's loans should increase and the overall general success of the IFC and its projects should enable it to sell more of its investments much more quickly. And as its lesser functions assist LDC projects too small to obtain IFC funding, the IFC will be able to focus on the larger projects.

Profitability

The IFC has developed a growth trend in its profitability. With larger and larger projects in more successful parts of the LDCs, this profit trend should continue for the foreseeable future. For the 1985-1989 period, the IFC doubled its net income three years in a row — from $25.4 million in FY1986 to $53.8 million in FY1987 to $100.6 million in FY1988 to $196.5 million in FY1989 ("IFC Finds Its Own Stride," 1989, p. 68; IFC, *Annual Report*, 1990, p. 5). Only in FY1990 did the trend retreat, as the IFC made a mere $157 million. However, the IFC disbursed more funds and approved more new investments during FY1990. With the added borrowing power as a result of the high debt ratings, the IFC is poised and ready to resume during the 1990s its increased investments and profitability of the latter 1980s.

Future Shift in the IFC's Emphasis

Two aspects of the IFC's operations have had changes in their emphases in the last few years. The changes will continue in the future but in a more aggressive manner. Some evidence exists to

TABLE 14-1. Profile of IFC Borrowings (amount in million US$, FY ended June 30)

	Market Borrowings			Currency Swaps Payable (Recbl)		Net Currency Obligations	
	Principal Amt.		Wgted. Ave. Cost				
	1989	1988	1989	1989	1988	1989	1988
US Dollars	657	655	8.63%	690	337	1,347	992
Deutsche mark	148	159	6.52%	48	41	196	200
Japanese yen	148	123	5.50%	(148)	(123)	-	-
Pounds sterling	63	69	9.13%	(63)	(68)	-	1
Swiss franc	60	66	4.75%	(9)	3	51	69
ECU	58	63	6.63%	(58)	(63)	-	-
Australian dollars	45	48	12.50%	(45)	(48)	-	-
Netherlands guilders	24	25	6.64%	(12)	(13)	12	12
Spanish pesetas	226	58	12.06%	(226)	(68)	-	-
Finnish markkaa	57	-	9.63%	(57)	-	-	-
Swedish kroner	75	-	10.50%	(75)	-	-	-
	1,561	1,276		45	(2)	1,606	1,274

Note: From "IFC Finds Its Own Stride," 1989, 15 September, <u>Asian Finance</u>, 15,

p. 70. Copyright 1989 by Asian Finance Publications Ltd. Reprinted by permission.

suggest that the geographical emphasis in project approvals and commitments has favored the Asian Region. This was the only geographic region which received more project investment in FY1990 than in FY1989. The interest by the IFC in the private sector in Asia probably stems from the fact that most of the nations of Asia, although considered developing in terms of per capita income, have had the fastest growing economies in the 1980s and the private sector in these countries has been extremely successful.

The evidence, however, points to the fact that Africa, particularly sub-Saharan Africa, has the greatest needs in terms of private sector development, outside of Eastern Europe — a special situation because of the decline of state control and communism in that region. Thus, the first shift in emphasis by the IFC over the next decade should be increased financial assistance to private sector projects in Africa.

The FIAS Conference on Foreign Investment in sub-Saharan Africa held in 1989 pointed to several adverse factors in the poorly developed private sectors in African nations and the reasons why, for example, that foreign investment in Africa is so low. Sub-Saharan African private sector projects received only 12 percent of the IFC's investments in FY1990, down from only 16.1 percent in FY1989.

The IFC has become active in Africa through the work of three of its special operations. The Africa Project Development Facility has just completed its first five years of operations and its mandate has been extended for the period through 1995. The work of this facility along with AMSCo, the African Management Services Company, which acquires executive talent for African companies and trains local management, should result in an improvement in the business environment in Africa, leading to increased foreign direct investment. FIAS will play a role in directly advising African governments in methods which will enhance their private sectors and encourage needed capital in the form of foreign investment. In addition, the Africa Enterprise Fund will be able to fund projects in Africa too small to receive funds directly from the IFC.

Aside from moving more actively into Africa, the IFC may also keep its interest high in Asia. It has offices in the Philippines, Indonesia, Thailand, and India, and plans to locate an office in Pakistan. Top officials at the IFC have expressed a desire to be more active in India, Pakistan, Indonesia, and the Philippines (IFC, *Annual Report*, 1990, p. 70).

The second major shift by the IFC in the next decade will be toward more fee-based services in member LDCs. These services have been discussed in various sections of this monograph and include the work of the CFS, the International Securities Group, and the FIAS—the Foreign Investment Advisory Service, just discussed. FIAS began operations as recently as 1989 and is jointly administered by the IFC and MIGA, the Multilateral Investment Guarantee Agency, a newly-formed World Bank affiliate.

The FIAS operations will become more important in the next decade because of the expertise it is accumulating from its direct discussions with LDC governments. As has been mentioned, the IFC does not require government guarantee of its investments. But, from a practical standpoint, it does need government approval to enter a project. This can be facilitated by the discussions held between FIAS and local government officials. In addition, many LDCs need to implement changes in their investment and business laws in order to encourage foreign investment and the assistance of agencies and institutions such as the IFC. The FIAS is able to give such advice and to suggest changes in the operating methods and regulatory environment of many of these countries. This is a need which should remain in existence throughout the 1990s.

THE ROLE OF PERSONALITIES AT THE IFC

Throughout its 35 years of history, the IFC has changed directions and emphases. The catalyst for these changes usually has been the drive of the individual officially titled Executive Vice-President, essentially the chief executive officer, of the IFC. The present CEO of the IFC is Sir William Ryrie, a Scottish government bureaucrat who has been a United Kingdom treasury official and an executive director of the World Bank and the IMF for the United Kingdom. He has had much experience in development finance but little or none as a merchant banker. Sir William has been CEO of the IFC since 1984 and acquired the office at a time when the IFC was extremely obscure in the multilateral development community and was an agency which did not appear to have a clear sense of direction ("IFC's Boosted Role," 1985).

During his tenure, several changes have been implemented. The IFC has undergone a major internal management overhaul designed to strengthen the vision on the part of the IFC's top management of the breadth of the agency's operations. The IFC has begun to fund its operations with capital market issues and has obtained the highest debt ratings under Ryrie's leadership. Project sizes never dreamed of in the first 25 years of the IFC's operations are now being considered and approved. Most of the new operations analyzed in Chapter 6 have been developed during the Ryrie years.

Ryrie's presence has given the IFC the appearance of a highly diversified investment bank and, in fact, has put it on a par in terms of competition in some operational areas with Wall Street institutions. He has made the organization a much more viable and vibrant workplace for its small professional staff, so much so that many of these personnel could move to the private sector at much higher rewards but choose to stay with the IFC.

What will happen when Sir William steps aside? The IFC should continue to grow and become more efficient in its private sector financing operations. The organizational and philosophical style has been set in place for the next decade. The operations of the new functions such as the FIAS, CFS, the regional project development facilities, AMSCo, the Energy Program, and TA and TS programs will be digested during the next decade and will be rationalized in the form of more efficient services for the fulfillment of the IFC's major objectives. Ryrie has spent much of his time traveling throughout the world in an attempt to publicize the IFC's operations and to make the organization a much less obscure institution. In summary, Sir William Ryrie was the man for the times at the IFC and he has given the agency a better focus on its direction. He is not a merchant banker by experience but he has transformed the IFC into what resembles a global merchant bank for the developing world.

VALUE OF THE IFC TO THE UNITED STATES

From its very beginning, the IFC was viewed in the United States by the conservative Eisenhower Administration with its pro-business philosophy as a potentially beneficial global institution. During its history, both the World Bank and the IFC have had American businessmen and former Federal Government officials serving in official positions. These officials have been active in lobbying for support for the IFC as an institution whose operations are very much in the U.S. national interest (Cooper, 1976).

Several benefits have accrued to the United States from operations of the IFC. For example, the IFC has worked with more than 200 U.S. private companies, financial institutions, and official agencies to establish more than 220 ventures in more than 50 LDCs. The IFC has furnished more than $2 billion in financial assistance to these ventures, whose operations have generated more than $1 billion in sales of U.S. goods and services.

In addition to financing these ventures, U.S. financial institutions have made loans to such projects, have invested in equity positions in them, and have participated in syndications of the IFC's loans to such projects. Other U.S. service companies have provided engineering and other technical assistance to the ventures, or have extended suppliers' credits to them, or have participated in procurement contracts for machinery or plant and other equipment for the IFC-project recipient firms (IFC, *IFC and the United States*, n/a).

POSSIBLE GLITCHES

The IFC should continue to grow in terms of the number of approvals made, the amount of the IFC's investments, the average total project costs, the amount of syndications of its loans to international financial institutions, its net profits, its international capital market borrowings, and in the number of its non-investment, fee-based activities. And these operations should be even more successful than they have been in the past. The World Bank and other development finance institutions have already demonstrated jealousy in terms of the success the IFC has had in its private sector development activities.

However, some glitches could result in less than totally successful operations by the IFC. The bureaucratic tendency on the part of the IFC with regard to some of its functions may discourage use of its services by private enterprise in LDCs and participations in its syndications by international financial institutions. Commercial bankers in some countries believe they can undercut the IFC in the terms of loans considered for LDC private firms and also believe they can act faster in approving financial assistance to some of these firms. The withdrawal of John Templeton from participation in the venture with IFC to manage the Emerging Markets Growth Fund, allegedly because of red-tape encountered by Templeton from the IFC's bureaucrats, is a prime example of possible problems caused by too many rules and regulations formulated by officials of the IFC. Perhaps the agency is not as streamlined as Sir William Ryrie would like it to be.

The perceived jealousy on the part of the World Bank toward the IFC's private sector prowess might become a problem in the future. The IFC is a junior affiliate of the Bank and shares the same top management. It is possible that Bank officials might infringe upon IFC operations in private sector development. However, the Bank has its own agenda and its present policy to reduce poverty, if successful, should only lead to improved results on the part of the IFC's activities in member countries assisted under such a World Bank policy.

A third possible glitch in the future of the IFC might stem from the competition from other multilateral development finance institutions. The regional development banks which focus on Latin America, Africa, and Asia have a history of lending to private sector projects in their respective regions. They and the new European Bank for Reconstruction and Development, operating in what is essentially Eastern Europe, may concentrate their activities on private sector investments without overextending their staffs over several different investment and advisory functions, as the IFC has done in recent years.

CONCLUSIONS

It is difficult to characterize the IFC because of its multi-faceted development operations. Private investors in industrialized countries which consider investments in LDCs have such a favorable perception of the IFC that many of them will not make such investments without participation in the project by the IFC. Wall Street investment bankers think that the IFC impinges on their territory because of the constant build-up of its investment and advisory services, including the growth in its approvals, disbursements, projects considered, syndications, capital market funding, fee-based services, and other activities meant to facilitate the implementation. of its major objective.

No other institution has the history or record of the IFC with regard to its major focus on private sector development in member LDCs without government guarantee. The regional development banks usually demand some sort of government guarantee. Of course, the World Bank and IDA demand such guarantees for their loans, do not engage in any equity operations, and do not make fee-based advisory services available to private enterprise. If the total value of the more than $60 billion of project costs on a book value basis could be measured, including their market value as well as social value, the grand total would be many times their book value.

Finally, the fact that the IFC has a relatively small professional staff, given the number and variety of its services, must be reiterated and re-emphasized. The agency's staff has relatively little turnover. It has been demonstrated in the writings of the staff and by interviews with some of them that they are quite willing to stay with the IFC for much less remuneration than could be obtained in the private sector because they perceive that their activities actually create benefits for LDCs, such benefits which are strikingly obvious when project approvals are analyzed on an ex-post basis. Although some believe the IFC remains a relatively obscure institution, from the viewpoint of the development profession, it is considered a very successful development finance institution.

The IFC of 1990 bears little resemblance to the institution which began operations in 1956. The concept put into effect 35 years ago as the IFC was an idea kept alive by informal discussions among internationalists, many of whom were Americans. The result was formulation of U.S. foreign policy by many who were officials of foreign embassies and international multilateral institutions, or were foreign service officers, among others. Thus, U.S. foreign policy in this case may very well have been formulated by foreign elements unattached to the U.S. Government. At any rate, a great development agency might never have evolved were it not for that other great institution, the Washington cocktail reception.

Bibliography

Books

Acheson, A. L. K., Chant, J. F., and Prachowny, M. F. J. (Eds.) (1972). *Bretton Woods revisited*. Toronto: University of Toronto Press.

African Development Bank. (1989). *Twenty-five years of development financing*. Abidjan, Ivory Coast: African Development Bank.

Asia 1989/1990: Measures and magnitudes. (1989). Hong Kong: Asian Finance Publications Ltd.

Baker, James C. (1968). *The International Finance Corporation: Origin, operations, and evaluation*. New York: Praeger.

Bello, Walden, Kinley, David, and Elinson, Elaine. (1982). *Development debacle: The World Bank in the Philippines*. San Francisco, Calif.: Institute for Food and Development Policy.

Bergsman, Joel, and Edisis, Wayne. (1988). *Debt-equity swaps and foreign direct investment in Latin America* – Discussion Paper No. 2. Washington, DC: International Finance Corporation.

Business International. (April 1987). Europe introduction. *Investing, licensing & trading overseas*. Geneva: Business International.

Business International. (November 1987). FFO regional development banks. *Financing foreign operations*. Geneva: Business International.

DeWitt, R. Peter, Jr. (1977). *The Inter-American Development Bank and political influence*. New York: Praeger.

Diamond, William, (Ed.) (1968). *Development finance companies: Aspects of policy and operation*. Baltimore, MD: The Johns Hopkins University Press.

Economics Department. (1989). *The development contribution of*

IFC operations — Discussion Paper No. 5. Washington, DC: International Finance Corporation.

Economics Department. (1990). *Exporting to industrial countries: Prospects for businesses in developing countries*. Washington, DC: International Finance Corporation.

Economics Department. (1989). *Prospects for the business sector in developing countries* — Discussion Paper No. 3. Washington, DC: International Finance Corporation.

Encyclopedia of banking and finance. (1983). Boston: Bankers Publishing Company.

Euh, Yoon-Dae, and Baker, James C. (1990). *The Korean banking system and foreign influence*. London: Routledge.

Gustafson, Douglas. (1968). Promoting broader ownership of private securities in the low income countries. In Diamond, William (Ed.) *Development finance companies: Aspects of policy and operation*. Baltimore, MD: The John Hopkins University Press.

Inter-American Development Bank. (1985). *Basic facts about the Inter-American Development Bank*. Washington, DC: Inter-American Development Bank.

International Bank for Reconstruction and Development. (1955). *Articles of agreement of the International Finance Corporation and explanatory memorandum as approved for submission to governments*. Washington, DC:

IBRD. International Bank for Reconstruction and Development. (May 1955). *The proposed International Finance Corporation*. Washington, DC: International Bank for Reconstruction and Development.

International Development Advisory Board. (1951). *Partners in progress*. Washington, DC: U.S. Government Printing Office.

International Finance Corporation. (1964). *Accounting and financial reporting*. Washington, DC: International Finance Corporation.

International Finance Corporation. (1990). *The Africa project development facility*. Washington, DC: International Finance Corporation.

International Finance Corporation. (1956). *Articles of agreement*. Washington, DC: International Finance Corporation.

International Finance Corporation. (1990). *Emerging stock markets factbook 1990*. Washington, DC: International Finance Corporation.

International Finance Corporation. (1990). *FIAS: Foreign investment advisory service*. Washington, DC: International Finance Corporation.

International Finance Corporation. (1970). *General policies*. Washington, DC: International Finance Corporation.

International Finance Corporation. (1989). *How IFC works with commercial banks*. Washington, DC: International Finance Corporation.

International Finance Corporation. (date n/a). *How to work with IFC*. Washington, DC: International Finance Corporation.

International Finance Corporation. (1982). *International Finance Corporation after 25 years*. Washington, DC: International Finance Corporation.

International Finance Corporation. (date n/a). *IFC and the United States*. Washington, DC: International Finance Corporation.

International Finance Corporation. (1989). *IFC in East Asia and the Pacific*. Washington, DC: International Finance Corporation.

International Finance Corporation. (1990). *IFC in Eastern Europe and Yugoslavia*. Washington, DC: International Finance Corporation.

International Finance Corporation. (1990). *IFC news digest*. Washington, DC: International Finance Corporation.

International Finance Corporation. (1971). *IFC 1956-1971: The record of fifteen years*. Washington, DC: International Finance Corporation.

International Finance Corporation. (1973). *IFC: What it is, what it does, how it does it*. Washington, DC: International Finance Corporation.

International Finance Corporation. (1990). *International securities group*. Washington, DC: International Finance Corporation.

International Finance Corporation. (1990). *Investing in mining: The IFC experience*. Washington, DC: International Finance Corporation.

International Finance Corporation. (1964). *Private development finance companies*. Washington, DC: International Finance Corporation.

International Finance Corporation. (1990). *Quarterly review of emerging stock markets – First quarter 1990.* Washington, DC: International Finance Corporation.

International Finance Corporation. (1989). *What IFC does.* Washington, DC: International Finance Corporation.

International Monetary Fund. (July 22, 1946). *Articles of agreement of the International Monetary Fund.* Washington, DC: International Monetary Fund.

International Securities Group. (date n/a). *Linking emerging and international capital markets.* Washington, DC: International Finance Corporation.

Kendrick, David A., Mieraus, Alexander, and Alatorre, Jaime. (1984). *The planning of investment programs in the steel industry.* Baltimore, MD: The Johns Hopkins University Press.

Lewis, John P., and Kapur, Ishan (Eds.). (1973). *The World Bank Group, multilateral aid, and the 1970s.* Lexington, MA: Lexington Books.

Marsden, Keith, and Bélot, Thérèse. (1988). *Private enterprise in Africa: Creating a better environment* – World Bank Discussion Paper 17. Washington, DC: World Bank.

Mason, Edward, and Asher, Robert E.. (1973). *The World Bank since Bretton Woods.* Washington, DC: The Brookings Institution.

Matecki, Bronislaw. (1957). *Establishment of the international finance corporation and United States policy: A case study in international organization.* New York: Praeger.

Moffitt, Michael. (1983). *The world's money.* New York: Simon & Schuster.

Moody's. (1990). *Moody's international stock guide.* New York: Moody's.

Morris, James. (1963). *The road to Huddersfield: A journey to five continents.* New York: Pantheon Books.

Nankami, Helen. (1988). *Techniques of privatization of state-owned enterprises: Volume II selected country case studies.* Washington, DC: World Bank.

Pfeffermann, Guy P. (1988). *Private business in developing countries: Improved prospects* – Discussion Paper No. 1. Washington, DC: International Finance Corporation.

Pfeffermann, Guy P., and Madarassy, Andrea. (1989). *Trends in private investment in thirty developing countries* — Discussion Paper No. 6. Washington, DC: International Finance Corporation.

Please, Stanley. (1984). *The hobbled giant: Essays on the World Bank*. Boulder, CO.: Westview Press.

Rotberg, Eugene H. (1973). The World Bank: A financial appraisal. In Mason, Edward S., and Asher, Robert E. (Eds.) *The World Bank since Bretton Woods*. Washington, DC: The Brookings Institution.

Syz, John. (1974). *International development banks*. Dobbs Ferry, N.Y.: Oceana Publications.

United Nations. (1953). *Report on a special United Nations fund for economic development*. New York: United Nations.

United Nations. (1962). *The United Nations development decade: proposals for action*. New York: United Nations.

United Nations Economic and Social Council. (May 3, 1947). *Document E/1245/revision 1*. New York: United Nations.

United Nations Economic and Social Council. (May 25, 1953). *Document E/2441*. New York: United Nations.

United Nations Economic and Social Council. (June 3, 1954). *Document E/2616*. New York: United Nations.

U. S. Congress. (August 11, 1955). *International Finance Corporation Act, Public Law 350, 84th Congress, 1st session*. Washington, DC: U.S. Government Printing Office.

U.S. House of Representatives. (1961). *Staff memorandum on international lending agencies, 87th congress, 1st session*. Washington, DC: U.S. Government Printing Office.

Weaver, James H. (1965). *The International Development Association*. New York: Praeger.

Wells, Louis T., Jr., and Wint, Alvin G.. (1990). *Marketing a country: Promotion as a tool for attracting foreign investment* — FIAS Occasional Paper 1. Washington, DC: International Corporation.

World Bank. (1985). *Convention establishing the Multilateral Investment Guarantee Agency and commentary on the convention*. Washington, DC: World Bank.

World Bank. (1989). *Developing the private sector: A challenge for the World Bank Group*. Washington, DC: World Bank.

World Bank. (1976). *Development finance companies*. Washington, DC: World Bank.

World Bank. (1990). *The World Bank: A financial summary*. Washington, DC: World Bank.

World Bank. (1967). *The World Bank Group in Mexico*. Washington, DC: World Bank.

World Bank. (1990). *World development report 1990*. Oxford, England: Oxford Press.

World Bank Group. (1971). *Profiles of development*. Washington, DC: World Bank.

Articles

Action on IFC. (1955, April 23). *Business Week*, p. 128.

African Development Bank report focuses on five-year lending program debt relief. (1989, June 26). *IMF Survey*. 18, pp. 202-203.

African Development Bank lending increased 31.2 percent in 1989. (1990, July 30). *IMF Survey*. 19, p. 231.

African Development Bank discusses reasons for Africa's weak economic performance. (1989, June 26). *IMF Survey*. 18, pp. 202-204.

Aiding the less developed nations, a cooperative venture. (1959, October 19). *Department of State Bulletin*, pp. 531-541.

Antoine, Guy C. (1988, December). IFC's initiatives in sub-Saharan Africa. *Finance & Development*, 25, pp. 37-38.

Asia-Pacific region's growth rises in 1988, remains above developing country coverage. (1989, May 15). *IMF Survey*. 18, pp. 153-154.

Baker, James C. (1980, June). The IFC and European banks: Key factors in development aid. *Journal of World Trade Law*. 14, pp. 264-270.

―――. (1968, October-December). IFC in the developing countries: A method of indirectly financing foreign trade. *Foreign Trade Review*. 3, pp. 289-298.

Bank. (1956, March). *United Nations Review*. 2, p. 3.

Bank of America group sets $300 million loan to Mexico steel firm. (1980, September 19). *The Wall Street Journal*, p. 39.

The Bank's new baby. (1956, August). *Fortune*. 54, p. 62.

Bear Stearns sets up fund for investing in Hungarian stocks. (1989, July 12). *The Wall Street Journal*, p. C17.

Bennet, William L. (1965). Developing private enterprise internationally. *Commerce*. 62, pp. 9-10.

Bennett, Keith W. (1972, November 23). Mexico's growth—Building solidly, but fast. *Iron Age*, pp. 69-71.

Bod, Peter Akos. (1990, September/October). Raising capital for Eastern Europe. *World Link*. 3, pp. 90-91.

Bohn, John A. (1990, September/October). Rating Eastern Europe. *World Link*. 3, p. 93.

Booklet outlines policies of International Finance Corporation. (1956, September 17). *Department of State Bulletin*, pp. 456-457.

Bovard, James. (1988, June 21). World Bank unit's lip service to private sector. *The Wall Street Journal*, p. 30.

Charter of new finance corporation now is force. (1956, August). *United Nations Review*. 3, p. 23.

Chowdhury, Amitabha. (1990, 15 September). Gulf crisis can shatter global aid programmes. *Asian Finance*. 16, pp. 36-46.

Clausen, A.W. (1982, October). IFC: finding "bankable" ventures. *The Director*. 36, p. 44.

Cooper, Charles A. (1976, April). World Bank affiliates spur growth, serve U.S. interest. *Treasury Papers*. 1, pp. 8-9.

Cooper, Roger. (1981, November). A calculator in one hand and the Koran in the other. *Euromoney*, pp. 44-64.

———. (1982, December). Dar al-maal al-islami has yet to prove its worth. *Euromoney*, pp. 123-126.

Cox, Tom. (1988, July 29). World Bank: development's foe . . . *The Wall Street Journal*, p. 10.

Damiba, P. C. (1989, September 20-22). Statement. Paper presented at FIAS Conference on Promotion of Foreign Investment in sub-Saharan Africa, Washington, DC.

Delamaide, Darrell. (1990, November). Now for the acid test. *Euromoney*, pp. 40-47.

Despite slowdown, Asia's growth outperformed other regions of world. (1990, July 2). *IMF Survey*. 19, pp. 197-198.

Dodero, Ing Giorgio. (1986, March). World Bank updates guidelines, rules for bidding, procurement. *Power*. 130, pp. 51-52.

Donlan, Thomas G. (1985, May 13). Troubled portfolio: IFC investments go sour. *Barrons*. 65, pp. 16, 18.

Donors agree to provide $15.2 billion for International Development Association. (1990, January 8). *IMF Survey*. 19, p. 8.

Dumaine, Brian. (1984, November 12). Frontier investing. *Fortune*. 110, pp. 143-144.

Eastern Europe: A significant role for IFC. (1990, Summer). *IFC Investment Review*, pp. 1-3.

Ehrlich, Paul Charles. (1989, March 29). IFC demands Thai loan repayment. *American Metal Market*. 97, pp. 2, 10.

Emerging Markets. (1990, 15 October). *Asian Finance*. 16, p. 8.

Farnsworth, Clyde H. (1989, April 27). Third world markets sizzled in '88. *The New York Times*, p. D6.

FIDE, CPDF sign agreement. (1990, June 9). *Tegucigalpa This Week*, pp.1+.

Field, Michael. (1981, July). Merchants and rulers of Arabia. *Euromoney*, pp. 81-90.

Finance Corporation. (1957, September). *United Nations Review*. 4, p. 5.

The financial problems of a developing world economy. (1960, October 17). *Department of State Bulletin*, pp. 607-617.

Finn, Edwin A., Jr. (1986, July 14). A shot in the foot. *Forbes*. 138, p. 80.

Foreign portfolio investment for development: an IFC initiative. (1986, June). *Finance & Development*. 23, p. 23.

Friedland, Jonathan. (1989, January). Money—who needs it? *Far Eastern Economic Review*. 143, p. 69.

Galactic resources names lead manager for mine financing. (1989, May 31). *The Wall Street Journal*, p. C14.

Garner, Robert L. (1961, October 15). The challenging task ahead. *Vital Speeches*. 28, pp. 13-18.

———. (1960, May). Industrialization of an ancient art-craft in Iran. *United Nations Review*. 6, pp. 20-21.

Gaud, William S. (1971, July 1). Overseas private investment in today's world. *Vital Speeches*. 37, pp. 566-569.

Gill, David, and Peter Tropper. (1988, December). Emerging stock markets in developing countries. *Finance & Development*. 25, pp. 28-31.

Graffam, Robert D., and Peter Tropper. (1990, Summer). Emerging stock markets. *IFC Investment Review*, pp. 4-6.

Hartigan, Martin. (1989, September 20-22). An externally funded mechanism to promote intra-regional trade and investment in Africa. Paper presented at FIAS Conference on Promotion of Foreign Investment in sub-Saharan Africa, Washington, DC.

————. (1989, September 20-22). FIAS foreign investor surveys. Paper presented at FIAS Conference on Promotion of Foreign Investment in sub-Saharan Africa, Washington, DC.

Huchne, L. H. (1964). The IFC creation, record & outlook. *Public Finance*. 19, pp. 142-155.

Hungarian Fund Aid. (1989, July 13). *The New York Times*, p. n/a.

Hürni Bettina. (1981, September/October). IFC: The new five-year programme. *Journal of World Trade Law*. 15, pp. 461-465.

Inter-american Development Bank lending soars in 1989. (1990, April 16). *IMF Survey*. 19, pp. 117-118.

International finance. (1956, February). *United Nations Review*. 2, p. 2.

International Finance Corp., assailed as too cautious, makes first investment. (1957, June 22). *Business Week*, p. 125.

International Finance Corporation. (1985, March). *The Banker*. 135, pp. 66-67.

International Finance Corporation. (1955, November 21). *Department of State Bulletin*, pp. 858-859.

The IFC approach. (1990, Summer). *IFC Investment Review*, p. 3.

The IFC at fifteen. (1971, July). *The Morgan Guaranty Survey*, pp. 9-11.

International Finance Corporation begins operations. (1956, August 6). *Department of State Bulletin*, pp. 248-249.

IFC's bid for bigger job abroad. (1961, February 25). *Business Week*, pp. 59-61.

IFC's boosted role. (1985, September). *The Banker*. 135, p. 63.

IFC brightens battered Africa. (1990, November). *Euromoney*, p. 11.

IFC designated as public international organization. (1956, October 22). *Department of State Bulletin*, p. 634.

IFC: Finding "bankable" ventures. (1982, October). *The Director*. 36, p. 44.

IFC finds its own stride. (1989, 15 September). *Asian Finance*. 15, pp. 68-70.

International Financial Corp. to fund Mobil's condensate project in Nigeria. (1988, October 14). *Platt's Oilgram News*. 66, p. 3.

The IFC at a glance. (1988, December). *Finance & Development*. 25, pp. 39-40.

IFC goes into new markets for nascent enterprises. (1990, 15 September). *Asian Finance*. 15, pp. 60-61.

IFC: Growth and diversification. (1988, December). *Finance & Development*. 25, pp. 22-24.

IFC investment in Mexico. (1957, September 2). *Department of State Bulletin*, p. 396.

IFC to loan $14.5M to Utexafrica for modernization of mill in Zaire. 1988, May 12). *Daily News Record*. 18, p. 12.

IFC negotiating with 12 banks to finance Nigerian condensate project. (1989, May 12). *Platt's Oilgram News*. 67, p. 3.

IFC in the news. (1990, Summer). *IFC Investment Review*, p. 7.

IFC plans program expansion. (1983, September 14). *Journal of Commerce and Commercial*. 357, p. 6A.

International Finance Corporation presents first annual report. (1957, November). *United Nations Review*. 4, p. 43.

IFC provides $39.5-million financing for Yugoslav gas. (1984, July 20). *Platt's Oilgram News*. 62, p. 3.

IFC reports high level of investments in 1960. (1961, January 16). *Department of State Bulletin*, pp. 90-91.

IFC revels in a banner year. (1988, 15 September). *Asian Finance*. 14, pp. 70-72.

International Finance Corporation: Ryrie wastes no time. (1985, March). *The Banker*. 135, p. 66.

The IFC's small but key role in Third World development. (1980, October 6). *World Business Weekly*. 3, pp. 49-50.

IFC starts to roll. (1956, September). *Américas*. 8, p. 14.

IFC and World Bank issue year-end financial statements. (1957, August 19). *Department of State Bulletin*, p. 316.

IFC and World Bank loans. (1957, October). *Américas*. 9, p. 2.

Int'l finance loan to help NTM modernize. (1987, July 6). *Daily New Record*. 17, p. 8 (Section 1).

International Financial News Survey. (1967, January 13). 19, p. 7.

IMF financial support for members reaches highest level since 1983/1984. (1990, September 24). *IMF Survey*. 19, pp. 273, 277-279.

Investing abroad. (1957, July 6). *Business Week*, p. 120.

Japanese firms boost Lysine. (1988, July 4). *European Chemical News*. 51, p. 25.

Jones, Peter, C. (1988, December). Corporate debt restructuring in LDCs. *Finance & Development*. 25, pp. 34-36.

Kassem, Omar. (1981, December). Arab aid funds represent the spirit of Islam. *Euromoney*, pp. 140-146.

Khouri, Rami. (1987, May). The spread of banking for believers. *Euromoney*, pp. 145-148.

Kramer, Jack. (1981, May 18). The World Bank widens its free enterprise window. *Business Week*, pp. 66, 70.

Kuhn, W. E. (1982). The Islamic Development Bank: Performance and prospects. *Nebraska Journal of Economics and Business*. 21, pp. 49-63.

Lawrence, Richard. (1966, August 28). IFC debuts plan to lure investors. *The Journal of Commerce*. 369, p. n/a.

———. (1987, September 15). World Bank affiliate to help Third World to tap markets. *Journal of Commerce*. 373, p. 1A.

Loan package for Argentina OCS venture. (1988, March 2). *Platt's Oilgram News*. 66, p. 2.

A look into 1991. (1990, 15 December). *Asian Finance*. 16, pp. 20-22.

Lure for private investors. (1955, June). *Américas*. 7, p. 2.

Mahindra Ugine Steel Company. (1968, February 15). *Monthly Newsletter of the Indian Investment Centre*. 5, pp. 1-10.

Malloch, Theodore. (1990, September/October). The road from serfdom. *World Link*. 3, p. 92.

Marsden, Keith. (1989, September 20-22). The role of foreign direct investment. Paper presented at the FIAS Conference on the

Promotion of Foreign Investment in sub-Saharan Africa, Washington, DC.

Matecki, B. E. (1956, May). Establishment of the International Finance Corporation: A case study. *International Organization*. 10, pp. 261-275.

Members quotas guide their access to IMF resources. (1990, August). *IMF Survey*. 19, pp. 4-5.

Mendels, M. M. (1966, June). IFC: Investment banker to world free enterprise. *Industrial Canada*, p. 2.

Mexican headache for international banks. (1977, January 22). *The Economist*. 262, p. 99.

Mexico plans to merge 3 major steel firms in bid to boost output. (1977, May 11). *The Wall Street Journal*, p. n/a.

Mexico's growth—building solidly, but fast. (1972, November 23). *Iron Age*, pp. 69-71.

A mood of self-content. (1956, September 29). *Business Week*, pp. 30-31.

More risk capital for abroad. (1955, June 11). *Business Week*, p. 113.

Nellis, J. (1989, September 20-22). The prospects for privatization in sub-Saharan Africa. Paper presented at the FIAS Conference on Promotion of Foreign Investment in sub-Saharan Africa, Washington, DC.

New finance corporation starts operations. (1956, October). *United Nations Review*. 3, p. 42.

New steps toward establishing International Finance Corporation. (1955, December). *United Nations Review*. 2, p. 46.

New verve for worldwide financing. (1966, July 9). *Business Week*, pp. 106-108.

On the economic front. (1957, October). *Américas*. 9, p. 2.

Owen, Henry. (1988, July 29). . . . or development's friend. *The Wall Street Journal*, p. 10.

Parker, Marcia A. (1984, July 9). Third World investments. *Oil & Gas Journal*. 82, p. 41.

Pfeffermann, Guy, and Bond, Gary. (1989, December). IFC and development. *Finance & Development*. 26, pp. 41-43.

Pfeffermann, Guy, and Weigel, Dale R. (1988, December). The

private sector and the policy environment. *Finance & Development*. 25, pp. 25-27.

Pinckney, Annette. (1989, September 20-22). Foreign direct investment and the private investment climate in sub-Sahara Africa: A critical review. A paper presented at the FIAS Conference on Promotion of Foreign Investment in sub-Saharan Africa, Washington, DC.

The price of cheap money. (1989, July 8). *The Economist*. 312, p. 61.

Promote the private sector. (1986, September 27). *The Economist – World Bank Survey*. 300, pp. 550-556.

Purposes of proposed International Finance Corporation. (1955, May 23). *Department of State Bulletin*, pp. 844-847.

Raising capital for Eastern Europe. (1990, September/October). *World Link*. 3, pp. 17, 90, 91.

Robust income helps big jump in net disbursements. (1990, 15 September). *Asian Finance*. 16, p. 50.

Rosen, Martin M. (1967, November 7). IFC and the growing need for private investment in the low income countries. Address to the Seminar on International Development. Toronto: York University.

_____. (1964, February 18). Industrial promotion. Address at the first international meeting of Financial Institutions for Development. Caracas, Venezuela.

_____. (1967, December 15). A successful development effort: The International Finance Corporation. *Vital Speeches*. 34, pp. 153-157.

Rozenthal, A. A. (1957). IFC and private foreign investments. *Economic Development and Cultural Change*. 5, pp. 277-285.

Ryrie, Sir William. (1989, September 20-22). Keynote address. Paper presented at the FIAS Conference on Promotion of Foreign Investment in sub-Saharan Africa, Washington, DC.

Schissel, Howard. (1986, January 29). Negotiations seen deciding future of Ivory Coast's oil industry. *Petroleum/Energy*. 367, p. 10A.

Schmitt, Bill. (1986, June 4). IFC investing $10M in Peru mine firm. *American Metal Market*. 94, p. 5.

Sethness, Charles. (1988, December). Capital market development. *Finance & Development*. 25, pp. 32-33.

Siconolfi, Michael. (1991, January 25). First Hungary fund hit by setbacks as Soros resigns. *The Wall Street Journal*, pp. C1, C17.

Smith, Kenneth S. (1985, April 29). World Bank, IMF—Do they help or hurt third world?" *U.S. News & World Report*, pp. 43, 48.

A step closer to fulfillment: Charter for International Finance Corporation drafted. (1955, June). *United Nations Review*. 1, pp. 80-81.

Stern, Ernest. (1990, June). Mobilizing resources for IDA: The ninth replenishment. *Finance & Development*. 27, pp. 20-23.

Thant, U. (1963, March). North versus south. A paper presented at the fifth World Conference, Society for International Development. New York.

3rd World focuses on privatization. (1986, September 15). *The Journal of Commerce*. 369, p. 2A.

Turner, John N. (1983, January). International harmonization: A professional goal. *Journal of Accountancy*. 155, pp. 58-66.

U.S. completes action required for membership in IFC. (1956, January 9). *Department of State Bulletin*, p. 54.

U.S. growth in economy. (1989, June 22). *The New York Times*, p. n/a.

Vielvove, Roger. (1987, October 5). Third World operations. *Oil & Gas Journal*. 85, p. 38.

Violet, William J. (1983, Spring). The development of international accounting standards: An anthropological perspective. *The International Journal of Accounting*. 18, p. 12.

Werber, Marilyn. (1988, September 2). Loan spurs Venezuela DRI output. *American Metal Market*. 96, p. 1.

Westlake, Melvyn. (1990, September). A private quarrel. *Euromoney*, pp. 39-41.

The whiff of politics that hangs over Arab banks. (1981, July). *Euromoney*, pp. 57-63.

Wilson, Neil. (1989, October). I'll do it my way. *The Banker*. 139, pp. 35-36.

World Bank affiliate to help glass factory lift output in Turkey. (1989, January 23). *The Wall Street Journal*, p. B4.

Government Hearings

rency on H.R. 6765. Washington, DC: U.S. Government Printing Office.

Personal Communications

Hamilton, Francis de C. (August 22, 1990). Personal interview. Washington, DC: International Finance Corporation.

Hartigan, Martin. (August 22, 1990). Personal interview. Washington, DC: International Finance Corporation.

Hinchey, Paul R. (August 22, 1990). Personal interview. Washington, DC: International Finance Corporation.

Hussain, Syed I. (June 10, 1967). Personal correspondence from the director and managing director of Packages, Ltd.

Kirk, Mark S. (August 22, 1990). Personal interview. Washington, DC: International Finance Corporation.

Lobl, A. C. (August 22, 1967). Personal correspondence from a director of Papel e Celulose, S.A., Saõ Paulo, Brazil.

Mistry, P. O. (July 13, 1967). Personal correspondence from the secretary of Mahindra Ugine Steel Company, India.

Parmar, Judhvir. (January 18, 1967). Personal interview. Washington, DC: International Finance Corporation.

Raj, James S. (February 23, 1968). Personal interview. Washington, DC: International Finance Corporation.

Talvadkar, Vivek V. (August 22, 1990). Personal interview. Washington, DC: International Finance Corporation.

Annual Reports

The Africa Project Development Facility. (1990B, October 31). *Report on operations for the 12 months ended October 31, 1989*. Washington, DC: International Corporation.

African Development Bank. (1985). *Annual report*. Abidjan, Ivory Coast: African Development Bank.

Asian Development Bank. (1985). *Annual report*. Manila: Asian Development Bank.

_____. (1989). *Annual report*. Manila: Asian Development Bank.

Inter-American Development Bank. (1989). *Annual report*. Washington, DC: Inter-American Development Bank.

International Finance Corporation. (1960). *Annual report*. Washington, DC: International Finance Corporation.

———. (1961-62). *Annual report*. Washington, DC: International Finance Corporation.

———. (1962-63). *Annual report*. Washington, DC: International Finance Corporation.

———. (1963-64). *Annual report*. Washington, DC: International Finance Corporation.

———. (1964-65). *Annual report*. Washington, DC: International Finance Corporation.

———. (1965-66). *Annual report*. Washington, DC: International Finance Corporation.

———. (1982). *Annual report*. Washington, DC: International Finance Corporation.

———. (1983). *Annual report*. Washington, DC: International Finance Corporation.

———. (1984). *Annual report*. Washington, DC: International Finance Corporation.

———. (1987). *Annual report*. Washington, DC: International Finance Corporation.

———. (1988). *Annual report*. Washington, DC: International Finance Corporation.

———. (1989). *Annual report*. Washington, DC: International Finance Corporation.

———. (1990). *Annual report*. Washington, DC: International Finance Corporation.

———. (1989). *Annual report of the World Bank and International Development Association*. Washington, DC: World Bank.

World Bank. (1990). *Annual report of the World Bank and International Development Association*. Washington, DC: World Bank.

Packages Ltd. (1966). *Annual Report*. Pakistan: Packages Ltd.

Unpublished Materials

Baker, James C. (1990). International accounting standards. Unpublished paper presented at the Association for Global Business Annual Meeting, Orlando, Florida.

International Finance Corporation. (date n/a). Part II: Control of

IFC's portfolio. An unpublished working paper. Washington, DC: International Finance Corporation.

Kim, Daniel. (1982). The securities exchange in a developing country: Evolution, organization, empirical tests, and evaluation of the Korea stock exchange. Unpublished doctoral dissertation. Kent, OH: Kent State University.

Kuiper, E. T., Gustafson, Douglas, and Mathew, P. M. (1967). Some aspects of policy and operation of development finance companies. Unpublished manuscript. Washington, DC: International Finance Corporation.

Lee, Soo-Chul. (1989). Tests of weak-form stock market efficiency on the Korea stock exchange. Unpublished doctoral dissertation. Kent, OH: Kent State University.

Press Releases

International Finance Corporation. (September 8, 1961). Press release No. 60. Washington, DC: International Finance Corporation, pp. 1-2.

International Finance Corporation. (June 19, 1962). Press release No. 62/6. Washington, DC: International Finance Corporation, pp. 1-2.

International Finance Corporation. (August 22, 1964). Press release No. 64/14. Washington, DC: International Finance Corporation, pp. 1-2.

International Finance Corporation. (May 31, 1966). Press release No. 66/9. Washington, DC: International Finance Corporation, pp. 1-2.

International Finance Corporation. (September 28, 1967). Press release 67/7. Washington, DC: International Finance Corporation, pp. 1-2.

International Finance Corporation. (February 10, 1972). Press release, No. 72/1. Washington, DC: International Finance Corporation, pp. 1-3.

International Finance Corporation. (March 15, 1972). Press release, No. 72/3. Washington, DC: International Finance Corporation, pp. 1-2.

Miscellaneous Materials

Cia. Fundidora de Fierro y Acero de Monterrey, S.A., Mexico (Fundidora). (November 1960). A report furnished by Fundidora company officials. Monterrey, Mexico: Fundidora. World Bank/ IDA Annual Report, various issues.

Ross report of investor's Mexican letter. (April 20, 1967). An advisory business service. 11, p. 2.

U.S. House of Representatives. (1955). Report No. 1299 of July 20, 1955, 84th congress, 1st session. Washington, DC: U.S. Government Printing Office.

Index

Asian Finance Corporation, 149
Athens Stock Exchange, 210
Atlantic Development Group. *See*
  ADELA Investment
  Company, S.A.
Australia, IFC operations in, 29,205

Baker, James, 261
Bamerical International Financial
  Corporation, 192
Banca Commerciale Italiana Group,
  51,136
Banca Serfin, 106
Banco Aboumrad, 135
Banco Comercial Mexicano, 135
Banco de Comercio, 135
Banco de Industria y Comercio, 135
Banco del Desarrollo Economico
  Español, S.A.
  (BANDESCO), 73-74,86
Banco de Londres y Mexico, 135
Banco Hispano-Americano, 134
Banco Industrial, S.A., 83
Banco Nacional de Desarrollo, 141
Banco Nacional de Mexico, 134,135
Banco Portuguêz de Investimento,
  87
BANDESCO. *See* Banco del
  Desarrollo Economico
  Español, S.A.
Bangladesh, IFC operations in
  Foreign Investment Advisory
    Service projects, 119
  Industrial Promotion and
    Development Company
    investments, 85
  Multi-Country Loan Facility
    loans, 105,125
Bank(s). *See also* names
  of specific banks
  national development. *See*
    National development banks
  regional development. *See*
    Regional development banks

Bankers International Financing
  Company, Inc., 213
Bankers Trust Company, 213
Bank for International Settlements, 5
Bank Handlowy, 249,250
Bank of America, 137,139,192
Bank of Finland, 86
Bank of Montreal, 141
Bank of Toyko, 77
Banque de Paris et des Pays-Bas,
  134
Banque Indosuez, 105,125
Banque Ivoirienne de
  Développement Industriel
  (BIDI), 85,86
Banque Nationale de Paris, 198
Banque Nationale pour le
  Développement Economique
  (BNDE), 77,85,86
Banque pour le Commerce et
  l'Industrie, 51
Barbados, 114
Barclays D.C.O., 194
Barclays of London, 61
Barclays Overseas Development
  Corporation Ltd., 194
Bear, Stearns & Company, 216-217
Belisce-Bel Tvornica Papira,
  Poluceluloze i
  Kartonaze-Belisce, 220
Biafra, 193
Bibliography (EMDB), 101
Black market, 250,253
Bogosu Resources gold project, 198
Bolivia
  IFC operations in
    Banco Industrial S.A., 83
    privatization, 234
    Technical Assistance Trust
      Funds program, 144
  terms of trade, 270
Bondweek, 42
Botswana, IFC operations in, 111
BPI Agricultural Development Bank
  of the Philippines, 85